Alternative and Activist New Media

Digital Media and Society Series

New technologies are fundamentally altering the ways in which we communicate. This series from Polity aims to provide a set of books that make available to a broad readership cutting-edge research and thinking on digital media and their social contexts. Taken as a whole, the series will examine questions about the impact of network technology and digital media on society in all its facets, including economics, culture and politics.

Alternative and Activist New Media

Leah A. Lievrouw

polity

First published in 2011 by Polity Press

Polity Press
65 Bridge Street
Cambridge CB2 1UR, UK

Polity Press
350 Main Street
Malden, MA 02148, USA

ISBN-13: 978-0-7456-4183-6
ISBN-13: 978-0-7456-4184-3(pb)

A catalogue record for this book is available from the British Library.

Typeset in 10.25 on 13 pt FF Scala
by Servis Filmsetting Ltd, Stockport, Cheshire
Printed and bound in Great Britain by MPG Books Group, Bodmin, Cornwall

The publisher has used its best endeavours to ensure that the URLs for external websites referred to in this book are correct and active at the time of going to press. However, the publisher has no responsibility for the websites and can make no guarantee that a site will remain live or that the content is or will remain appropriate.

Every effort has been made to trace all copyright holders, but if any have been inadvertently overlooked the publisher will be pleased to include any necessary credits in any subsequent reprint or edition.

For further information on Polity, visit our website: www.politybooks.com

Contents

List of Tables and Figures

Tables

Figures

Acknowledgements

I would like to acknowledge the support, assistance, inspiration, and advice of the colleagues and friends who encouraged me in the process of researching and writing this book. I begin with thanks to my UCLA Information Studies doctoral students Lilly Nguyen and Alla Zollers, who provided incisive and constructive comments on early outlines and proposals. Alla's expertise on tagging and folksonomies, in particular, was a key influence on my thinking about the commons knowledge chapter; she served as my research assistant in the early days of the project with financial support from a Faculty Research Grant from the UCLA Academic Senate.

By extending an invitation to spend a sabbatical term at the ICT & Society Center at the University of Salzburg (Austria), Dr. Ursula Maier-Rabler, the Center's Director and a longtime colleague and friend, gave me an ideal opportunity to elaborate and "test" my ideas with the outstanding group of multinational, multidisciplinary graduate students who participated in my mediation seminar there in 2009. The gracious hospitality of Ursula and the Center's extraordinary staff (especially Elke Holzmann and Esther Nowy, who were on call to help with absolutely anything, from scouting apartments to securing visas to locating sources for bubble-wrap) was more than matched by the intellectual diversity and energy of the Center's students and faculty.

I also owe sincere thanks to my editor at Polity, Andrea Drugan, for her patience and unfailing good humor in the course of a project that took rather longer than either of us expected. Her encouragement and unflagging enthusiasm for this volume helped to ensure that the process of writing my first sole-authored book has been a delight. And I especially appreciate the assistance of copy editor *extraordinaire* Justin Dyer.

And, of course, the biggest thanks must go to my spouse, travel partner, private chef, guide to culture, and greatest "motivator," Dan Danzig. His constant, good-humored reminders to "hit those keys!" always kept me on task when endless academic chores and distractions loomed large.

CHAPTER 1

Introduction

Throughout most of the twentieth century a handful of firms and institutions dominated the media and information industries, especially in the U.S., Europe, and other affluent regions of the world. An industrial-style system of mass production and distribution delivered all kinds of cultural materials – books, newspapers, cinema, music, television and radio programs – to mass audiences, and helped generate a "mainstream" media culture in which people were viewed mainly as collective "publics," markets, or audiences. Small presses, alternative and underground newspapers, independent filmmakers and musicians, pirate and low-power radio struggled to provide divergent points of view and cultural choices, but their successes were often short-lived. Lacking the enormous resources needed to compete in heavily capitalized and concentrated media markets, most remained on the cultural margins, were absorbed by larger players, or disappeared altogether.

Over the last three decades, however, the proliferation and convergence of networked media and information technologies have helped generate a renaissance of new genres and modes of communication and have redefined people's engagement with media. The big corporate actors and institutions still exist, of course, but their dominance is no longer as assured as it was, as their market prerogatives and business models come under threat from an array of rivals for people's time, money, and attention. Media *audiences* and *consumers* are now also media *users* and *participants*, immersed in complex ecologies of divides, diversities, networks, communities, and literacies. This changing landscape has created unprecedented opportunities for expression and interaction, especially among activists, artists, and other political and cultural groups around the world who have found new media to be inexpensive, powerful tools for challenging the givens of mainstream or popular culture. Websites, mobile telephones, digital photography, video, and audio, blogs, wikis, file-sharing systems, social media, and open-source software all permit social groups with diverse interests to build and sustain communities, gain visibility and voice, present alternative or marginal views, produce and share their own do-it-yourself (DIY) information sources, and resist, talk back, or otherwise confront dominant media culture, politics, and power.

At the same time, this emerging new media ecology[1] has posed complex problems of social equity and solidarity, privacy and security, political and economic participation, freedom and control, expert versus lay/popular knowledge, and more. In the contemporary media context, the familiar processes-and-effects perspective that has animated traditional mass communication research and scholarship, and the production–consumption dynamics of critical media studies, tell only part of the story. Today, a lively and contentious cycle of capture, co-optation, and subversion of information, content, personal interaction, and system architecture characterizes the relationship between the institutionalized, mainstream center and the increasingly interactive, participatory, and expanding edges of media culture (a relationship that media designer and critic Peter Lunenfeld [forthcoming] has aptly called "the war between uploading and downloading").

From the days of the pre-browser internet of the 1970s and 1980s to today's Web 2.0, a tension has grown up between what I have called the competing *pipeline* and *frontier* visions of the internet and other new media systems (Lievrouw, 2006a, 2008). On one hand, the pipeline or center view sees traditional and new media alike as just so many "factories" for the manufacture and distribution of cultural products intended for consumption on an industrial scale. On the other hand, the frontier or edge view regards media more as venues for participation, speech, interaction, and creativity, and considers the vast and growing archive of media products and content as a trove of resources to be re-fashioned and re-presented by users "rummaging in the universal media archive . . . [where] all the data in the world . . . make up one lovely big amusement park' (Lovink, 1997, p. 59). The pipeline view tends to see media technologies and content in terms of property and gatekeeping, production and consumption; the frontier view is more likely to value reputation, credibility, creativity, reciprocity, voice, and trust as well as ownership, and to see media and information technologies as opportunities to create and communicate as well as consume. These contrasting views have helped to shape the popular understanding of the proper cultural and economic role of new media over the last three decades, as well as the technical design of the systems themselves. Disputes about what new media are for, who gets to use them, and who decides have set the stage for the current rise of alternative and activist new media projects.

This book explores these contending views by highlighting several major families or *genres* of contemporary new media projects that have adopted an explicitly alternative, activist, or oppositional perspective. I review the cultural and conceptual roots of these projects in alternative media, new social movement theories, and activist art, and the distinctive features of alternative and activist new media projects that can be traced to these historical antecedents. In the next chapters, important examples of each genre demonstrate how the creators of particular alternative and activist projects have employed the capabilities and features of new media to enlist support and participation, or to achieve their aims for social, political, or cultural change.

More broadly, the book also has a theoretical aim, to which I will return in the concluding chapter. I hope to show that alternative and activist new media projects provide strong empirical support for a theoretical perspective on communication processes, creative work, and media culture – the *mediation* perspective – that has developed within the communication field in recent decades in response to the rise of new media and information technologies based on networked computing and telecommunications (Lievrouw, 2009). New media have challenged the field's traditional distinctions between interpersonal/ group interaction, on one hand, and mass communication, on the other, and between the behaviorist, "administrative" approach of American media research and the cultural, "critical" approach of British/European media studies. Scholarship within the discipline has been segregated along these lines since the field's inception.

Mediation, in contrast, can be understood in both senses of the word, i.e., the use of technological channels to extend or enhance communication, and the interpersonal process of participation or intervention in the creation and sharing of meaning. From the mediation perspective, interpersonal interaction and media, and behavior and culture, are complementary and mutually determining aspects of the whole phenomenon of communication, rather than analytically separate and competing domains. Furthermore, mediation is comprised of two interrelated modes of communicative action that contrast with the production–consumption dynamics and linear "effects" or feedback models associated with mass media. One mode is *reconfiguration*, where users modify and adapt media technologies and systems as needed to suit their various purposes or interests. The second mode – and here I borrow a term from Jay Bolter and Robert Grusin (1999) – is the *remediation* of content, forms, and structures of communication relationships, where users borrow, adapt, or remix existing materials, expressions, and interactions to create a continually expanding universe of innovative new works and ideas.[2] Elsewhere, I have proposed that reconfiguration and remediation are hallmarks of contemporary communication processes, creative work, and media culture (Lievrouw, 2006a, 2008). Reconfiguration and remediation allow people to work around the fixity of traditional media technologies and institutional systems, and to negotiate, manipulate, and blur the boundaries between interpersonal interaction and mass communication. They are also vital, even definitive, strategies in new media art and activism.

Mediation is not a new concept in communication study. Attempts to theorize the intersection between technologically mediated communication processes and interpersonal interaction date back at least as far as Elihu Katz and Paul Lazarsfeld's *Personal Influence* and the two-step flow theory of mass media effects (Katz & Lazarsfeld, 2006 [1955]). However, the need for a theoretical bridge between interpersonal and mass communication processes became acute in the 1980s and 1990s as new media diffused into everyday life, work, and leisure. Some researchers sought to move away from a view of "media" as relatively fixed, stable, and depersonalized institutional entities that exert effects *on* people, in order to focus on what people do *with* media to engage with communication systems and each other. By the late 1980s, the term "mediation" had been adopted by researchers and critics to indicate the new approach, which reframed people's engagement with media in terms of agency, communicative action, representation, and interaction (notably Gumpert & Cathcart, 1986, 1990; see also Altheide & Snow, 1988; Anderson & Meyer, 1988; Hawkins, Wiemann & Pingree, 1988; Lievrouw & Ruben, 1990; Livingstone, 2009; and Meyer, 1988). In the final chapter, I return to this theme to discuss mediation as a possible way ahead for understanding people's uses of new media technologies to make, share, and change society and culture.

In the remainder of this chapter, I lay out some definitions to help frame the discussions in the rest of the book. I begin with a definition of new media that comprises technical artifacts, communicative practices, and institutional arrangements, discuss the characteristics that make new media "new," and consider how this definition applies in the alternative/activist new media context. I review the main points of media genre theory and relate these to emergent forms of new media activism, and close with a brief overview of the subsequent chapters.

New media defined

In order to understand alternative and activist new media projects, we should first decide what we mean by the term "new media." The phrase has become something of a cultural placeholder – people often use it without having a clear or specific idea what it means or includes (and doesn't). In everyday use, the boundaries of what people mean by new media are uncertain. By new media, do we mean the latest technical gadgets, novel forms of entertainment, sophisticated ways to find information, or (by far the most common usage) just anything having to do with the internet? Clearly, a more careful definition is essential if the aim is to describe new media generally and alternative/activist new media in particular.

In the field of communication, scholars have taken several approaches to defining media and communication technologies over time. One common approach categorizes media according to their technical *features* or capabilities, especially those that correspond to human senses and behavior: for example, still versus moving images, sound or silent, one-way versus two-(or more) way transmission, text versus pictures, signals sent through wires or over-the-air (broadcasting), paper or screen (e.g., Durlak, 1987; Pool, 1983; Schramm, 1977; Steuer, 1995). Another approach, widely used in introductory communication textbooks, defines communication technologies according to the *content* they produce, how that content is perceived by people who receive or consume it, and how the content affects them – whether in the form of television programs, printed newspapers or books, feature-length movies, computer games, or other forms. A third approach considers different media systems (i.e., the technologies and the organizations that own and operate them) as *institutions* or industries that may be regulated and governed to achieve various social, cultural, or economic objectives (such as return on shareholder investment, speech and press freedoms, universal service obligations, political participation, or the maintenance of public culture or morals), as well as the transmission of content.

Whatever the approach, communication scholars historically have tended to view the communication process itself as a separate matter from the devices and methods that people use to do it. That is, media and communication technologies have been defined instrumentally, as the means to an end or an intervention in an otherwise undistorted process of "real" human expression and interaction, rather than an essential and integrated aspect of communication itself. With new media, however, it is not so easy to make these simple distinctions. Not only do new media combine and remix features and capabilities from all types of media and information technologies and content, they also blur the usual divisions between media producers and consumers, and between those who design systems and those who use them. Indeed, one of the most striking things about new media – why we can keep calling them "new" – is that they are the product of the continuous interweaving of innovative activities, services, systems, and uses that blend or even eliminate familiar distinctions between telephone calls, movies, letters, newspapers, television, photography, or music, for example.

My colleague Sonia Livingstone and I have proposed a different kind of definition for new media – one that, as I hope to show in the next section, may be particularly useful for analyzing alternative and activist media projects (Lievrouw & Livingstone, 2002, 2006). To begin with, we define new media as information and communication technologies and their social contexts, which include three main components:

(1) the material *artifacts* or devices that enable and extend people's abilities to communicate and share meaning;
(2) the communication activities or *practices* that people engage in as they develop and use those devices; and
(3) the larger social *arrangements* and organizational forms that people create and build around the artifacts and practices.

For example, in the case of mobile telephones, this definition would include the system's hardware and software components (handsets, relay towers, satellites, and undersea cables, switching systems, computers that track calls and generate bills each month), how people use them (voice calls, texting, web access, voicemail, subscribers who use long-term service contracts or pay-as-you-go, top-up cards), and the ways that systems and users are organized (private-sector corporations and their customers, government regulations on rates and competition, whether calls can be monitored by law enforcement agencies or anxious parents).

Of course, all communication systems, not just new media, include these three elements. From handwritten letters enclosed in stamped envelopes and delivered to recipients via postal mail, to massive computerized financial systems that execute instantaneous trades in global markets, we might identify the artifacts, practices, and social arrangements involved in any given system. The next step in defining new media is to say what makes their artifacts, practices, and arrangements different from those of other technological systems, including earlier types of media. Here, we can point to four key factors that distinguish new media.

Two factors have to do with the ways that new media have tended to develop over time – how they have been designed and shaped by society and their users. One is that over time, new media have developed as *hybrid* or *recombinant* technologies – they resist stabilization or "lockdown" and change continuously as a result of combining existing, older systems (e.g., video recording) and innovations (software that makes it easy to upload videos on YouTube). The important point here is that new media are the product of people's ideas, decisions, and actions, as they merge old and new technologies, uses, and purposes. This doesn't mean that a technology will work exactly as it is "supposed" to, that we can always predict how a system might be used or redesigned later, or that some technologies will not become entrenched, routine, and difficult to change.[3] But it does mean that people direct and guide technological change – technologies don't just evolve by themselves, in some inevitable direction.

A famous example is the ARPANET, the early prototype and

predecessor of today's internet (Abbate, 1999; Lievrouw, 2006b). The ARPANET was designed by engineers and scientists working for the Advanced Research Project Agency of the U.S. Department of Defense, who linked long-distance telephone systems and computers so that they could share scientific data-processing capacity across a select network of scarce, expensive, and complex mainframe computers. The system was designed to re-route data to different computers automatically if part of the system failed (e.g., by coming under military attack). Those engineers and scientists never expected that a simple program that allowed project workers to exchange, store, and forward telegraphic "electronic mail" messages would quickly become the most heavily used feature of the system (Newell & Sproull, 1982), and thus the world's first "killer application," or that email would launch a whole new era of computer-mediated communication and pave the way for other forms of digital expression and interaction (see Figures 1.1 and 1.2).

Certainly, some technologies and uses become stable and routine; we can hardly imagine a world without email today. But because it is relatively easy to tinker with new media technologies (indeed, most have been designed deliberately so that they can be modified), and to create and improvise new uses and types of content, they tend not only to change more rapidly than media systems have in the past, but also to keep changing – which is why, in recent decades, we have continued to think about new media as "new," as a moving target.

Another factor that distinguishes new media from mass media is that newer systems have been designed and developed as continuously reorganizing, unfolding, point-to-point webs of technologies, organizations, and users – as a *network of networks*. In this respect, the architecture of new media systems is much more like the telephone and early telegraph than it is like publishing or broadcasting. This is unsurprising, given that new media have been built on the foundation of the global telecommunications system, from the ARPANET onward.

In today's global networks, any point can connect with any

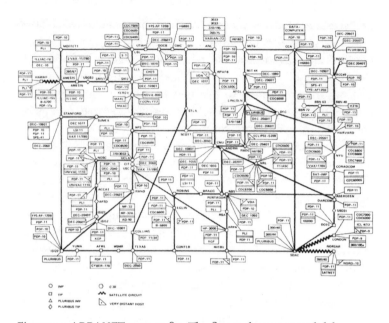

Figure 1.1. ARPANET map, 1980. The figure shows research labs
and other ARPA sites (small circles on the grid) and the number and
models of computers connected at each site.

Source: Newell, A. and Sproull, R.F. (1982). 'Computer networks:
Prospects for scientists.' *Science*, 215(4534), Feb. 12, 843–52. Reprinted
with permission from AAAS.

other point, telephone-style; it is technically possible for any user
to retrieve and exchange messages or programs from any other
user or site on demand. The power of networked architecture
is illustrated by the quintessential feature of new media, the
hyperlink, which not only connects one location, document, or
resource to another online, but also opens a wide and highly
contingent path of subsequent linking where users may move
among sites, resources, and people with few technological barriers. This contrasts dramatically with traditional mass media
systems, in which relatively few, large creators or producers generate media "products" for mass distribution and consumption.

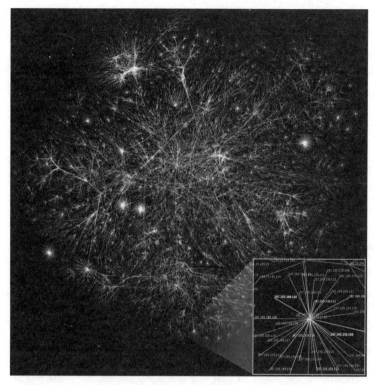

Figure 1.2. Detail from Matt Britt, "Partial Map of the Internet," 2005.

Source: Wikimedia Commons, http://commons.wikimedia.org/wiki/
File:Internet_map_1024.jpg

Mass media are designed around the assumption that there is (and should be) a fairly direct and linear path from the origin of a message to its destination, from producer to consumer, from beginning to end of a program, or from one type of product to another, as in mass market publishing, cinema, or television broadcasting, for example.

The networked architecture of new media is also designed to allow a variety of technologies (telephone, video, recorded sound, text documents, databases) and users to connect and disconnect from the network, as different uses and purposes require. While there is no question that some elements of networked new media have become relatively more centralized and stable over time, and that legacy media industries have adapted some of their products to new media platforms, the persistent openness of the system to innovation (including sabotage or work-arounds) from any place in the network marks a crucial difference from more traditional systems (indeed, this tension between control and openness is at the heart of the contending pipeline and frontier perspectives noted at the start of the chapter). The word "network" has become a commonplace – even clichéd – way to describe both interlinked technological systems and the patterns of social relationships and organizing that they reflect and support. Again, this constitutes a significant change from mass media systems and industries, which are structured mainly around hierarchical, top-down forms of organization, to ensure centralized control, to facilitate the reliable mass production and distribution of media products to mass audiences, and to capture and return steady streams of revenue back to the producers.

The two other factors that make new media new have to do with their consequences or outcomes for society and culture. The first is the sense of *ubiquity* that they encourage – the seeming presence of new media everywhere, all the time, which affects everyone in societies where they are used, whether or not every individual uses them directly.[4] Of course, new media are *not* available everywhere, for everyone, to anything like the same degree. Indeed, the serious and persistent unevenness and inequity of access across geographic areas and social groups has become the subject of numerous studies and enduring debates surrounding various "digital divides" (Norris, 2001; Warschauer, 2004). But over the last few decades, and especially since the introduction of web browsers in the early 1990s (which made more diverse sources of online information accessible to more people than ever before), many people have come to assume, rightly or wrongly, that new media technologies and applications will eventually be accessible for everyone – that they should be regarded as public goods on a par with electricity, water, a telephone service, or other necessities of life in developed societies.[5] Whether and how this assumption will actually be realized in the form of greater access for people in disadvantaged areas or groups is still an open question.

The fourth factor that distinguishes new media from other communication systems is that they are fundamentally *interactive*. They give users an unprecedented degree of selectivity and reach in their choices of information and cultural resources, and their personal interactions and expressions. To some extent the sense of interactivity derives from the networked, point-to-point architecture of new media systems mentioned previously – an infrastructure modeled on telephone systems rather than broadcasting. The immediacy, responsiveness, and social presence of information and other people that new media users experience constitute a qualitatively different experience of engagement with media, and create different expectations about what new media can and should be for, when compared with conventional mass media systems. At the same time, interactive and highly selective systems can promote a sense of solipsism and self-centeredness, cultural fragmentation and pastiche, and the belief that immediate access to quick information that fits one's personal interests and preferences is more valuable or desirable than the in-depth knowledge of the expert – what some critics have called the "Daily Me" (Negroponte, 1995; Sunstein, 2007; see also the parody documentary *EPIC 2015*, discussed in Chapter 5).

Interactivity has long been acknowledged as a distinguishing feature of new media and information technologies, and indeed has been the focus of a large body of literature in communication studies (for example, treatments of the concept in early new media studies include those by Rafaeli [1988], Rice & Associates [1984], and Rogers [1986]). However, it is particularly important in the process of social/political change because it supports or provides conditions for *participation*, which is an essential element of alternative and activist new media (as we will see throughout this book). Mass media systems may have enormous persuasive power, but people's principal mode of engagement with mass media is basically receptive (even from the "active audience" perspective; see Chapter 8). Exposure to or reception of a message may or may not provoke action on the part of the receiver; indeed, the preponderance of classical media effects research has been devoted to understanding just what conditions or predispositions are needed to convert message reception into action. In contrast, new media systems do not just deliver content; people must actively use them to do something, i.e., search, share, recommend, link, argue, and so on. Use is an action by definition, which may encourage new media users toward more involved social and cultural participation online and off. We might argue that it is a much shorter step from use/interaction to participation than from exposure/reception to participation.

Like interactivity, participation has been a core concept in new media studies. For example, Mark Deuze (2006) argues for three distinctive modes of engagement with new media: participation, remediation, and *bricolage*. (We will return to the concept of remediation in the closing chapter; *bricolage* as a communicative strategy in alternative and activist new media is discussed in Chapter 2.) Participation, Deuze says, makes people "active agents in the process of meaning-making" (p. 66), and new media promote participation in this fundamentally constructive and interactive sense. Thus they also provide the necessary platforms for participatory journalism, participatory democracy, and so on. Henry Jenkins (2006), focusing on the production and circulation of popular culture "goods" via new media, says that although interactivity and participation are "words that are often used interchangeably" (p. 133), they are distinct concepts. Interactivity refers to "the ways that new technologies have been designed to be more responsive to consumer feedback" (p. 133), while participation depends on "cultural protocols and practices" (p. 23).

Participation can also be seen as the point at which an individual's knowledge, or capacity to act, is actually transformed into communicative action (Lievrouw, 2001). Interactivity is a necessary cultural, social, and technological condition that supports interac*tion*, which in turn is a necessary condition for participation. We might think of interactivity as a feature of media infrastructure (articulating artifacts, practices, and social arrangements) and participation as a particular form of action supported by that infrastructure; but one depends on the other. "Interactive" new media offer more opportunities for communicative action, and interaction, than do most traditional mass media formats, and thus more opportunities for participation.

Examples of participation are found throughout this book. But to return to the four main features that make new media new – recombination, networked architecture, ubiquity, and interactivity – they also influence each other. The design and use factors (recombination, networks) help shape the social consequences of the system (ubiquity, interactivity). In turn, the social consequences also influence continued use and future design choices. Again, using the example of mobile telephones, so-called "third generation" (3G) or "app" phones have been designed to link a range of new and existing network services (voice calls, text messaging, web browsing, email, delivery of music and video on demand). As these services become a routine part of people's mobile phone use, users' expectations will naturally affect the design and marketing of even newer features and services.

To summarize, new media (like other communication technologies) can be defined as the combination of material artifacts, people's practices, and the social and organizational arrangements involved in the process of human communication (see Figure 1.3). However, they differ from other media forms and systems in four important ways: in terms of their design and use, they are continuously *recombinant* and complexly and dynamically *networked*; in terms of their social consequences, people now take new media for granted as being pervasively *ubiquitous* and *interactive* (with interactivity being a necessary condition for social, political, and cultural participation). Over time, design and use factors, on one hand, and social consequences, on the other,

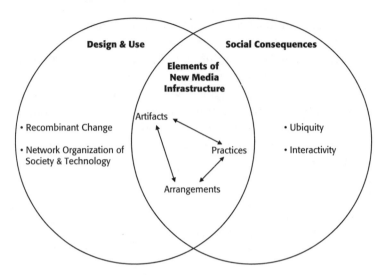

Figure 1.3. New media defined.

continue to influence each other mutually as the technology – an ensemble of artifacts, practices, and arrangements – develops.

Defining alternative/activist new media

The definition above gives a broad sense of what new media are and how people perceive and use them. But what makes certain uses of new media "alternative" or "activist"?

Over the last decade, a number of writers have explored the uses of media, including new media and information technologies, in political, social, and cultural movements. As noted by communication scholar John Downing (2008), this body of work has shifted from a focus on the uses of communication technologies, especially mass media, by mainstream political campaigns and parties to a greater emphasis on citizen, activist, or community engagement with issues and movements through the internet and related technologies (see also Silver, 2003). Other work has focused on *tactical media*, a response to the post-1989 fall of communism in Europe, the failure of left-revolutionary movements, and the ostensible "victory" of market capitalism. Tactical media theorists, notably Geert Lovink and David Garcia, have suggested that, amid the cultural fragmentation and radical subjectivity of postmodernity, the only tenable way forward for political activism is smaller, episodic, nomadic, rapid-response moments of "resistance," not revolution (Cubitt, 2006; Garcia & Lovink, 1997). Critics, however, contend that such an approach – essentially all tactic and no strategy – is too easily co-opted by mainstream political and economic interests, and that diffuse "resistance" is no substitute for more fundamental, revolution-ary change: "tactical media ceded too much to the neo-liberal triumphalists" (Ray, 2006, p. 32).

Generally speaking, analysts have treated alternative and activ-ist new media projects as the latest incarnation of a long historical line of oppositional, radical, underground, or anarchist media, including newspapers and small-press publishing, pirate or underground radio, and public-access video. Various writers have noted the experimental quality of alternative and activist projects that employ both mass media and new media forms and tools, the diversity of viewpoints and values being expressed, the eclecticism or subcultural quality of their audiences, the amateur or volunteer nature of participation, and the marginality of these projects in opposition to entrenched media institutions (Atton, 2002, 2004; Downing et al., 2001; McCaughey & Ayers, 2003; Meikle, 2002; van de Donk et al., 2004; Vegh, 2003). Sandra Braman (2002), for example, identifies four characteristics of alternative media and argues that all are found in tactical media: "The use of medium as content, the rejection of ideology, the merging of politics and art, and appreciation of the ability of digital information to directly make things happen."

However, few of these observers have tried to define what, if anything, distinguishes alternative projects that use conven-tional mass media from the new media/online variety. Some scholars have applied concepts from classical mass communi-cation research (e.g., uses and gratifications theory) or media studies (the triad of production, text, and audience) to new media cases. Others have tended to gloss the differences between mass and new media as a simple matter of greater opportunities for interactivity, participation, or feedback, without probing deeply into what these phenomena are or why they are significant. Some writers have been reluctant to say which projects or issues are actually alternative or activist and which are not. For example, in the preface to their edited collection on cyberactivism, Martha McCaughey and Michael Ayers (2003, p. 14) refuse to define what "counts" as "legitimate online activism" because projects that seem radical or oppositional from one point of view may seem insufficiently committed or effective from another perspective. Downing, who has published extensively on the topic of radical media, argues that "context and consequences must be our primary guides in defining radical alternative media given the range of issues, actors, interests, and meanings involved" (Downing et al., 2001, p. x).

One scholar who has made some clear distinctions, however, is Chris Atton, whose careful analyses of alternative mass media and the "alternative internet" (Atton, 2004) outline the differences between mainstream and alternative projects. He has suggested that over time, alternative media have sought to be participatory, emancipatory, non-commercial, authentic (i.e., faithful to a community's point of view or experience), and anti-institutional. They combine both "creative expression and social responsibility" (Atton, 2002, pp. 13–14), in a way that departs from most mainstream media. Moreover, the alternative internet merges the political and the cultural across a diverse, even idiosyncratic, range of projects, although some (such as Indymedia sites or right-wing blogs) may lean more toward the political, while others (such as culture jamming projects or artworks that defy copyright laws) lean toward the cultural. Ultimately, however, Atton focuses on the explicitly oppositional quality of alternative and activist new media projects, and, crucially, the nature of such projects *as actions in their own right*, rather than communication *about* other "real" actions (what Stefan Wray [1998] has called activism of the deed vs. activism of the word).

Thus, Atton defines the alternative internet as "a range of media projects, interventions and networks that work against, or seek to develop different forms of, the dominant, expected (and broadly accepted) ways of 'doing' media" (Atton, 2004, p. ix).

Taking a cue from Atton's description, then, we might recast the general definition of new media above to propose that **alternative/activist new media employ or modify the communication artifacts, practices, and social arrangements of new information and communication technologies to challenge or alter dominant, expected, or accepted ways of doing society, culture, and politics.** Their creators take advantage of the recombinant, networked nature of new media infrastructure, and the ubiquity and interactivity that they offer users, to create innovative projects in which people extend their social networks and interpersonal contacts, produce and share their own "DIY" information, and resist, "talk back" to, or otherwise critique and intervene in prevailing social, cultural, economic, and political conditions. That is, alternative/activist new media projects do not only reflect or critique mainstream media and culture, they constitute and intervene in them.

New media and genre theory

In Chapters 3 through 7, the discussion will turn to five basic genres of contemporary alternative and activist new media projects: *culture jamming, alternative computing, participatory journalism, mediated mobilization,* and *commons knowledge.* Each of these forms relates to a different domain of social life, culture, or technological practice. For example, culture jamming borrows, comments on, and subverts elements from popular culture, such as entertainment, advertising, art and music, literature, cinema, and so on. Alternative computing simultaneously critiques and reconfigures the infrastructure of information and communication technologies (ICTs). Volunteer or amateur participatory journalism projects employ the ethics and practices of professional news reporting and editorial opinion to cover communities, stories, and points of view that are neglected by the mainstream press. Mediated mobilization extends and activates the power of "live," local social relations and organizing – such as kinship and social support networks, professional affiliations, or expert advice networks. Commons knowledge projects reorganize and categorize information in ways that can challenge or reframe the established, expert knowledge classifications of mainstream cultural institutions and disciplines. Before looking at those genres individually, however, it is useful to say what a genre is, and how genres play a role in media in general and in new media in particular.

To begin with, the concept of *genre* has a long history in the study of communication, from Aristotle's classification of different types of rhetoric and their power to influence or persuade listeners, to the analysis of major literary forms like poetry and fiction, to the categorization of films and television shows according to their style, format, and content (e.g., westerns, action films, situation comedies, game shows, reality programs, or news). Since the 1990s, scholars have also looked at various types of online communication as genres, including email, personal websites, FAQ (frequently asked questions) pages, blogs, and online newspapers. These studies have sought to understand the similarities of online genres with more traditional types of media content, but perhaps more importantly, they have examined how new genres may be evolving and departing from more familiar forms, as people understand and use them differently and as new technological tools become available.

Basically, a genre is a type of expression or communication that is useful and/or meaningful among the members of a given community or within a particular situation.[6] Genres have both *form* and *purpose*: that is, they have typical material features or follow certain format conventions, and they allow people to express themselves appropriately, and to achieve their various purposes or intentions, in a given situation. Although a genre's characteristics may depend to a great extent on the communication technologies or media that are used to produce it, genre and medium are not the same thing – often, a genre may originate in one medium and then be carried over into others. For example, westerns were once a popular genre of print fiction that was later adapted to cinema and television. In fact, one of the most interesting aspects of genres is how people adapt and modify them as new communication technologies become available in different social contexts (Yates & Orlikowski, 1992).

Genres have several other important characteristics that are relevant for alternative and activist new media projects. First, they help 'mediate' or facilitate communication among members of communities. As Phil Agre (1998, p. 81) puts it, genres are the "meeting point between the process of producing media materials and the process of using them." The authors of an analysis of Web genres note that "Genres are useful because they make communications more easily recognizable and understandable by recipients" (Crowston & Williams, 2000, p. 203). Remarking on one-way mass media like cinema and television, Denis McQuail has observed that "The genre may be considered as a practical device for helping any mass medium to produce consistently and efficiently and to relate its production to the expectations of its audience . . . a mechanism for ordering the relations between producers and consumers" (McQuail, 2005, p. 370).

Thus, genres are the means for creating and maintaining community and social context, and the cultural products of those communities and contexts. But they can also be so specific to a certain group's worldview or situation that outsiders may not understand them – so genres can also act as boundaries or markers that exclude outsiders and reinforce the power of insiders, as with youth subcultures, for example (Hebdige, 1979). Sonia Livingstone has pointed out that "different genres are concerned to establish different world views" (Livingstone, 1990, p. 155). Daniel Chandler (2000) observes that "Any text requires what is sometimes called 'cultural capital' on the part of its audience to make sense of it." Indeed, "recognition of a particular genre is one sign of membership in a particular community" (Crowston & Williams, 2000, p. 203).

Another important point about genres is that they are not fixed or static, but active, dynamic modes of communication and expression that change with their users' circumstances and interests. Some genres (the mystery novel, the television situation comedy, the scientific journal article, the newspaper editorial, the email message) have remained fairly stable over time because they have remained consistently meaningful and useful to the people who use them, and therefore feel no need to modify them. But other genres may change as rapidly as the communities that create and circulate them. Dramatic recent examples include the blending of personal web pages, instant messaging, tagging and bookmarking, and entertainment in social media like Twitter or Facebook, as well as DIY "mash-ups" of music and video clips such as those exchanged among high-school-age fans of Japanese *anime* (Ito, 2009 [2008]). And, as these examples suggest, genres do not stand alone: members of a community commonly employ a variety of complementary genres in their interactions, which have been called genre systems (Bazerman, 1995) or genre repertoires (Orlikowski & Yates, 1994).

To illustrate these preliminary points about genres, then, we can outline the five main genres covered in this book, along with the social/cultural domains they concern and some of their typical forms and purposes (see Table 1.1).

Culture jamming is a genre which critiques popular/ mainstream culture, particularly corporate capitalism, commercialism, and consumerism. Here, media artists and activists appropriate and "repurpose" elements from popular culture to make new works with an ironic or subversive point – put another way, culture jamming "mines" mainstream culture to critique it. As a strategy for making political art, culture jamming predates the internet. (As we will see in the next chapter, many of its signature tactics originated in European Dada and Situationism.) Early culture jamming projects borrowed elements from mass media and pop culture sources, especially print and broadcast advertising and corporate image communications (e.g., logos, slogans, and products); classic

Table 1.1. Genres of alternative and activist new media			
Genre	*Social domain*	*Forms*	*Purposes*
Culture jamming	Popular culture, mainstream media, corporate advertising	Appropriated images, sound, text from popular culture	Cultural critique, political and economic commentary
Alternative computing	Computing, telecoms, media infrastructure (hardware and software)	Hacking, open source system design, file sharing	Open access to and use of information and IT
Participatory journalism	Reporting, news, commentary, public opinion	Online news services, blogs, Indymedia	Covering under-reported groups and issues, investigative reporting
Mediated mobilization	Social movements, identity, cultural politics, lifestyles	Social media, mobs, virtual worlds, blogs	Activist mobilization, lifestyle examples ("prophecy")
Commons knowledge	Expertise, academic/technical disciplines and institutions, Socially sanctioned knowledge	Tagging, bookmarking, wikis, "crowdsourcing"	Mobilizing "outsider," amateur knowledge, comprehensive collection and organization of diverse, arcane knowledge

examples include the work of the Canadian magazine and web-site *Adbusters* (http://www.adbusters.org). However, with the birth of the World Wide Web, the same media strategies were quickly adopted by online activists and digital media artists in the 1990s, including the launching of "memes," and so-called "guerrilla" or "viral" marketing. Culture jammers must also contend with an ongoing cycle of "reverse jamming," where radical or oppositional messages and styles are reappropriated or recuperated (Hebdige, 1979) by mainstream marketers to give their products a cool, countercultural, or anti-establishment image. More of the background and strategies of culture jamming will be explored in Chapter 3.

The genre of *alternative computing* relates to the hardware, software, and institutional power and gatekeeping of the material

ICT infrastructure. It is the province of highly skilled programmers and engineers who oppose and work around commercial
or political restraints on access to information or information
technology. In the words of media activist Mark Dery, it can be
thought of as "outlaw computer hacking *with the intent of exposing institutional or corporate wrongdoing*" (Dery, 1993, emphasis in
the original) – a practice that is often referred to as hacktivism.
Thus alternative computing combines technical expertise with
explicit ethical commitments (i.e., it is not undertaken solely
for personal gain or amusement, or for criminal purposes; see
Nissenbaum, 2004). The range of activities that can be classed as
alternative computing includes the development and distribution
of free and open source software, to the extent that open source
software designers intend it as a critique of proprietary technologies (see the GNU Manifesto of the Free Software Foundation,
http://www.gnu.org), as well as the planting of hidden bits of
code or "Easter eggs" in software programs to acknowledge the
contributions of otherwise uncredited programmers or produce
unexpected system responses, and publicly demonstrating the
susceptibility of well-known software to viruses or security
breaches (often over the system owner's objections).

Alternative computing also includes the development of programs or systems that elude or sabotage state or commercial
surveillance and censorship, encrypt data and communications,
or disable digital rights management or copy protection schemes,
in the name of preserving users' privacy, government or corporate accountability, or freedom of information, for example.
More extreme tactics include sabotage directed against organizations that activists consider to be engaging in exploitative, unjust,
or corrupt activities, such as "ping-storm" or denial-of-service
attacks that overload an organization's servers, "Google bombs"
that manipulate an organization's page rankings in the results
returned by search engines, or the redirection of searchers to
"spoof" web pages that mimic an organization's original site,
but with critical content, to political or ironic effect. As we will
see in Chapter 4, alternative computing is often traced to the

libertarian, countercultural values that developed among highly skilled programmers in the 1960s and 1970s, self-described *hackers* who considered computing to be a force for progressive social transformation and personal expression (Nissenbaum, 2004; Turner, 2006).

Participatory journalism projects, and particularly Indymedia, are web-based alternative, radical, or critical news outlets and services that adopt the practices and philosophy of public, civic, citizen, participatory or "open source" journalism to provide alternatives to mainstream news and opinion. This genre includes online news services, where news is gathered and published in much the same way as conventional print and online publications, as well as news and opinion web logs ("blogs"), where authors and readers contribute opinions and debate current events and issues. Both types of projects critique the traditions and prerogatives of establishment journalism and the press (so-called "mainstream media"), particularly the mainstream's marginalization or exclusion of local, minority, unpopular, or fringe communities, issues, and views. Often staffed by volunteers with a personal or political interest in the stories and issues they cover, Indymedia sites cultivate connectivity and interactivity within their home communities, and seek to break down the distinctions between news providers, on one hand, and readers/ citizens, on the other. In Chapter 5 we examine the Independent Media Centers (IMCs) that launched the Indymedia movement.

A fourth genre, *mediated mobilization*, relates to the domain of political/cultural organizing and social movements. It takes advantage of web-based social software tools like social network sites, personal blogs, flash mobs, and email listservs, as well as DIY digital media, to cultivate interpersonal networks online and to mobilize those networks to engage in live and mediated collective action. The example of the global justice movement discussed in Chapter 6 shows that new media technologies have emerged as powerful virtual arenas where people with similar interests can seek, find, and assess information and each other across geographic distances and social/cultural boundaries.

People develop relationships, seek and give advice and guidance, and amass and trade "reputation capital" online – all of which has had important consequences for social, cultural, and political movements. (As the discussion of social movement theory in the next chapter suggests, the internet and related technologies would seem to be ideally suited to the identity-focused needs and interests of new social movement activism.) The growing articulation of live and online/mediated interpersonal and group communication and collective action is the focus of Chapter 6.

The final genre, *commons knowledge*, relates to the content of culture itself – the nature of knowledge and expertise, how information is organized and evaluated, and who decides. Traditionally, top-down, hierarchical classification systems or taxonomies based on expert disciplinary knowledge, such as those used in library catalogs, have helped determine what kinds of information are worth collecting and how different types and areas of knowledge relate to each other. But the sheer volume and idiosyncrasy of information online has driven the creation of new tools, such as search engines and tags, that use searchers' own language, rather than the predetermined *controlled vocabularies* (search terms or technical language) approved by experts, to locate and retrieve relevant resources. This reliance on everyday language and users' own schemes for rating and classifying information has fostered the growth of folksonomies – organic, dynamic, bottom-up classification schemes for organizing and categorizing diverse, arcane, local, personal, or amateur information sources, which often challenge or critique expert disciplinary taxonomies. In Chapter 7, Wikipedia serves as a case study to show how wikis, tagging, and other tools for online collaboration have opened the way for grass-roots alternatives to expert consensus.

Alternative and Activist New Media is intended as an introduction to new media activism and a broad summary of this emerging area of study and practice. Obviously the book cannot cover every case, political debate, or cultural controversy in depth; readers are encouraged to consult the references for other works that deal with particular media technologies, activist projects, or social causes and movements at greater length.

The book is organized in a sort of hourglass scheme. It begins with a broad overview of theory and history in Chapters 1 and 2, followed by five chapters dealing with the individual genres sketched above. Each of these five chapters provides a general background discussion of the genre in question, and uses one major example to illustrate the main points. In the final chapter, the discussion broadens again to consider the mediation perspective in communication study, particularly the aspects of reconfiguration and remediation as defining modes of communicative action across the genres. The book closes with a brief consideration of mediation as a useful way forward for theorizing and empirical research about communication and technology, and new media and society.

CHAPTER 2

The Roots of Alternative and Activist New Media

It can be tempting to assume that new media, and particularly the internet, have transformed the nature of human communication and culture and made all previous modes of expression and interaction obsolete. As noted in Chapter 1, we tend to equate "new" with unprecedented, and to forget that successful innovations are almost always built on the foundations of existing techniques and systems. This applies not only to media and information technologies themselves, but also to *how* people use them, and what they use them *for*.

In this chapter we explore two important sources of influence on today's alternative and activist uses of new media, one cultural and one social/political. The first is the legacy of activist art, especially the work of Dada and the Situationist International, which combined radical politics with provocative new uses of media, performance, and language. The second is the study of social movements as mechanisms or agents of social change, particularly the identity-centered *new social movements* perspective and subsequent theory developed since the 1960s. Both streams have origins in the early twentieth century, and both have helped shape the ways that today's activists, artists, and movements use new media technologies to express their ideas, articulate their interests, organize resources and people, and achieve their purposes.

Obviously, a single chapter cannot possibly capture the range and depth of scholarship that already exists about Dada, the Situationists, or new social movements. Each topic is the subject of an exhaustive literature in its own right, and readers who are particularly interested in them can find many more detailed sources in the References. Instead, the purpose of this chapter is to introduce some basic background regarding these political and cultural movements, and to show how their core ideas and strategies have resurfaced as defining features of today's alternative and activist new media projects. We begin with historical sketches of Dada, the Situationist International, and the development of social movement studies, particularly the rise of new social movements, and then review themes, ideas, and recent literature that link these movements and online activism. At the end of the chapter, we return to the discussion of genres that began in Chapter 1, and lay out a conceptual framework for understanding alternative and activist new media genres derived from their historical and intellectual precedents in activist art and new social movements.

Cultural roots: Dada and Situationism

Cultural critics and scholars have long recognized the ties between today's "remix culture" – the sampling, fragmentation, juxtaposition, and recombination of disparate elements of text, image, and sound to create new works – and the availability of easy-to-use digital media technologies (e.g., Manovich, 2007). But as numerous critics and historians have pointed out, the cultural sensibility of radical discontinuity and rupture of everyday experience that is commonplace in contemporary media culture can be traced as far back as Dada, which emerged in Europe at the time of World War I (Dickerman, 2005; Hopkins, 2004; Hughes, 1991; Lippard, 1971). In the 1950s and 1960s, a related sensibility – and some of the same tactics – were revived in France among the artists and writers of the Situationist International, in response to pervasive consumer culture, military/colonial powers, and the disabling, ideological "spectacle" generated by global systems of mass communication and cultural domination. The critique by the Situationist International has found a fertile new arena in activist new media (Best & Kellner, 1999; Downing et al., 2001).

As we will see, many of the techniques, styles, and strategies worked out in Dada and Situationism have been absorbed into what might be called the "house style" of today's digital culture, especially of alternative and activist projects whose aim is to overturn dominant, taken-for-granted meanings of everyday life and politics. Dada and Situationism were by no means the only cultural precursors of digital media that used fragmentation, discontinuity, incongruity, or juxtaposition as communicative strategies; we might think of Cubism, Futurism, Surrealism, Conceptual Art, Pop Art, and other twentieth-century approaches as well. However, Dada and Situationism are particularly relevant for the present discussion because of their explicitly political objectives, their critique of dominant economic and political regimes, and their ready appropriation and adaptation of popular media technologies and content to confront and intervene in mainstream culture and politics.

Early twentieth-century media culture: Dada

> And so Dada was born of a need for independence, of a distrust toward unity. Those who are with us preserve their freedom. We recognize no theory. We have enough cubist and futurist academies: laboratories of formal ideas. . . . Let each man proclaim: there is a great negative work of destruction to be accomplished. We must sweep and clean. . . . Freedom: Dada Dada Dada, a roaring of tense colors, and interlacing of opposites and of all contradictions, grotesques, inconsistencies: LIFE.
> Tristan Tzara, *Dada Manifesto 1918* (Tzara, 1971 [1918], pp. 15, 20)

Dada was conceived and played out between about 1915 and 1925 by an international roster of artists and writers across half a dozen European cities and New York, in the shadow of what was then called the "Great War" (Dickerman, 2005; Lippard, 1971). The origins of the word itself would be debated in later years among surviving Dadaists and art historians, but all agreed that it was deliberately chosen for its absurd, childish quality, and as a word that meant little or nothing in any of the languages of the artists involved (Dachy, 2006 [2005]; Hopkins, 2004). The founders of Dada were profoundly shocked by the slaughter and waste of modern, mechanized warfare. Several of them had served in the war (Otto Dix, Max Ernst, Louis Aragon, Hannah Höch, Hans Richter), and some sustained serious physical and psychological injuries. Others fled to neutral Zurich to avoid the conflict or to New York before the United States entered the war, or claimed disabilities that exempted them from military service. Some observers have argued that the alienation between the older generation who promoted and glorified the war and the younger men sent to fight it produced the twentieth century's original "generation gap" (Hughes, 1991).

The Dadaists were also outraged by what they saw as the dehumanization associated with industrial mass production and the associated rise of mass consumerism, which, along with the war, seemed utterly to have superseded the values and aspirations of nineteenth-century European high culture. As Donald Egbert (1970, p. 296) describes it, "[Dada] wanted to shock in order to reveal the demonic vacuum at the heart of a self-destroying civilization." The emerging media culture from the teens to the 1930s (a period made famous by the critic Walter Benjamin as the "age of mechanical reproduction") grew up around radio and the wireless telegraph, illustrated newspapers and magazines, newsreels, propaganda, and marketing techniques, all of which were used to present the war with a new and disturbing immediacy, and consumer goods as the fulfillment of irresistible desires. Consequently the Dadaists rejected idealistic notions of "art for art's sake" and transcendence, in favor of an "anti-art" stance that proclaimed art to be inseparable from the subjective experience of everyday life: "the implicit question the dadaists posed for themselves was how to reimagine artistic practice in this age of media and technological warfare" (Dickerman, 2005, p. 7).

Dada was technologically innovative: artists adopted and merged new media technologies like photography, cinema, and mass-produced typography and printing with high-art forms like painting, sculpture, and theater. Taking a cue from the earlier Cubist technique of collage (where artists glued mundane materials like newsprint, oilcloth, or woven-cane chair seats into paintings), the Dadaists developed techniques of abstraction and photo-montage, assembling fragments of photographs and text into disjointed and sometimes random imagery that lampooned the savagery and absurdity of war, politics, and popular culture (Figure 2.1).[1]

In fact, chance, randomness, and "accident" comprised a central theme in the Dada aesthetic, reflecting the senselessness that, from the Dada viewpoint, had come to dominate modern life (Egbert, 1970; Hughes, 1991). Tristan Tzara, self-proclaimed Dada leader and author of the *Dada Manifesto 1918* quoted above, wrote poems by clipping words out of newspapers, shaking them in a bag, and sticking them down in the order they were drawn out. Similarly, Hans Arp cut out "irregular pieces of paper, allowed them to fall, and used the resulting chance arrangement as a point of departure for pasting them into collages" (Egbert, 1970, p. 295).

Dadaists fabricated sculptures using all kinds of found objects, from clothing to machine parts. These culminated with Marcel Duchamp's famous *readymades*: bottle racks, bicycle wheels, or urinals signed and exhibited as the artist's original work, and as scathing commentaries on industrialism and mass consumption. Beginning with the movement's launch at the Cabaret Voltaire in Zurich in 1916, Dada artists and writers held events, or "provocations," that combined art installations, poetry readings, outlandish dramatic presentations and musical performances, and political commentary, and demanded audience participation. They interrupted public cultural events and religious services, and accosted priests and officials in the street. Dadaists published experimental journals of Dada poetry, images, and essays, adopted multiple aliases and pseudonyms, created new identities and alter egos. The so-called "gratuitous gesture" became a central Dada tactic – using art to disrupt the commonplace and compel new ways of seeing reality (Lippard, 1971).

Figure 2.1. *Festival Dada* by Hanna Höch.

Source: Christie's Images/Corbis.

Guy Debord and the Situationist International
In the 1950s and 1960s, the French philosopher, critic, and filmmaker Guy Debord and a small band of other artists and writers drawn from a range of earlier groups and collectives (including the Lettrist International, the CoBrA [Copenhagen–Brussels–Amsterdam] artists, and the International Movement for an Imaginist Bauhaus; Ford, 2005) formed the Situationist International (SI) in Paris. Their critique of post-war French society and its capitalist and colonialist foundations blended the early twentieth-century shock tactics of Dada and Surrealism (the latter of which itself had been a response to capitalist accumulation) with the complex political economy of post-Stalinist Marxism.

The Situationists recognized that the modern consumer culture that had dismayed the proponents of Dada in the early twentieth century had not been overcome. Rather, it had evolved into a new, pervasive, spectacular form, in which the images of consumption and commodities, even more than the goods themselves, produced and circulated in an endless cycle of representation and manipulation of desires by mass media industries and technologies, had come to dominate culture and to substitute for authentic personal experience, creativity, and cultural participation. Debord summarized the point: "An earlier stage in the economy's domination of social life entailed an obvious downgrading of *being* into *having*. . . .The present stage, in which social life is completely taken over by the accumulated products of the economy, entails a generalized shift from *having* to appearing. . . .The spectacle is *capital* accumulated to the point where it becomes image" (Debord, 1994 [1967], § 17, p. 17, § 34, p. 24, emphasis in the original).

The all-encompassing spectacle, reinforced and reproduced in politics, education, leisure, and private life, generated a new form of alienation that superseded reality, immobilized people's ability to act for themselves, eliminated the possibility of resistance to political, cultural, and economic domination, and reduced people to mere spectators in their own lives and societies. For anyone in media-dominated, spectacular society, the new form of alienation "works like this: the more he contemplates, the less he lives; the more readily he recognizes his own needs in the images of need proposed by the dominant system, the less he understands his own existence and his own desires. . . .The spectator feels at home nowhere, for the spectacle is everywhere" (Debord, 1994 [1967], § 30, p. 23).

The only way to confront and destroy the power of the spectacle, said the Situationist International, was for people to construct their own alternative, disruptive *situations* in everyday life that overturned the dominant, media-driven representations of culture and politics. In an essay originally published in 1961, "Instructions for Taking Up Arms," Debord declared:

> Revolution has to be reinvented, that's all. . . .People's creativity and participation can only be awakened by a collective project explicitly concerned with all aspects of lived experience. The only way to "arouse the masses" is to expose the appalling contrast between the possible constructions of life and its present poverty. . . . We don't claim to be developing a new revolutionary program all by ourselves. We say that this program in the process of formation will one day practically contest the ruling reality, and that we will participate in that contestation. (Debord, 1981c [1961], pp. 63–5)

Like the Dadaists, the Situationists believed that there should be no separation of art from everyday life and experience: "The Situationist project . . . demanded an overcoming of all forms of separation, so that individuals could directly produce their own life, culture, and forms of social interaction" (Best & Kellner, 1999, p. 133).

In their writings, films, and other works, the Situationist International used several main strategies for constructing situations. The first was the *dérive*, literally a "drift," in which, in an "attempt to discover lost intimations of real life behind the perfectly composed face of modern society' (Marcus, 2002, p. 7), participants would wander through urban streets and spaces, making observations, encounters, and interpretations that challenged taken-for-granted views of life and action, and indeed redefining the meaning of urban space as a subjective cultural experience (Sadler, 1998). In the early 1950s, Debord and his Lettrist International colleagues "used to drink too much and plan [such] systematic rambles" (Jappe, 1999, p. 45). The *dérive* was a somewhat similar strategy to that of the strolling *flâneurs* in late nineteenth-century Paris celebrated by Charles Baudelaire and Walter Benjamin (Benjamin, 1968 [1955]), and more recently has been compared to the experience of navigating among information sources and social networks online (Hartmann, 2004). Debord described the method in the second issue of the group's journal, *Internationale Situationniste*: "In a dérive one or more persons during a certain period drop their usual motives for movement and action, their relations, their work and leisure activities, and let themselves be drawn by the attractions of the terrain and the encounters they find there' (Debord, 1981a [1958], p. 50).

Although the Situationists had largely abandoned the *dérive* strategy by the early 1960s (Ross, 2002a), in his 1978 film *In girum imus nocte et consumimur igni*, Debord would reflect, "We did not seek the formula for changing the world in books, but in wandering. Ceaselessly drifting for days on end, none resembling the one before. . . .We did not go on television to announce our discoveries. We did not seek grants from academic foundations or praise from newspaper intellectuals. We brought fuel to the flames" (Debord, 2003 [1978]).

A second, and better-known, strategy advocated by the Situationists was *détournement*, which used Dada-style techniques of collage and montage to create new works from "found" cultural materials, but with even greater emphasis on subverting or inverting the original meanings of the borrowed images, texts, or other elements. As early as 1956, Debord and his Lettrist associate Gil Wolman had argued that the new strategy should go beyond the simple ironies of the Dadaists:

> The literary and artistic heritage of humanity should be used
> for partisan propaganda purposes. . . . Since the negation of

the bourgeois conception of art and artistic genius has become pretty much old hat, [Duchamp's] drawing of a mustache on the *Mona Lisa* is [now] no more interesting than the original version of that painting. We must now push this process to the point of negating the negation. (Debord & Wolman, 1981 [1956], p. 9)

Thus *détournement* recombined and juxtaposed fragmentary materials and elements from existing sources to achieve new, incongruous, and subversive meanings. It was a strategy of "diverting elements of affirmative bourgeois culture to revolutionary ends, of distorting received meanings" (McDonough, 2002, pp. xiii–xiv), "a collage-like technique whereby preexisting elements were reassembled into new creations" (Jappe, 1999, p. 48). The concept also "entails the notion of detour, the intent to circumvent an obstacle, and contains elements of game playing and warfare. *Détournement* turns the reader or public into a warrior" (Kaufmann, 2006 [2001], p. 37) (see Figure 2.2).

Many of the most famous examples of SI-inspired *détournement* were created in connection with the "events" of May 1968 in France, by students whose angry protests over oppressive university policies and conditions sparked widespread demonstrations and strikes that paralyzed the nation and eventually helped unseat Charles de Gaulle as head of state (Bourges, 1968; Quattrocchi & Nairn, 1998 [1968]; Ross, 2002b; Seale & McConville, 1968; Touraine, 1971a [1968]).[2] The students embraced the advice of Réné Viénet, a founding member of the SI, who insisted that any effective Situationist media strategy should détourn the media technologies, techniques, and images of the spectacle itself, for example, by:

1 *Experimentation in the détournement of romantic photo-comics* as well as "pornographic" photos. . . . we bluntly impose their real truth by restoring real dialogues by adding or altering speech bubbles . . . .
2 *The promotion of guerrilla tactics in the mass media* . . . .
3 *The development of situationist comics.* Comic strips are the only truly popular literature of our century . . . .
4 *The production of situationist films.* . . . We should appropriate

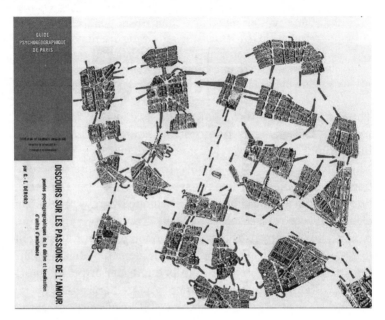

Figure 2.2. Paris détourned.

the first stammerings of this new [film] language; and above all its most consummate and modern examples . . . newsreels, previews, and above all, filmed ads.

(Viénet, 1981 [1967], pp. 213–15, emphasis in the original)

Using graffiti, posters, comic book art, and improvised costumes and street theater, students put the principle of *détournement* into practice, with slogans like "Never work!," "Beauty is in the street," "I take my desires for reality because I believe in the reality of my desires," and, perhaps most poetically, referring to the cobblestone *pavés* that protesters dug out of the Paris streets to throw in clashes with police, "Under the paving stones, the beach" (Ford, 2005; Gray, 1998 [1974]; Viénet, 1992 [1968]) (Figure 2.3).

Debord's insistence on the construction of confrontational – even violent – situations as a method for reclaiming authentic social life and cultural experience in the face of the alienating

Figure 2.3. May 1968 Paris graffiti.

Source: Gray, C. (ed. and trans.) (1998). *Leaving the 20th century: The incomplete work of the Situationist International.* London: Rebel Press, p. 24. (Originally published by Free Fall Press, 1974.)

spectacle and commodity culture found a ready audience among student protesters and their allies. The SI's ideas moved from the obscure fringes of the avant-garde to the lecture halls of universities in Strasbourg and Nanterre, and ultimately to the walls and barricades in the Paris streets and the student-occupied Sorbonne.

Many of the main grievances of the students were articulated, and the revolt anticipated, in a 1966 pamphlet entitled *On the Poverty of Student Life.* Written jointly by members of the SI and a radical student group at the University of Strasbourg, l'Association Fédérale Générale des Étudiants de Strasbourg (SI/ AFGES, 1981 [1966]), it was later distributed in Paris by the SI. The essay rejected the "failed" programs of classical Marxism and the anarchists, and argued that students, rather than industrial workers or the establishment left, were the proper agents of revolutionary social change in an emerging society dominated by media commodities and spectacle. Subjugated by impoverishment, the "protracted infancy" of student life imposed by their families and the state, overcrowded university facilities, and the growing alignment of higher education with employer and state interests, students had begun to see the whole system of higher education as a machine geared to produce spectators, rather than actors, in society. Their studies seemed to them merely a "rehearsal for [their] ultimate role as a conservative element in the commodity system. . . . the student is a product of modern society just like Godard and Coca-Cola" (pp. 320, 325). The essay noted admiringly that American students were already "refusing to accept the business and institutional roles for which their specialized studies have been designed to prepare them. . . . the rebelling American youth are already seeking a coherent revolutionary alternative from within the "affluent society"' (pp. 328–9).

The role of students as the central agents of revolt against spectacle and commodity culture was also analyzed in depth by Alain Touraine, a French labor sociologist and professor at the University of Nanterre. The student revolt had flared first at Nanterre, in March 1968, before spreading to Paris and elsewhere in France in May and June. As we will see later in this chapter, Touraine was an important early proponent of new social movement theory. He recognized that the fundamental conflicts and dynamics of what he was the first to call postindustrial or "programmed" society were mainly knowledge-based and cultural. Touraine argued that in the changing post-war social context, actors' subjectivity and self-expression would play a greater role in social change than the classic economic, institutional, or class relations and determinisms associated with industrial society – a shift that would spur the development of new social movements.

On a more practical level, Touraine was actively involved as a mediator between students and the Nanterre university administration during the events of 1968, often defending the students. As one of his colleagues recalled: ". . . at the centre of the turmoil . . . one would find him on the barricades with the student revolutionary leaders, then dialoguing with records and ministers on the radio, while engaged in impossible negotiations in the middle of the night during the time when Parisians thought the insurrection would gain victory' (Crozier, 1996, p. 15). Like Debord and the SI, Touraine saw the student protests as symptomatic of the increasingly industrial-style training and socialization of creative professionals in the university. In *The May Movement*, he asked, "What do students have in common with workers in aerospace, radio and television technicians, and managerial circles in industry? All are – or will be in the future – highly trained, white-collar workers who share an opposition to those who direct and exploit their expertise" (Touraine, 1971a [1968], p. 7). In a passage that seemed to echo Situationist views, Touraine insisted that creative social actors resist domination by appeals to "imagination against pseudorationality, to sexuality against the art of compromise, to creativity as opposed to the automatic passing on of traditions and codes" (Touraine, 1971b [1969], p. 11).

Social/political roots: social movement theory

A second important resource for understanding contemporary alternative and activist new media projects is social movement theory, and particularly the emergence of *new social movement theory* and subsequent, related perspectives on collective action developed since the 1960s. The "new" social movements perspective contends that the ideologically driven, society-wide movements of the industrial age – the labor movement, antiwar/ peace movements, and civil rights, for example – gave way in the postindustrial, postmodern era of the 1960s to the 1980s to smaller-scale movements more focused on wide-ranging issues or concerns (e.g., green/environmentalism, animal rights, anti-nuclear, anti-globalization, consumer rights), or group identity or lifestyle (e.g., the women's movement, gay rights, national/

ethnic/language/ cultural/religious identity movements). Today, many of these elements have become hallmarks of global-scale movements against economic inequity, cultural domination, and political injustice.

Theorists noted that participants in new social movements (NSMs) also tend to be drawn from the ranks of better-educated, creative "knowledge workers," who frame their grievances in symbolic and cultural terms rather than as a struggle over material goods or economic class interests. Alberto Melucci, a leading theorist of NSMs, observed in the late 1990s that "In the last thirty years emerging social conflicts in complex societies have not expressed themselves through political action, but rather have raised cultural challenges to the dominant language, to the codes that organize information and shape social practices" (Melucci, 1996, p. 8). That is, the participants in NSMs have been precisely those members of society who are most involved in the production and circulation of culture, including media culture and information technology.

In the discussion of mediated mobilization in Chapter 6, we focus more closely on studies that address the relationship between social movements and new media, particularly in the process of movement mobilization. Some researchers contend that new media have provided a platform ideally suited to the concerns with cultural codes, values, creativity, the search for identity, and meaning and personal experience that typify NSMs. Here, we take a longer-term view of how ideas about social movements have evolved over time.

Social movements: changing views about change
For many people who witnessed the social, political, and cultural upheavals of the 1960s and 1970s, the era represents something of a "golden age" for social movements and social change, particularly in the U.S. and Europe. The civil rights, antiwar, student, and green movements have had lasting consequences for politics and culture on both sides of the Atlantic. Movement leaders built on the experience and legacy of earlier movements,

for example by adopting some of their organizational strategies (such as the community and trade union organizing used in the labor movement) and operational tactics (such as the educational and nonviolent civil disobedience techniques used by anticolonial movements and women's suffrage activists). Debates will continue regarding the significance of "the sixties." But the period will certainly continue to be seen as a time of intense political and social activism that produced important changes in cultural attitudes, the distribution of political power, and legal rights and protections for underrepresented groups and interests; it also generated a range of new approaches to the study of social movements.

Collective behavior theory   Not surprisingly, given the social and political shifts of the time, the 1960s and 1970s also saw an upsurge in theorizing and research into the nature and course of social movements. Existing theories seemed inadequate to explain the power and influence of the most important movements of the day, notably the civil rights and student/antiwar movements. The classical "collective behavior" view of social movements that had prevailed up to that point was developed in the 1920s and 1930s by the interactionist "Chicago School" sociologists, including Robert Park, Ernest Burgess, and Herbert Blumer, who themselves had been influenced by European theories of mass psychology and mass society elaborated by Gustave Le Bon, Gabriel Tarde, and others at the turn of the century (Diani & Eyerman, 1992; Neidhardt & Rucht, 1991). Both lines of thought defined collective behavior as a sudden, spontaneous, disorganized outbreak of crowd behavior that defied "normal" social conduct. As Aldon Morris (2000, p. 445) put it, movements were thought to arise "in highly charged contexts characterized by mass enthusiasm, collective excitement, rumor, social contagion, and mass hysteria."

The Chicago sociologists' views differed slightly in emphasis from those of European theorists. Where Europeans saw the breakdown of social order and the anarchy of the mob, at least some Americans (like Robert Park, and, later, Ralph Turner and Lewis Killian) saw opportunities for the creation of new values and new institutional order in spontaneous mass movements. However, both perspectives tended to focus on the emotional or irrational quality of mass movements, their spontaneity or random appearance, the marginality or alienation of the participants, the "contagion" of ideas and actions among susceptible social groups, and the manipulability of the crowd or "mass," especially by media and propaganda. Blumer's seminal 1939 classification of types of collective behavior was later summed up as: "(1) crowdlike behavior such as panic and riots, (2) mass behavior which is collective but not organized, (3) public and public opinion, (4) propaganda, psychological warfare and communist tactics, and (5) social movements" (Neidhardt & Rucht, 1991, p. 423).[3]

In the late 1950s, however, Ralph Turner and Lewis Killian (1957) proposed a variation on the classic account of social movements in their book *Collective Behavior*. They rejected the idea that movements were sudden, irrational eruptions of collective will (what Hank Johnston, Enrique Laraña, and Joseph Gusfield [1994] would later deride as the "volcanic" view of social movements). Rather, as Turner (1969, p. 390) later argued, movements are generated by the emergence of new norms or values around which people may mobilize: ". . . any major social movement depends upon and promotes some normative revision." Thus, according to Turner and Killian, social movements represent the first stage of social reorganization around new values and expectations that social conditions should change according to those values.

Resource mobilization theory   By the 1960s, *Collective Behavior* had become a standard text in American social movement studies. However, to many scholars the collective behavior approach, even as amended by Turner and Killian, still had a number of problems, not least its failure to describe or understand the larger organizational and institutional contexts of social change, or to see social movement participants as rational agents with the ability to pursue their interests and to weigh the costs and benefits of participation. To these critics, "The actor in social movements and in protest action was not under the sway of sentiments, emotions, and ideologies. . . but rather . . . the logic of costs and benefits as well as opportunities for action." Thus the tactics and strategies of movements could be seen as a "rational game" (Johnston, Laraña & Gusfield, 1994, p. 5). A group of American researchers, led by Mayer Zald, Doug McAdam, John McCarthy, Charles Tilly, Sidney Tarrow, and their associates, advanced a variety of approaches under the rubric of *resource mobilization theory*, whose common theme was the application of concepts from organization theory to social movement studies (Diani & Eyerman, 1992; Gusfield, 1994; Klandermans, 1991; Morris, 2000; Morris & Herring, 1987; Neidhardt & Rucht, 1991). Sociologist Joseph Gusfield distinguished the two points of view:

> From the point of view of collective behavior theorists, what was important about a movement was its consequences for change. For resource mobilization theorists, the movement had to be studied as a form of organizational behavior, that is, gathering and utilizing resources. . . . [resource mobilization theory] brought utilitarian considerations of costs and benefits into the picture. (Gusfield, 1994, p. 61)

Adherents of the resource mobilization view held that the most effective social movements are those whose leaders and organizers are able to recognize the political, organizational, economic, and technological "opportunity structures" available to the movement, to identify incentives for action, and to capture and use those opportunities and incentives. As opposed to the collective behavior approach, which tended to cast movements as entities that behave like individuals with "mass" motivations, emotions, and beliefs, resource mobilization theory focused on *how* movements organize themselves, how participants make choices and use resources from the network of larger social and institutional structures beyond the movement itself to achieve their goals, and how movements persist over time.

Resource mobilization theory certainly helped to reorient the study of the major social movements of the post-war era, especially the civil rights and antiwar movements. It shifted focus away from a view of movements as spontaneous, disorganized outbreaks of irrational "mob psychology" and toward a view that highlighted the deliberate and strategic decisions of movement participants as they identified and secured resources to support movement needs and aims. Resource mobilization quickly came to dominate social movement research: by the early 1980s one study found that about 70 percent of all published research articles on social movements to that time were written from the resource mobilization perspective (Morris & Herring, 1987).

New social movement theory   However, resource mobilization theory's emphasis on rational choice, organizational strategies, and "opportunity structures" left some analysts unpersuaded, particularly those who believed that the student and counter-culture movements of the late 1960s signaled an important cultural shift away from the hierarchical social relations and bureaucratic control structures of industrialism, and toward a new "postindustrial" or "programmed" society built on the foundations of networked information technologies, media culture, and an emerging class of highly educated, creative "knowledge workers" (Diani & Eyerman, 1992; Eyerman, 1992; Johnston, Laraña & Gusfield, 1994; Klandermans, 1991; Melucci, 1989, 1994, 1996; Morris, 2000; Morris & Mueller, 1992; Offe, 1985; Touraine, 1971a [1968], 1971b [1969], 1977 [1973], 1981 [1978]; Turner, 1969). For European theorists like Alain Touraine, Claus Offe, Alberto Melucci, and Mario Diani, among others, neither American approach – collective behavior or resource mobilization – had much to say about the agency and action of the people actually engaged in novel, "unconventional" forms of social activism, such as the feminist, gay rights, new age, anti-nuclear, animal rights, and environmental movements. They proposed that these new collective actions could be seen as "new social movements" (NSMs).

As Melucci (who studied with Touraine) would later point out, collective behavior presented movements as "action without actors," while resource mobilization and other structural accounts like Marxism saw movements as abstract "actors without action." Or, put another way, collective behavior could hypothesize the *why* of movements but not the *how*, while resource mobilization and structural frameworks could account for the *how* but not the *why* (Melucci, 1989, pp. 18–22). In the process of conceptualizing social movements as autonomous entities, abstract "forces," or organizational maneuvers, theorists had lost a clear sense of the people engaged in the everyday activities and practices involved in social movements and social change.

Thus, theorists have argued that a number of key characteristics distinguish NSMs from previous types of movements. Many of these characteristics have become core elements of more recent social movement research. Different writers have emphasized different factors, but, broadly speaking, the literature highlights the following features as distinctive. The first three have to do with new social movement *actors*, while the remainder concern the nature of *action* in movements.

Participants and constituencies. A central tenet of NSM theory is that new social movements arose in the context of larger social shifts in the late twentieth century from industrial to "postindustrial" or information society. During this period, information and service industries, dominated by "information work" and "knowledge workers," emerged as the key economic sector. In contrast to previous social movements (especially the labor movement), which identified the industrial working class as the prime collective "actor" and economic/class inequalities and grievances as the drivers of social and economic change, new social movements were seen to be organized more around the shared identities, professions, interests, values, and experiences of individual actors.

Alain Touraine was one of the first analysts to identify well-educated, creative, "white-collar" knowledge workers as pivotal

CHARACTERISTICS OF NEW SOCIAL MOVEMENTS

New Social Movement Actors

- *Participants and Constituencies*
  Knowledge/information workers, professionals, well-educated, creative workers

- *Collective Identity*
  Independence from institutional structures and categories (e.g., class); focus on construction and sharing of common subjectivity, worldviews, and experiences; identification with personal attributes, e.g., age, gender, sexual orientation, ethnicity, language, professional background; emphasis on cultural, symbolic causes

- *Meaning and Symbolic Production*
  Construction and control of information, symbolic resources, representations of group interests, expertise, norms, values

New Social Movement Action

- *Movements as Social Networks*
  Loosely affiliated, informal, anti-hierarchical networks of interpersonal relations; micromobilization; small, diverse groups in *ad hoc* linkages; segmented, diffuse, decentralized, autonomous organizational forms; focus on particular, local concerns; constant flux and reorganization

- *Everyday Life*
  Movement activities integrated into daily life rather than intense, episodic events; action linked to lifestyle, personal issues; conflation of personal and collective concerns; action by example, prefigurative action, "prophecy," acting by personal example

- *Use of Media and ICTs*
  Extensive, sophisticated use of media and ICT (information and communication technology), communication and representation as a principal field and form of action in itself

- *"Unconventional" Action Repertoires*
  Reliance on expressive, creative, *ad hoc* disruption and resistance; small scale, decentralized action; "sub-institutional," "extra-parliamentary" exertion of power, spontaneous action

> - *Permanent, Transnational Campaigns*
>   Movement action extends over time and space, consistent with daily life experience (vs. focused on specific grievances, events, or remedies in particular times/places); continuous realignment and reorganization within a broad field of interests and values; movements and action as ordinary, everyday modes of change and perpetual engagement

actors and agents of social change in postindustrial societies. The shift from industrial to postindustrial societies would depend "much more directly than ever before on knowledge, and hence on the capacity of society to call forth creativity" (Touraine, 1971b [1969], p. 5). As he noted in *The Voice and the Eye* (perhaps reflecting on the alienation experienced by students who participated in the events of May '68), actors in new social movements are the "fraction of the *professionals* who perform the role that used to be played by qualified workers in industrial society. They speak in the name of knowledge against an apparatus that seeks to subject knowledge to its own interests" (Touraine, 1981 [1978], p. 22, emphasis in the original). They are "the new middle class and . . . well-educated young people working in the civil service" (Klandermans, 1991, p. 27). Or, as Ron Eyerman put it, "new social movements are to a great extent peopled by the highly educated and the content of their critique of modern society builds on both their educational experience and their occupational expectations" (Eyerman, 1992, p. 47).

Collective identity. The role of identity and subjective experience in movement formation and action is another defining feature of NSMs. Instead of representing an overarching, collective "class interest" or ideology, participants in NSMs seek to articulate their subjective experiences and interests and to maintain their independence from institutional domination. In emerging movements, creative, articulate actors resist domination by sharing these subjective experiences and values with one another to construct a collective (if localized) identity. Contemporary "opposition movements defend identity and community but imagine at the same time a society more favorable to initiative, personal development, and interpersonal communications" (Touraine, 1992, p. 74).

Participants in NSMs are more likely to identify with and organize around their youth, gender, sexual orientation, ethnicity, language, or professional background than with abstract categories like class. Beginning in the 1960s, analysts began to find that "an increasing number of movements and conflicts articulated grievances that were not based on economic and class interests . . . [but] were based on less 'objective' elements such as identity, status, humanism, and spirituality" (Johnston, Laraña & Gusfield, 1994, p. 21). The values and causes they support are often cultural or symbolic, and more closely linked to their identity than to broad economic grievances or class conflicts. "[A]scribed characteristics such as sex, age, skin color, even neighborhood and religion, contribute to the establishment and delimitation of communities, the creation of sub-culturally protected communications groups which further the search for personal and collective identity" (Habermas, 1981, p. 36).

The focus on identity thus marks a major departure from more traditional movements. In postindustrial society, "The freedom to have which characterized . . . industrial society has been replaced by the freedom to be" (Melucci, 1989, pp. 177–8) and as a consequence the "search for identity, the quest for self . . . [in which] we seek to fit back together the scattered fragments of a human experience" (Melucci, 1994, p. 112), has become a central feature of everyday life.

Meaning and symbolic production. Given the role of educated, creative "knowledge workers" and the importance of collective identity in NSMs, the construction of meaning and the control of information, symbolic resources, and representations constitute the central task of NSMs. "[New] social movements create new systems of meaning which make visible to society as a whole that new conflicts and issues have emerged" (Diani & Eyerman, 1992, p. 9). The stakes in NSMs have more to do with knowledge, culture, and the perpetual struggle of control over symbolic production and expertise than with maintaining social integration, order, or balance (as collective behavior theory proposes), or exploiting class structures, power relations, or the exchange of material resources (as stressed by resource mobilization and Marxist accounts). "The new social movements express concerns that are more cultural than economic. They aim at changing norms and values rather than productive and distributive relations" (Eyerman, 1992, p. 45).

Again, Alain Touraine was the first to articulate the need for a theory that would integrate people's subjective cultural meanings, experiences, and identities with larger-scale institutional processes (Alexander, 1996, p. 213). In Touraine's view, participants in NSMs "define themselves by their opposition to the social and cultural forces that dominate the production of symbolic goods" (Touraine, 1992, p. 66). However, among NSM theorists, Alberto Melucci is perhaps the most strongly associated with this emphasis on meaning construction in NSMs and their opposition to what he calls "dominant codes" of society:

> In the last thirty years emerging social conflicts in complex societies have not expressed themselves through political action, but rather have raised cultural challenges to the dominant language, to the codes that organize information and shape social practices. . . . It is the individual and collective reappropriation of meaning of action that is at stake in the forms of collective involvement which make the experience of change in the present a condition for creating a different future. (Melucci, 1996, pp. 8–9)

As we will see later in this chapter and in Chapter 6, symbolic production has become one of the principal theoretical concerns in the analysis of social movements, particularly the global justice movement.

Movements as social networks. Another key characteristic of new social movements is their mode of organizing, which takes the form of loosely affiliated, informal, anti-hierarchical "networks of networks" of interpersonal relations, linked to one another and to larger-scale, geographically dispersed social and cultural networks (Diani, 2003). This view, which emphasizes "micro-mobilization," contrasts with the tendency within resource mobilization theory to view networks as relatively centralized and stable, and as resources to be exploited like any others. New social movement theorists frame "social movements as social networks" (Diani & Eyerman, 1992, p. 9). They are not merely structures to be exploited instrumentally, but "'invisible' networks of small groups submerged in everyday life" that support individual participants' needs, collective identities, and part-time membership. Such networks act as "laboratories in which new experiences are invented . . . [and] given new names" (Keane & Mier, 1989, p. 6), and are particularly powerful as environments for recruiting participants. For Anne Mische, this means that previous frameworks are now outmoded: "What we need is a more dynamic conception in which social networks are seen not merely as locations for, or conduits of, cultural formations, but rather as composed of culturally constituted processes of communicative interaction" (Mische, 2003, p. 258).

In terms of organizational form, NSMs "tend to be segmented, diffuse, and decentralized . . . [with] considerable autonomy of local sections . . . [in] sharp distinction with the hierarchical, centralized organization of the working-class movement" (Johnston, Laraña & Gusfield, 1994, pp. 8–9; see also Klandermans, 1991). Among movement participants, "High value is placed on the particular, the provincial, small social spaces, decentralized forms of interaction and de-specialized activities, simple interaction and non-differentiated public spheres" (Habermas, 1981, p. 36). Organizing is woven into local, everyday experience, but is also undertaken with a global sensitivity, an awareness of being part of a larger world system that is itself in a constant state of flux and reorganization (Keane & Mier, 1989).

Everyday life. Another characteristic, closely associated with the social-network character of NSMs, is that rather than being episodic, extraordinary outbursts of action in response to specific situations or events, new movements are deeply enmeshed and acted out in the everyday lives of movement participants. Indeed, as the preceding points about identity and subjectivity suggest, participants' own lifestyles, values, and practices figure prominently in movement actions. The causes supported by movement activists often deal with the most personal or intimate aspects of life (e.g., sexual orientation, reproductive rights, dietary practices, or child rearing); more broadly, they reflect participants' shifts "from materialist to post-materialist values" (Klandermans, 1991, p. 27). In many ways, the personal/individual and the collective aspects of life are conflated in NSMs, with causes and movements enacted by individual behavior rather than in formally mobilized groups, and the movement becoming a focus for members' self-definition and the confirmation of personal identity (Johnston, Laraña & Gusfield, 1994).

Consequently, participants in new social movements also tend to "practice what they preach" in their everyday lifestyles, as a sign or message to the rest of society: ". . . actors self-consciously practise in the present the future social changes they seek" (Keane & Mier, 1989, p. 6). Social movement theorists and activists often refer to this type of activity as *prefigurative*, that is, it models the desired or ideal social conditions for others in society; it is also a mainstay of anarchist political thought (Downing, 2003, 2008). For example, in a posting on an Indymedia discussion list, one activist describes the project as "practice for the real thing . . . prefigurative politics" (quoted in Pickard, 2006b, p. 330; see also Atton, 2002; Downing, 2008). Melucci refers to this practice of movement values and identity as *prophecy*, that is, "the message that the possible is already real" (Melucci, 1994, p. 125), or creating "the experience of change in the present [as] a condition for creating a different future" (Melucci, 1989, p. 9).

Use of media and ICTs. New social movements are also distinguished by their extensive and sophisticated uses of media and information technologies, not just as tools or channels for relaying information to participants or the wider public, but as the actual field of action where movement concerns are articulated and struggles played out (Rucht, 2004). For the creative "knowledge workers" at the center of NSMs, new media and the Internet have become essential resources for action and the principal contested landscape of meaning, identity, knowledge, and values. "It is difficult to overestimate the influence of major communications industries and widespread formal education in understanding contemporary social movements" (Gusfield, 1994, p. 71).

Alain Touraine argues that in postindustrial or "programmed" society, communication has become more valuable than material wealth. "Programmed society . . . views itself as a network of relations, and the forms of behavior it rates highest are those which reinforce the ability to communicate more than to save and invest" (Touraine, 1981 [1978], p. 15). Information and information technologies are "crucial resources" for NSMs (Melucci, 1994, p. 112); the shift toward cultural concerns in NSMs is partly attributable to "the impressive development of communication technologies, [and] the creation of a global media system" (Melucci, 1996, p. 8). Melucci also identifies three distinctive "models of communicative action" that NSMs use to assert their interests and "subvert the logic of dominant codes": *prophecy* (see above); *paradox*, which movements use to demonstrate that dominant cultural codes are exhausted and no longer authoritative; and *representation*, the production and enactment of new media technologies and forms (Melucci, 1994, p. 125).

"Unconventional" action repertoires. NSMs also tend to reject traditional methods of organizing and institutional/political channels in favor of *ad hoc*, radical, creative, expressive, or disruptive action, which theorists refer to broadly as "unconventional" action (Cammaerts & van Audenhove, 2005; Dahlgren, 2005). "New social movements make extensive use of unconventional forms of action. They take a dissociative attitude toward society, as indicated by their antagonism toward politics. They

prefer small-scale, decentralized organizations, they are anti-hierarchical, and they favor direct democracy" (Klandermans, 1991, p. 27) and "forms of action [that] do not enjoy the legitimacy conferred by established political institutions" (Offe, 1985, p. 828).

A deep-seated mistrust of mainstream channels for social change – including government, political parties, cultural and educational institutions, mainstream media, and even traditional social movements – seemed to explain NSMs' attitude and approach toward action. "The new social movements are expressions of the rejection of the politics of administration and its representatives in both labor and capital" (Eyerman, 1992, p. 48). This alienation from mainstream institutions of both left and right was "related to the credibility crisis of the conventional channels for participation in Western democracies" and encouraged NSMs to create "alternative forms of participation and decision making" (Johnston, Laraña & Gusfield, 1994, p. 8), what Jürgen Habermas has called "sub-institutional, extra-parliamentary forms of protest" (Habermas, 1981, p. 33; see also Carroll & Hackett, 2006; Scott & Street, 2000). One retrospective overview of social movement theory in the 1980s noted that in NSMs "Representative democracy was dismissed in favour of grass-roots models of political participation; conventional lobbying and pressure activities were replaced by unconventional and confrontational techniques" (Diani & Eyerman, 1992, p. 7).

Some analysts have suggested that NSMs' turn away from more conventional forms and avenues of protest led them toward "radical mobilization tactics of disruption and resistance" (Johnston, Laraña & Gusfield, 1994, p. 8). Traditional social movement theory, notably resource mobilization theory, tended to overlook or downplay "the more expressive, spontaneous, and disruptive role of conflict and violence" that can appear in NSMs (Mueller, 1992, p. 18). Other observers have worried about a further turn toward violence or suppressive tactics. Touraine warns that, perhaps ironically, "the most important collective movements today are . . . the movements calling for identity, specificity and community that link cultural demands and state power and suppress, generally in a violent way, public space and social movements" (Touraine, 1992, p. 61).

Permanent, transnational campaigns. In a sense, the final characteristic of new social movements, which deals with space and time, is the culmination of the others discussed to this point and has become perhaps the most prominent aspect of "post-NSM" theorizing since the 1990s. In contrast to traditional social movements, which respond to specific grievances or events in a particular place and time, organize people and resources into formal structures, articulate specific goals and demands, and tend to disband when those goals and demands are met, NSMs tend to become "permanent" or "transnational" campaigns that extend over time and across geographic and national boundaries. For participants in NSMs, the "reappropriation of time, of space, and of relationships in the individual's daily experience" is crucial (Melucci, 1980, p. 219). Because they are expressions of activists' ongoing experiences, identities, meanings, lifestyles, and relationships, NSMs do not demobilize and remobilize in sequence, as traditional movements tend to do. Instead, they realign and reorganize continually around diverse objectives and issues within the larger landscape of activists' values and interests. In NSMs, "remote and unrelated experiences are juxtaposed" and movements coexist (Melucci, 1994, p. 117).

For example, in early work Alain Touraine insisted that, far from being disorganized, episodic breaks in social order, in postindustrial society social movements had become the primary, usual, and ongoing mode of social change. The purpose of movements is not to restore some ideal "lost balance" or social order and then quietly fade from the scene, but to generate perpetual struggle, change, and re-creation, "society's self-production" (Touraine, 1981 [1978], p. 8). As Melucci (1994, p. 116) puts it, "movements are not occasional emergencies in social life located on the margins of great institutions. . . . In complex societies, movements are a permanent reality."

Social movement theory: recent developments   More recent theorizing about social movements in the wake of new social movements has taken a decisively communicative turn. The new social movements of the 1960s to 1980s are now seen by some as a transitional form that was peculiar to postindustrial society, bridging the period between the class-based mass movements of industrial society and the adaptable, reorganizing, global-scale movements characteristic of network society today (Wieviorka, 2005). However, the influence of NSMs on current theory is clear: today's movements are commonly depicted as heterogeneous, decentralized, and distributed social networks, and research focuses on their fundamentally cultural and subjective qualities, especially rhetorical and discursive processes of issue and action framing, representational strategies, and symbolic repertoires, as well as the use of new information and communication technologies. Some "culturalist" theorists have even posited that movements exploit "discursive opportunity structures" similar to the political and economic opportunity structures advanced in resource mobilization theory (e.g., Johnston & Noakes, 2005).

Manuel Castells (2009), for example, expanding on his influential theory of network society and identity, considers the relation between communication and power. Power "is primarily exercised by the construction of meaning in the human mind through processes of communication enacted in global/local multimedia networks," and "the ability to successfully engage in violence or intimidation requires the framing of individual and collective minds" (p. 414). This is accomplished by the constitution of, and especially *switching* among, communication and media networks in different social, economic, and cultural domains – that is, powerful actors are able to adapt and "program" these networks according to their interests. Social movements challenge this power, and effect social change, by "reprogramming" networks to introduce and diffuse new values and hopes to the wider society.

Michael Hardt and Antonio Negri (2004) propose the *multitude* as the prime agent of political resistance and social change in a global context where media and information technologies and a white-collar information workforce are predominant. Rather than organizing sustained movements and campaigns around well-articulated issues, media representations, or identities, or acting as a coherent, mobilized force, the multitude is an "imminent," nomadic, emergent, always-becoming entity made up of innumerable networked "singularities" (people acting in concert in the name of their various concerns, grievances, commitments, values, relationships, and so on). Using global media and information networks, the multitude organizes and disorganizes rapidly and unpredictably, "swarm"-style, in response to the oppressive, totalizing operations of "Empire" – a postmodern form of global sovereignty "composed of a series of national and supranational organisms united under a single logic of [late capitalist] rule" (Hardt & Negri, 2002; see also Hardt & Negri, 2000).

In a sweeping synopsis, Jeffrey Alexander (2006) critiques the materialism and realism of classical "revolutionary" models of social movements, the "retreat into microsociology" and hyper-subjectivity of collective behavior theory (p. 233), the functionalism and instrumentalism of resource mobilization theory, as well as what he sees as the defensive stance, overemphasis on the vulnerability of actors, and the "updating" of revolutionary models in new social movement theory. (Indeed, in the global justice and anti-capitalist movements some observers see a resurgence of class-driven revolutionary movements and a "new wave of sustained class conflicts" over the distribution of resources and wealth [della Porta & Diani, 2006, p. 10].)

In contrast, Alexander suggests that social movements today are fundamentally cultural, and that their success depends on a group's ability to represent and communicate its particular concerns to the wider society, to "present themselves as typifying sacred values, as the bearers of social, national, and even primordial myth, as cultural innovators who can create new norms and new institutions" (p. 229). Using Habermas's phrase, Alexander contends that the "will formation" necessary to create social movements can only emerge from the loyalties, norms, and solidarities among members of a particular civil sphere. The key problem for movements is "translating" the particular concerns of the sphere to the wider society by using "significant idioms, codes, and narratives . . . transcending, overarching symbolic frameworks" that appeal to "the obligations created by civil society" more broadly (pp. 229–30). Such translation requires leaders with "creativity and imagination":

> Successful translation allows movements that emerge as protests in one . . . particular subsystem, sphere of justice, or segmented community – to be taken up by the civic public. . . . Domination in a particular sphere is challenged not because it violates a particular institutional culture but because it is constructed as violating the collective representations of civil society. (pp. 231–2)

Alternative and activist new media: a genre framework

In Chapter 1, the concept of media genres was discussed and five contemporary genres of alternative and activist new media projects were introduced. To close this chapter, we now consider some common themes in activist art and new social movement theory that have re-emerged as features across different genres of online activism. The correspondence of genres, themes, and features is not exact; the scheme proposed here is meant more as a broad sketch than as a faithful "map" of the territory of new media activism, and not every genre exhibits every feature. However, all of the genres have at least a few in common with one another. The genres, themes, and features are summarized in the framework shown in Table 2.1.

At the most general level, three major themes link activist art movements, new social movements, and online activism: the *scope* or size of activist projects; the *stance* of movements and projects relative to dominant/mainstream society and culture; and the nature of projects as *action* and activists as *agents* of change.

Table 2.1. A genre framework for alternative and activist new media

Features	Culture jamming	Alternative computing	Participatory journalism	Mediated mobilization	Commons knowledge
• Scope					
Small-Scale: low-cost, limited size, small group, "micromedia"	++	++	++		+
Collaborative: DIY, shared effort, credit; volunteer	++	+++	++	++	+++
• Stance					
Heterotopic: "outsider" re: mainstream, marginality, counter-sites	++	+++	+	++	++
Subcultural Literacy: insider knowledge, solidarity, recuperated meanings	++			+	
Ironic: humor, satire, play, parody, appropriation	+++	+		+	
• Action & Agency					
Interventionist: alters existing conditions, direct action	++	+++	++	+++	++
Perishable: short-lived, nomadic, rapid response, ephemeral, temporary	++	+	+++		++

Scope

Scope includes two related features. The first is the small scale of activist projects. From "provocations" at the Cabaret Voltaire in 1916, to the graffiti slogans of May '68 in Paris, to the spoof corporate website posted in 2002 by the Yes Men on the eighteenth anniversary of the deadly gas leak at the Dow Chemical plant in Bhopal, India, activist art, new social movements, and new media activists have tended to mount relatively small, low-cost projects. Today's alternative and activist new media projects have been called "micromedia" (Peretti, 2001a). Media theorists David Garcia and Geert Lovink have characterized such efforts as *tactical media*, small interventions rather than coherent, carefully planned campaigns, "what happens when the cheap 'do it yourself' media . . . are exploited by groups and individuals who feel aggrieved by or excluded from the wider culture" (Garcia & Lovink, 1997). Or, as Sean Cubitt puts it, "Tactical media are addressed to what is doable now, to the effective and to the short term . . . 'winning' is not an option" (Cubitt, 2006, p. 42).

Indymedia projects, for example, are often sustained by a handful of volunteer staff members and donated equipment. Many of the most popular political blogs are produced and hosted by private individuals or small teams. Even the relatively large Wikipedia project (http://www.wikipedia.org), a collaboratively built, non-profit reference work that thrives on intramural disputes among volunteer contributors and editors, is generated and maintained by a core collective of just several thousand participants worldwide, and depends on charitable donations for its main financial support (see Beschastnikh, Kriplean & McDonald, 2008).

To a degree this preference for small-scale projects may be attributable to the fact that few artists and activists have access to large, reliable sources of funding and staff. However, the "micromedia," DIY aesthetic would also seem to reflect a basic attitude among activists about supersized modern culture. For example, the rejection of mass production, consumer culture and consumption, and industrialized violence that defined Dada re-emerged in the countercultural, confrontational manifestos and constructed situations of the Situationist International. New social movements, from environmentalists to gay rights advocates to anti-globalization protesters, have inherited a similar distrust, and even hostility, toward large-scale, dominant power structures and institutions.

The scale of activist projects may also be limited because the audience for any minority, oppositional view is likely to be small by definition, at least in a movement's early stages. In addition, activists place a high value on flexibility and rapid action: the Dadaists numbered no more than a few dozen artists and writers at the peak of the movement (Dickerman, 2005). The SI, which never included more than eight or ten core members, became notorious for its frequent, abrupt ostracisms and expulsions of collaborators whose philosophical or political views diverged from the core (Wark, 2009). One effect of the small scale of most activist sites online, and the distinctively personal (not to say idiosyncratic) roles that their creators play in these projects, is that they tend to give visitors and contributors a sense of familiarity or intimacy, of being an insider who knows the players personally.[4]

Given the small scale of artists' and activists' projects, it is unsurprising that they also tend to be *collaborative*, the product of group effort, rather than individually produced, solo works. In this respect they are part of a larger trend toward a "new collectivism" associated with postmodern art and activism (Stimson & Sholette, 2007a). Like the most memorable Dada and Situationist efforts, and the communitarian values underpinning new social movements, the "new collectivism," and alternative and activist new media projects, are predicated on an assumption of community, interactivity, and participation in their design, organization, and operation. Chris Atton (2004), for example, has described the "social authorship" or social creativity of alternative internet sites and actions. The power of new media "lies less in the information that it [sic] carries than in the communities that it creates" (Schrage, 2001). In their analysis of Indymedia journalism, Sara Platon and Mark Deuze (2003, p. 337) have observed that

"The potential for immediate interaction between users on the internet surpasses all other media. . . . [Indymedia] also has an increased potential for (re)connecting media formats and forms of journalism with different types of community."

For example, the readers and contributors to the non-profit, liberal/progressive blog and discussion group *Daily Kos* (http://www.dailykos.com) frequently treat the site as a perpetual conversation with each other and the blog's founder, Markos Moulitsas. In 2006 the *Daily Kos* community launched its own annual live meeting, YearlyKos, where 1,200 influential bloggers and online political activists met face-to-face. In 2007 YearlyKos was considered such a choice gathering of "netroots" activists that seven of the eight Democratic presidential candidates made appearances. By 2008 the meeting (renamed Netroots Nation) had grown to about 2,000 attendees, although a center-right blogger who attended the meeting noted that this number was still small relative to the enormous field of progressive political activists online, and seemed to be restricted to a hand-picked "elite" of participants (Nalle, 2008).

Stance

A second general theme that bridges activist art movements, new social movements, and online activism has to do with their sense of separation or difference from dominant culture and mainstream social beliefs or values – that is, how they situate themselves, or the "space" they occupy, relative to the rest of society. The *stance* of alternative and activist new media projects can be seen in three main characteristics.

First, these projects are *heterotopic*, that is, they act as "other spaces" or "countersites" for expression, affiliation, and creativity apart from the dominant culture (Lievrouw, 1998).[5] A heterotopia, according to Michel Foucault (1986, p. 24), is "a kind of effectively enacted utopia in which . . . all the other real sites that can be found with the culture are simultaneously represented, contested, and inverted. Places of this kind are outside of all places, even though it may be possible to indicate their location in reality." This definition certainly resonates in the context of activist art and new social movements, as well as newer online projects. Dada, for example, had a very specific physical geography that included several major European cities and New York. Only a handful of artists and writers worked in each place, and the emphasis of the work varied from city to city. (German Dada, for instance, was decisively political and revolutionary in its aims, while the Zurich, Paris, and New York contingents emphasized absurdity, playfulness, randomness, and the "gratuitous gesture"; Dickerman, 2005; Hopkins, 2004; Lippard, 1971). Nonetheless, through steady streams of correspondence, travel, and collaboration the Dadaists established a relatively coherent aesthetic that took a defiantly oppositional, "outsider" stance toward dominant art, culture, and politics. Similarly, the SI believed that only the deliberate fabrication of shocking situations and "counter-spectacles," in opposition to dominant economics and politics, could offer "spectators" a way to reclaim authentic experience and autonomy. And as Touraine, Melucci, and other theorists have argued, new social movements have been effective not because they try to restore cherished social values, but because activists themselves have demonstrated and exemplified new, alternative, "other" values and practices for the rest of society, out of a "desire to erect communities conceived as a refuge within an increasingly thicker social network. Marginality, considered for so long a failure of integration, becomes thus the hallmark of an opposition, a laboratory in which a new culture and a social counterproject are being elaborated" (Touraine, 1988 [1984], p. 106).

Likewise, borrowing a term from Arjun Appadurai, online activists and artists create diverse "mediascapes" or "cartographies" (Holmes, 2007) where they can "congregate" and share minority or marginalized views. Maren Hartmann (2004) has argued that "being online" constitutes a sort of *cyberflânerie* analogous to the strolling of nineteenth-century *flâneurs* in Paris or Berlin or the *dérives* of the Situationists, redefining and reshaping the meaning of cultural spaces as they go. Projects can serve as "counterpublic" arenas where marginal or oppressed groups may not only articulate their exclusion from and opposition to other groups, places, or views, or their solidarity with each other, but also engage in discourse and build strategies that can overcome exclusion (Asen, 2000).

Critics have noted the potential for social fragmentation or separatism, and the loss of civic or public culture, in the diversity of online sites (e.g., Mitchell, 2003; Sunstein, 2007). Others worry that separation from mainstream discourse and the concerns of the larger society tends to reinforce extremist values and opinions. However, such "cyber-separatism" or "nanoaudiences" (Kahn & Kellner, 2005) may be balanced by the growing ability of underrepresented groups to seek greater visibility and legitimacy for their interests on a global scale by going online, as in the widely analyzed use of websites by the Zapatista movement in Mexico in the 1990s (which is discussed further in Chapter 6).

A related point in critique and commentary about alternative/ activist new media is the nomadic quality of social and cultural engagement via new media and information technologies, particularly the possibilities for oppression, and for autonomy and resistance, available to the "nomads" and "data dandies" who traverse digital networks. "The Net is for the electronic dandy what the metropolitan street was for the historical dandy. Strolling along the data boulevards cannot be prohibited and ultimately jams the entire bandwidth" (Lovink, 1997, p. 64; see also Critical Art Ensemble, 1994; *Economist*, 2008a). Hakim Bey's concept of Temporary Autonomous Zones (TAZ) (2003) has been invoked as a model for new media activism by a number of scholars.

Given their heterotopic nature, perhaps it is unsurprising that, like activist art and new social movements, many alternative/ activist new media projects have a *subcultural* quality, or that online activists cultivate what Richard Kahn and Doug Kellner (2003) have called subcultural literacy. Chris Atton (2004, p. xi) notes that the study of the alternative internet can basically be considered "the study of subcultures." Like anti-nuclear activists using *agitprop* street theater, publishers who distributed John Heartfield's photo-montages lampooning German militarism in the 1920s and 1930s (Getty Center, 2006; see http://www.getty.edu/art/exhibitions/heartfield/), or Situationists setting out on their rambling *dérives*, online activists expect their audiences to share a degree of insider knowledge, a "hyper self-reflexivity about the nature of pop culture" (Collins, 1995, p. 2), that has also been described as an "aesthetic of poaching, tricking, reading, speaking, strolling, shopping, desiring" (Garcia & Lovink, 1997). Alternative and activist projects reinterpret the familiar with an acute sense of awareness of contemporary culture – and expect that others who are interested will "get it," too. Issues, images, buzzwords, and attitudes are selected, captured, subverted, co-opted, fragmented, recombined, and re-presented in unexpected (and ideally felicitous) ways.

In line with their heterotopic, "outsider" status and subcultural sensibilities, activist art, new social movements, and alternative/activist new media projects often have an acute sense of *irony* and *humor*, especially in their appropriation of mainstream cultural images and ideas to advance alternative or oppositional meanings. Online projects are often ironic, playful, humorous, campy, or parodic (Braman, 2002); or, as linguist Geoffrey Nunberg has commented about blogging, their participants often present themselves as "co-conspirators who are in on the joke" (Nunberg, 2004, quoted in Stimson & Sholette, 2007a, p. 2). New media activism has been called "immature . . . [celebrating] the possibility of ironic, humorous and contradictory political actions" (Peretti, 2001b). Such projects "do not take themselves that seriously . . . they know how to laugh" (Lovink & Richardson, 2001). As we have already seen, both Dada and the SI made extensive use of absurdity and black humor in their commentaries on art and modern life. A similar playfulness has carried over into the sensibility and style of many new media projects, and is often seen in their public communications and events (see Chapter 3). Although "Nothing can suck the air around it like political art: so many words, so much ideology worn so transparently on the sleeve, so much certainty, and so little of interest to look at" (Thompson, 2004, p. 10), a lot of alternative/activist art projects are straightforwardly funny, exploiting the absurd quality of much of mainstream culture, economics, and politics. Well-known collectives such as the Yes Men, ®™ark, and the Critical Art Ensemble, for example, seek to inspire outrage by pointing out and mocking the absurdity, or even producing a little humorous absurdity themselves.

A frequently used ironic device in online activism, as it has been in activist art and new social movements, is *bricolage*, the juxtaposition of unrelated elements to create new (and usually contrary or subversive) meanings. Dick Hebdige has traced the subversive and subcultural uses of *bricolage* to Dada and Surrealism. In his analysis of 1970s punk, he argues that *bricolage* is a signature element of subcultural style: "It is basically the way in which commodities are *used* in subculture which mark the subculture off from more orthodox cultural formations" (Hebdige, 1979, p. 103, emphasis in original). Debord and the SI put it more baldly: "Plagiarism is necessary, progress implies it" (Debord & Wolman, 1981 [1956], p. 10).

The Amsterdam media activist collective ADILKNO, which originated with the squatters' movement there in the 1970s (ADILKNO, 1994 [1990]), employed a range of media strategies and interventions, including "vague media," that seemed to borrow directly from the Dada and Situationist playbooks:

> Certain historical figures have found their natural milieu in vague media: Mao, Gysin, Manson, Reich, Jesus, Debord, Meinhof, Fromm, Hitler, Hendrix, Castaneda, Goldman, Marley and Longstocking, but also cookbooks, weapons, children's drawings, witches, blood, death's-heads and always animals. As long as it is cut up, overloaded with text, full and dark, with illustrations heavy and in black and white. (Lovink, 1997, p. 59)

In the online context, Mark Deuze (2003) emphasizes the role of *bricolage* in Indymedia sites that bring diverse materials together with a pastiche effect, and has also argued that along with participation and remediation, *bricolage* can be considered one of the "principal components" or defining features of digital culture (Deuze, 2006).

Other notable examples of ironic new media *bricolage* include spoof (parody) corporate websites; an online "exhibit" of artworks "borrowing" from copyrighted and trademarked materials, as a critique of intellectual property law hosted by the collective Illegal Art (see http://www.illegal-art.org and the discussion in Chapter 3); works by the band Negativland (http://www.negativland.com; see also Negativland, 2003); and David Rees's political comic strip-cum-rant, Get Your War On. This series, which Rees launched less than a month after the September 11 attacks in the U.S., borrows the Situationist technique of replacing dialogue "bubbles" in cliché comic strips or clip art with profane and paradoxical text (http://www.mnftiu.cc/mnftiu.cc/war.html).

Agency and action

A third theme linking activist art, social movement theory, and alternative/activist new media projects is action and agency – that is, the extent to which projects are conceived and executed as *action*, by participants who see themselves and their projects as *agents* of social change. Two characteristics are involved here. The first is that all three traditions are explicitly *interventionist*. Their creators seek to interrupt or alter existing conditions, to subvert common-sense or taken-for-granted meanings and situations, to "introduce noise into the signal" (Dery, 1993), or to create "a kind of temporary blockage in the system of representation" (Hebdige, 1979, p. 90). Contemporary artists and activists attempt to "create situations in the world at large" (Thompson, 2004, p. 10).

The Dadaists made their interventionist aims clear through their deliberately public events, propaganda, and provocation. In Europe between the wars it was still possible "to interpose one's art, even with no guarantees of effectiveness, between the official message and the audience" (Hughes, 1991, p. 81). Dada sought to launch "intervention[s] into governability, that is, subversions of cultural forms of social authority – breaking down language, working against various modern economies, willfully transgressing boundaries, mixing idioms, celebrating the grotesque body as that which resists discipline and control" (Dickerman, 2005, p. 11). The Dadaists' anarchic, iconoclastic methods were meant to achieve a "clean slate" or *tabula rasa* for reconceiving everyday life and culture (Lippard, 1971).

Today, activist projects online "push against" existing sites, events, and practices: "Culture jammers do not exist without corporate billboards" (Lovink & Richardson, 2001). Projects can either constitute intervention and action in themselves (such as the persistent and illegal posting of DVD decryption code on U.S. websites described in Chapter 4; Eschenfelder & Desai, 2004), or invite and encourage intervention by others (such as the continuous stream of proposals for staging cultural and political flashmob events throughout the world, posted at http:// www.flashmob.com; see also Rheingold, 2002).

As interventions and actions, alternative and activist projects, activist art and new social movements alike are often *perishable*, short-lived responses to rapidly changing cultural contexts and meanings. They are "capable of taking risks, even if this means they might self-destruct in the process" (Lovink & Richardson, 2001). Alternative and activist new media projects in particular are notable for their "mobility, [their] flexible response to events and changing contexts" (Meikle, 2000). Like the communication links and traffic flows on the digital networks that support them, activist projects online organize, disorganize, and reorganize more or less continuously, with a high rate of attrition as a result. In this respect they resemble earlier artistic movements, such as conceptual and performance art (both of which are often cited as direct descendants of Dada, and, to a lesser extent, Situationism), which were deliberately made not to leave material – thus collectable or commodifiable – traces or remnants.

An important influence on the perishability of alternative and activist new media projects may be the ephemerality of the Web itself.[6] At any time, a surprisingly large proportion of all websites are outdated, broken, abandoned, or inaccessible using standard web browsing techniques – comprising the so-called "invisible" or "dark" Web (Sherman & Price, 2001). One widely cited study from 2001 estimated that the "deep Web" was anywhere from 100 to 500 times the size of the easily accessible "surface" Web (Bergman, 2001). In 2000 a study by IBM researchers of the largest sample of the World Wide Web available at the time found that about 30 percent of all websites were either barely connected to, or entirely disconnected from, the rest of the Web, and that searchers actually found what they were looking for online only about 24 percent of the time (Broder et al., 2000). In 2003, another study found that nearly 70 percent of blogs had not been updated in the previous two months (Henning, 2003).

Of course, it is important to remember that throughout history, only a tiny fraction of *any* media artifacts – written manuscripts, letters, printed books, films, photographs, audio or video recordings, artworks, and so on – have ever been preserved. Indeed, not only is history "written by the victors" from selectively saved documentary evidence, it is becoming depressingly apparent that the deliberate, and selective, destruction of records is being revived in the digital age as a tool of repressive power, from the burning of ancient Islamic texts in the Sarajevo library to the deletion of inconvenient emails and other electronic records in corporate offices or an American presidential administration (Sanders, 1997), to denial-of-service "botnet" attacks launched against an opponent in advance of military action, as in the conflict between Russia and Georgia over South Ossetia and Abkhazia. It may be wishful thinking to expect that the situation for the preservation of digital media materials will be any different.

We can conclude this chapter with another thought from the Italian semiotician and scholar Umberto Eco. In a 1967 newspaper article, he predicted that media culture would soon require audiences to engage in "semiological guerrilla warfare":

> What must be occupied, in every part of the world, is the first chair in front of every TV set (and naturally, the chair of the group leader in front of every movie screen, every transistor, every page of every newspaper). . . . the battle for the survival of man as a responsible being in the Communications Era is not to be won where the communication originates, but where it arrives. (Eco, 1986, p. 142)

Eco was writing about television, but, if anything, his advice seems just as relevant today – with one proviso. In today's networked media culture, it is worth asking: where exactly do new media "originate," and where do they "arrive"?

CHAPTER 3

Monkeywrenching the Media Machine

Culture Jamming

In an article in the *New York Times* in 1990, cultural critic Mark Dery helped to lead culture jamming from the shadows of radical street subcultures, graffiti art, vandalized billboards and bus shelters to the bright stage of American popular culture.

> Cultural jamming is artistic "terrorism" directed against the information society in which we live. . . . most cultural jammers will never know the 15 minutes of celebrity augured by Andy Warhol. Walking a fine line between petty crime and conceptual art, they often labor undercover to make public statements. Their work owes its impact to the anonymity of the artist and the hit-and-run nature of the art. (Dery, 1990)

According to Dery, the San Francisco art-rock band Negativland coined the term "culture jamming" in 1984 "to describe billboard alteration and other underground art that seeks to shed light on the dark side of the computer age." Negativland themselves defined it as "media about media about media." Part satire, part hoaxing, part dystopian image factory, culture jamming projects turned the everyday stream of advertising, TV news, political spin, and cultural clutter inside out.

Eventually, Dery got more than his own metaphorical fifteen minutes when he expanded his *Times* report into an essay, "Culture Jamming: Hacking, Slashing and Sniping in the Empire of Signs" (Dery, 1993), published online in 1993, and later on his own website. It continues to be widely cited as an authoritative culture jamming manifesto; the Wikipedia entry for culture jamming calls the Dery piece "a seminal essay that remains the most exhaustive historical, sociopolitical, and philosophical theorization of culture jamming to date" (http://en.wikipedia.org/wiki/Culture_jamming).[1] In the essay Dery (1993) defines culture jamming as "media hacking, information warfare, terror-art, and guerrilla semiotics, all in one."

Culture jamming captures and subverts the images and ideas of mainstream media culture to make a critical point, or as media designer Jonah Peretti has put it, it is a "strategy that turns corporate power against itself by co-opting, hacking, mocking, and re-contextualizing meanings" (Peretti, 2001a, p. 1). Others have called it an "explicit attempt to monkeywrench the media machine" (Meikle, 2002, p. 131). It is closely related to other approaches that *détourn* popular culture to make a political or economic point, such as *tactical media*, in which activists employ a range of media technologies, including experimental film and video, local access cable television, or theater in public spaces, to intervene in and comment on political and economic conditions (Braman, 2002; Cubitt, 2006; Garcia & Lovink, 1997).

As a genre of new media activism, then, culture jamming takes the *form* of popular culture, but with the *purpose* of subverting and critiquing that culture. In this chapter we consider how culture jamming has moved from street art to online activism.

Culture jamming offline

Many early culture jamming projects reconfigured commercial images and public spaces, especially billboards and other advertising. In her book *Spray It Loud*, for example, Jill Posener details the reworkings of sexist and racist billboards in the UK (Posener, 1982). In 1977, the San Francisco group Billboard Liberation Front (BLF) began making late-night "corrections" to the typefaces and images of outdoor advertising for cosmetics, cigarettes, liquor, oil companies, military recruiting, and other products and organizations they found objectionable, a practice later characterized as "subvertising." Over time, the BLF expanded their efforts beyond San Francisco to lampoon the dot.com industries in a series of billboards in the Silicon Valley, and to reconfigure the marquee signs of gambling casinos (these and other examples can be seen at http://www.billboardliberation.com).

Taking a different approach, the political poster artist Robbie Conal and his assistants began regular late-night "guerrilla postering" sorties across Los Angeles in the 1980s. These projects, which Conal's group still conduct today, plaster construction sites, building walls, and billboards with haggard, unflattering portraits of powerful political figures with ironic captions, such as "Little White Lies" for the conservative U.S. Senator Jesse Helms, "Dough Nation" alongside the doughy face of then-President Bill Clinton, "Contra Diction" for former President Ronald Reagan, "Speak" for a grimacing image of Colonel Oliver North testifying in uniform, and, more recently, a smiling face of President Barack Obama with the words "Climate" in red type above the image, and "Change" in blue type below, and so on (Figure 3.1). Conal's website also outlines the do's and don'ts of guerilla postering.

Print media were also an early culture jamming target. The non-profit Canadian magazine *Adbusters* (http://www.adbusters. org), published by the Adbusters Media Foundation since 1989, is a glossy quarterly magazine which couples parodies of marketing, advertising, and popular media with critiques of consumer culture and political commentary. In 2000 the founding editor of *Adbusters*, Kalle Lasn, published a polemical call to media activism entitled *Culture Jam: How to Reverse America's Suicidal Consumer Binge – and Why We Must* (Lasn, 2000), which includes a brief primer on the philosophy and practice of culture jamming. *Adbusters* also sponsors a number of related projects, such as "Buy Nothing Day" and the "Black Spot" line of anti-brand shoes. In recent years *Adbusters*' efforts have expanded into other media, including television and the internet.

The possibilities for culture jamming projects have been as diverse as the messages and technologies available in the wider culture. New York City activist Andrew Boyd, in a comparison to the motivational speaker, has been called the "Tony

Figure 3.1. *Watching Bunny* by Robbie Conal.

Source: With permission from Robbie Conal.

Robbins" of the culture jamming movement (Caldwell, 2003). Boyd, who also helped create the spoof political fundraising group "Billionaires for Bush" (http://billionairesforbush.com/index.php), offers "Culture Jamming 101" seminars in which he shows aspiring culture jammers how to create their own projects (http://www.culturejamming101.com).

A wave of culture jamming "counter-surveillance" projects have also emerged as a political response to the growing use of closed-circuit television (CCTV) and surveillance cameras

ROBBIE CONAL'S GUERRILLA POSTERING AND ETIQUETTE GUIDE

(Source: Robbie Conal's Art Attack!
http://www.robbieconal.com//guerrilla.html)

WHAT WE WANT:

1 Mass distribution of our message: The most direct form of unmediated expression available – cheap – to underfolks like us. "Get the Shiznit to the Public", as the Chocolate Sunflower would put it.
2 Counter-infotainment: A surprise for people on their way to work in the morning. Critical ideas where people least expect them. To tickle the general public into thinking along with us about issues we think are important to the health of American democracy, the Constitution, our First Amendment rights, and the future of Hip-Hop Nation.
3 Empowerment: To take direct cooperative action on an issue that concerns us. For the general public who feel they have no avenues of resistance to the dominant power structure, no community support system, no ability to change their situation. To change apathy and cynicism to optimism.

WHAT WE DON'T WANT:

1 Don't Get Arrested (for no good reason). The non-violence in Non-violent Civil Disobedience – even our minor form of mischief – is NOT something you don't do: It's a principle.

PLEASE BE POLITE TO EVERYONE on the streets at night. Especially the police! Going to jail could ruin your evening. If you're hassling with the cops, you're not distributing our message. The Po-Po are just doing their job out there. The Guerrilla etiquette definition of conversation with the police is: They talk, we listen. Do what they tell you. Get off their beat. Go to another neighborhood. They'll ask you what you're doing. Tell them it's an ART PROJECT. Nothing else. If they want you to stop, take the posters down, whatever – just say OK, do it and leave quietly. Then go to another part of town (easy in LA, it's a big town) and continue your good work!

PS – This goes for "Rent a Cops" as well. They'll lose their jobs if posters are found on property they're guarding – jobs are scarce; postering sites are plentiful.

2 Don't alienate our Audience. This includes merchants, private property owners and people on the streets. Don't poster on store windows, walls, surfaces. Don't poster on city property (though the posters were originally scaled to the size of LA traffic light switching boxes –hint hint), church property or federal property (mailboxes). Discuss the poster and the issues with pedestrians if they ask, but don't talk too long and don't argue. If people want a poster give them one. If they want ten – give them one. If cars roll up and drivers or passengers want a poster, give them one. They're our audience – our people. Treat 'em right! [anecdotal evidence; "Lenny Lambchop" was getting up on telephone boxes in NYC lower east side around 2 am; the bars were letting out. Two beautiful working girls wobbled over to him and asked if they could have posters. "What are you gonna do with 'em?," he asked. One of the ladies, wearing a too short spandex something, replied, "I'm gonna put 'MEN WITH NO LIPS' up in my room." Concerned, L.L. said, "But we want lots of people to see them." The other woman winked, "Oh they will, honey, at least twenty people a night!" Good enough.]

on private property and in public spaces (Monahan, 2006). Experimental and parodic dance groups have performed for cameras inside cashpoint/teller machine lobbies (Markoff, 2002). One project uses inexpensive laser pointers to temporarily disable surveillance cameras in public spaces (Naimark, 2002). In 2001, the British television show *The Mark Thomas Comedy Product* held a "competition for the most inventive closed-circuit television performance" (Rimensnyder, 2001). The Institute for Applied Autonomy, an art/engineering collective, designs and creates "contestational robotics." Its "inverse surveillance system" application, iSee, maps the locations of CCTV cameras in urban areas so users can plan "paths of least surveillance." (http://www.appliedautonomy.com/isee.html).

The Surveillance Camera Players (SCP) are one of the most renowned surveillance jamming groups. They have staged performances of original and classical plays (including Jarry's *Ubu Roi*, Beckett's *Waiting for Godot*, and their own adaptations of Wilhelm Reich's *Mass Psychology of Fascism* and Orwell's *Nineteen Eighty Four*) before surveillance cameras on the street or in other locations, such as subway stations, for the benefit of whoever might be watching (Chavoya, 2004; see http://www.notbored.org/the-scp.html). Videos of their performances have been shown in major contemporary art exhibitions and have been posted on YouTube. Like the Institute for Applied Autonomy, the SCP also post maps of "walking tours" in New York and other cities that show where cameras are located, so that strollers can avoid them as they tour the city, and sticker otherwise inconspicuous cameras with "helpful" labels reading WE ARE WATCHING YOU. Branches of the SCP have been launched in other cities, including Tempe, Arizona, Stockholm, Bologna, and San Francisco, and similar groups have staged projects in Vilnius, Perth, Innsbruck, Paris, Istanbul, and Chicago (more details are described in the *SCP 10-Year Report, 1996-2006*, available at http://www.notbored.org/10-year-report-long.html).

Culture jamming goes online

By the 1990s, culture jamming had become a familiar tactic among media activists, and widely discussed among media scholars (Carducci, 2006; Harold, 2004; Wettergren, 2009). However, it entered a new and more vigorous phase with the introduction of the World Wide Web and browser technologies. The internet seemed ideally suited to the cut-and-paste, collage-style, hit-and-run tactics favored by media designers and artists making art with a point. Activists and artists quickly adopted digital media to reach new audiences, recruit support, and organize protests and collective projects.

For example, in their work, the collective Illegal Art address increasingly restrictive and punitive intellectual property laws as a restraint on creative work and free expression, particularly in the online context, and create "the 'degenerate art' of a corporate age: art and ideas on the legal fringes of intellectual property" (http://illegal-art.org). The masthead of their website/exhibit is assembled from letters cut from popular product logos, and they are widely known for their projects involving illegal audio sampling (see the discussion of *Deconstructing Beck*, below). Their satirical "End User License Agreement," modeled after a typical software license, specifies the conditions under which visitors to the Illegal Art website may "use" the exhibit, and includes the following provisions:

> This Website End User License Agreement accompanies the Web Pages and related explanatory materials ("Crap"). The term "Crap" also shall include any upgrades, modified versions, or repaintings of the Website licensed to you by either The Prince of Wales, a sentient washing machine, or my old Rabbi (the one who used profanity). Please read this Agreement carefully. At the end, you will be asked to accept this agreement and provide this Website with a warm, lingering, creepy hug. . . . 1.2 You may make and distribute unlimited copies of the Website, including copies for commercial distribution, as long as each copy that you make and distribute contains this Agreement and is created in one of the following media: carved out of ice, as in an ice sculpture centerpiece; smeared in mustard on the side of a white or off-white panel van; or taught to a parrot who is then condemned to fly the earth for eternity, incessantly repeating the mantra of this Website. (see http://www.illegal-art.org/contract.html)

Jonah Peretti's "Nike Media Adventure" demonstrates how going online can affect the visibility of even the smallest project (Peretti, 2001a, 2001b; see also Wasik, 2009). The designer wanted to comment on the firm's labor practices, and to test the concept of the *meme* – an idea, expression, image, practice or other bit of cultural "code" that is picked up and absorbed into the larger culture, such as fashion, slang, or new ways of doing familiar things. The concept was proposed by biologist Richard Dawkins in his 1976 book *The Selfish Gene* as a sort of cultural counterpart to the gene, with analogous abilities to diffuse, replicate, mutate, and hybridize its way into the "organism" of culture.[2]

Peretti responded to a marketing campaign by Nike that was intended to associate the brand with freedom and creativity. The company invited customers to customize their own running shoes by ordering pairs inscribed with their choice of words. Peretti ordered shoes bearing the word "sweatshop." In subsequent email correspondence with Peretti, the company refused to fill the order, or to acknowledge the implicit critique as the reason why they would not make the shoes. The firm's persistent evasiveness and resort to euphemism led Peretti to forward the whole text of the correspondence to ten friends, who passed it along to others, who did the same.

Almost immediately, the correspondence circulated so widely that it came to the attention of online news sites like Slashdot and Plastic.com. Mainstream print and broadcast news reporters monitoring online sites for leads picked up the story, and Peretti's exchange with the intransigent Nike was featured in prominent publications ranging from the *Village Voice, San Jose Mercury News,* and *USA Today,* to *Time, Business Week,* the *Los Angeles Times,* and the *Wall Street Journal.* Peretti appeared on NBC's *Today Show* and the story was covered by the BBC. In a matter of a few months Peretti's meme had spread across a large portion of Anglo-American popular culture both online and off, and Nike had attracted precisely the kind of adverse publicity they had hoped to avoid in the first place. In a story in *The Nation,* Peretti wrote about the power of memes, "viral marketing" and the power of using the internet as "micromedia" (Peretti, 2001a), and he has also graphed the rate of email traffic "hits" he received related to the correspondence with Nike (Peretti, 2001b). (The complete, annotated Nike email is available at http://www.shey.net/niked.html.)

Reverse jamming: the cycle of cross-appropriation

Ultimately, what makes culture jamming distinctive as a genre of alternative/activist new media is that it "mines" mainstream culture to reveal and criticize its fundamental inequities, hypocrisies, and absurdities, very much in the tradition of Dada and the Situationists. However, it is also part of an increasingly important dynamic of co-optation and cross-appropriation – what might be called *reverse jamming* – in which mainstream and alternative culture continually borrow, refashion, and reinterpret the other's images, attitudes, symbols, or practices, a process that is dramatically accelerated in the online context. Culture jammers hack the elements of mainstream culture, while marketers and media interests troll subcultures for new "memes" that can sell products, fashions, or ideas.

Scholars and critics have long been aware of these counterforces of appropriation between "authentic" social and cultural movements and groups, and commercial/marketing interests. In his study of 1970s punk, British cultural studies scholar Dick Hebdige (1979) shows how subcultures borrow, "recode," and invert mainstream imagery and practices in the construction of their own separate and oppositional styles and values. In turn, subcultural styles are co-opted, the underlying social rifts and breaks that they represent are repaired, and the mainstream culture is reintegrated through two forms of "recuperation":

> (1) the conversion of subcultural signs (dress, music, etc.) into mass-produced objects (i.e. the commodity form);
> (2) the "labeling" and re-definition of deviant behaviour by dominant groups – the police, the media, the judiciary (i.e. the ideological form).
> (Hebdige, 1979, p. 94)

Hebdige cites the observation of Henri Lefebvre: "That which yesterday was reviled today becomes cultural consumer-goods; consumption thus engulfs what was intended to *give meaning and direction*" (Lefebvre, 1971 [1968], p. 95, emphasis in the original). Consistent with the era of his study, he also identifies traditional mass media as the primary conduit of cultural influence.

In the context of new media, this cycle of cultural appropriation, repurposing, and reappropriation is clearly still at work, although there is a temptation to pay more attention to the user side and the supposedly newfound power of the periphery to confront the established center. Commenting on the greater opportunity for participation and DIY content production afforded to activists by new media, Chris Atton cautions that "Most accounts of radical media have treated such practices as unique and defining characteristics. . . . Little attention has been paid to how these practices might be employed by the mainstream media, or indeed to how radical media might borrow practices from the mainstream" (Atton, 2004, p. 9). Joshua Gamson (2003), for example, describes the emergence of gay subculture as a powerful market segment, and the "naturalization" of gay styles and symbolism through both mass and online media, as a two-way process of cross-appropriation between the subculture and the mainstream.

However, in the online context, the cycle may differ in one important respect from reverse jamming via traditional media. It may be more accelerated, as demonstrated by the Peretti–Nike case, where the whole episode, from email exchange to mainstream media coverage, transpired in a matter of weeks, and indeed mostly within a window of a few days (see Peretti, 2001b). This speed-up of co-optation between mainstream and subculture, or between center and periphery, has had important consequences in political communication, for example. Political campaigns can be disabled by the instant circulation of a candidate's thoughtless remarks or behavior via blog posts, tweets, or YouTube, as demonstrated by the failure of the 2006 U.S. Senate campaign of incumbent George Allen (R-Virginia) after amateur videos of his racist remarks at an informal campaign event were posted online. Since the 2008 Obama presidential campaign, such "viral" message generation – and deflection – has become a staple of political communication at every level in the U.S.

From a different perspective, for nearly two decades the essayist and cultural critic Thomas Frank has mounted a sustained and polemical critique of the symbiotic relationship between alternative subcultures and marketing. He argues that the 1990s and early 2000s have been notable for the rise of advertising strategies employing so-called "guerrilla" or "viral" marketing tactics, which deliberately harvest subcultural styles and ideas in order to design and sell products that appeal to consumers' senses of individuality, non-conformity, difference, rebellion, alternative lifestyle, and so on. This continual process of co-optation leaves no authentic or independent space for genuine cultural expression apart from the market, and in fact closes off the very possibility of dissent and difference (Frank, 1997).

Frank alleges that such tactics are not merely a matter of subcultural exploitation and rip-off; members of alternative or subcultural groups are often willing participants or "consultants" in the process of defining and circulating new, "cool" styles.[3] Marketers themselves invoke the theories and discourse of cultural studies, especially the "active audience" view that frames and celebrates consumption and media reception as so many acts of reinterpretation, "resistance" to hegemonic mainstream culture, and rebellion among audience members. As Frank puts it, this has encouraged a tendency "to understand consumption itself as democracy." Consequently,

> American audiences are growing more skeptical by the minute; fashion cycles that once required years now take months. . . . suddenly questions like the oppositional or subversive potential of *The Simpsons* aren't quite as academic as they once seemed. Given the industry's new requirements, the active-audience faith of the cult stud [cultural studies scholar] becomes less an article of radical belief and more a practical foundation for the reprioritized audience research being done by the new breed of marketing experts, who can be found commenting lucidly on the postmodern condition in highbrow business publications like the *Journal of Consumer Research*. (Frank, 2000, p. 305)

Today, culture jamming is a core tactic of political communication. The website of the Center for Communication and Civic Engagement at the University of Washington, which focuses on the study of political communication, includes a page on culture jamming with links to "classics" of the form, including the Billboard Liberation Front, *Adbusters*, the Jonah Peretti–Nike encounter, Andrew Boyd's Culture Jamming 101, and many others (http://depts.washington.edu/ccce/ polcommcampaigns/ culturejamming.htm). But as a communication style and strategy for attracting attention and "eyeballs," culture jamming has also become a standard feature in popular culture. Its ironic, parodic, "in on the joke" quality and use of pastiche have been appropriated by a number of mainstream entertainment programs, such as *The Simpsons, Family Guy, American Dad!, The Daily Show*, and *Colbert Report* in the U.S., for example.

This commonplace appropriation, of course, raises the question of whether culture jamming retains its power to shock and its credibility and effectiveness as a strategy of critique and protest, or (as Frank might suggest) whether its whole premise has been so thoroughly co-opted by mainstream/corporate culture and media that it is no longer a worthwhile form of activism. Another way to frame the question is to ask in what phase of the cycle of appropriation and reappropriation culture jamming itself may be.

Recent scholarship outlines a few important "lessons learned" from culture jamming and suggests that as a tactic of critique it still has a degree of subversive power. The first is that small interventions can make a big difference in popular perception, even briefly. The deliberate and strategic creation and circulation of elemental cultural notions – memes – that oppose or invert the status quo is a rhetorical and symbolic strategy with considerable power, and seems to be well suited to the fragmentation and rapid turnover of ideas, images, and discourse in the new media context. In some ways the "viral" approach to mediated communication has parallels with the recent interest in framing, and discourse and symbolic repertoires, in social movement theory – as well as marketing.

A second lesson can be drawn from the emotional or affective valence of culture jamming projects, particularly how effectively they have deployed humor, irony, fun, play, and absurdity as means of (even a weapon for) exposing social, political, and economic problems, attracting adherents, and moving them to action. Both humor and outrage can be effective persuasive tactics, and culture jamming seems particularly adept at combining the two.

The third lesson is the degree to which activist art and technology *collectives* have taken center stage in political and cultural opposition and organizing using new media (Holmes, 2007; Stimson & Sholette, 2007a). Artistic/political collectives are not new: we need only think of Dada, or the Situationist International and its predecessors, such as CoBrA, the Lettrist International, and the International Movement for an Imaginist Bauhaus, as noted in Chapter 2. But today's collectives may have greater potential reach or influence given their use of new media technologies as the platform both for making/performing/instantiating new works and for reaching interested publics.

For example, the argument has been made that collectives like the Electronic Disturbance Theater and Critical Art Ensemble serve as "research and development" or prototyping laboratories for inventing and trying out techniques of technological and cultural subversion (Rolfe, 2005) – a sort of countercultural "skunkworks" where creative artists and technologists cultivate new ideas and strategies for critique.[4] Some collectives, such as the Institute for Applied Autonomy, even portray themselves deliberately as "laboratories" for developing subversive techniques (Monahan, 2006). Eventually the techniques may be adopted by more "everyday" movement organizations, or become part of mainstream media culture, as suggested previously. Together, these three points suggest that the cycle of contention and cross-appropriation between mainstream and counterculture continues to be a powerful dynamic, and possibly more so in a new media context that is less constrained by geographic, cultural, and legal boundaries than in cultural settings dominated by highly regulated and structured mass media systems.

In the remainder of this chapter, we focus on what might be considered an omnibus case study, a project that has been one of the most creative, provocative, acclaimed – and studied – venues for activist culture jamming online: ®™ark.

®™ark: jamming under the "corporate veil"

In Renaissance emblems, the melancholicus was depicted as
someone with a gagged mouth, book in hand, sitting near a river.
[In digital art] he sits in front of a computer, wearing a corporate
mask, and contemplates Internet data streams.

(Cramer, 2009, p. 187)

Perhaps no culture jamming project has better filled the role of digital *melancholicus* than ®™ark (pronounced art-mark). Founded in 1991, its aim – in the wake of the dot.com crash (Moore, 2007) – was the creation and support of works that critique consumerism and corporate culture. The name itself is a portmanteau word combining the symbols for "registered" and "trademark" in U.S. law. ®™ark's founders added a twist: they established the project as a corporation so that it could operate with the same "individual" rights and shelter from liability enjoyed by other U.S. corporations. On the principle that "marketplaces can become an art form [where] buying and selling are means of self-expression" (Plewe, 2008, p. 977), ®™ark uses the imagery and jargon of business, with capital investment, products, target markets, a "bottom line," a corporate identity, and so on, but with the critical difference that ®™ark seeks to maximize "cultural dividends" rather than monetary profit. Its corporate video, *Bringing IT to YOU!*, notes, "As a privately held corporation, ®™ark allows investors to participate in blacklisted or illegal cultural production with minimum risk" (http://rtmark.com/bityscript.html). Or as one art critic puts it, "®™ark is a hacked corporation" (Stallabrass, 2003–4, p. 12).

Essentially, ®™ark is structured as brokerage that brings together artists and potential funders. Project proposals are organized into "mutual funds" that "offer high cultural dividends with risk levels tailored to the needs of diverse market sectors." ®™ark's publicity video winks at the style of financial reporting and prospectuses:

The ®™ark mutual funds, like their financial counterparts, enable laypeople with minimum time and knowledge to invest strategically by leveraging the wisdom and skill of specialized experts. ®™ark's mutual fund managers have shown substantial staying power by personally delivering the highest dividends even in the cultural bear markets of the '80s and early '90s. (http://rtmark.com/bityscript.html)

Through the funds, artist/entrepreneurs pitch their ideas and solicit underwriting from interested (but anonymous) investors (see http://rtmark.com/funds.html). Projects are identified by stock-ticker-style acronyms and listed in fund categories according to the fund's aims or concerns – health care, warfare, labor, intellectual property, environment, or corporate law, for example (see Figure 3.2). Each listing describes the proposed project and an estimated budget, and investors fund various projects through ®™ark rather than sending funds directly to artists. The "fund managers" are prominent artists and critics in their own right, including DJ Spooky (That Subliminal Kid) (the Frontier Fund), the band Negativland (the Intellectual Property Fund), moving image archivist Rick Prelinger (the Emerging Communications Fund), Critical Art Ensemble (the Biological Property Fund), the cultural organization Rhizome (the Net Fund), and the poet Andrei Codrescu (the Media Fund).

Because many proposals involve various types of sabotage or subversion of mainstream products, content, or organizational routines, the ®™ark structure offers artists and investors a "corporate veil" that maintains the anonymity of both investors and artist-workers, and "displaces liability from funder and worker." Indeed, the veil extends to ®™ark's principals themselves, who have used pseudonyms and computer-generated animations for all corporate communications in order to protect their anonymity.

®™ark established itself as a culture jamming force with its earliest, pre-internet projects. The Barbie Liberation Organization, for example, used money donated by a veterans' group to fund artists who switched voiceboxes in talking Barbie

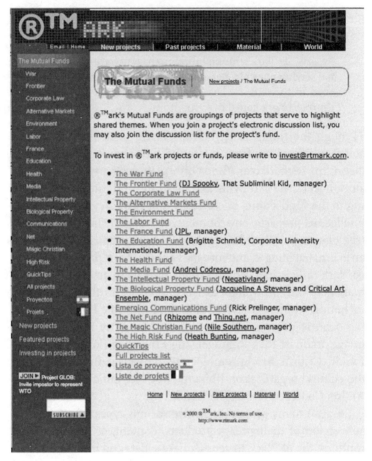

Figure 3.2. The ®™ark mutual funds.

Source: http://www.rtmark.com/funds.html.

and GI Joe dolls and replaced them on toy store shelves for sale (http://rtmark.com/blo.html). ®™ark also channeled funds from an investor in New York City to a programmer working for the company producing the video game SimCopter, so that the programmer could substitute "hundreds of near-naked kissing boys for buxom babes" (http://rtmark.com/simcopter.html).

In 1993 the group's reputation and influence expanded dramatically when it launched an online bulletin board to circulate information about prospective activist art projects in need of funding: "It's an open-ended system, and you can come to it with money, or you can come to it as a worker with an idea looking for money. . . . People submit ideas they want to carry out themselves but need to raise some capital to do it" (Guerrero, Myerson & Jain, 2003, p. 130). Early internet-based projects included *Deconstructing Beck*, an album of music by the Illegal Art collective, assembled from illegally sampled and remixed works by the popular musician (whose own works make extensive use of sampled music by other artists; http://rtmark.com/db.html). ®™ark provided support for the FloodNet application developed by the Electronic Disturbance Theater, which was used by the Zapatista movement in 1999 to mobilize thousands of participants in online denial-of-service attacks against Mexican and U.S. government web servers.

Also in 1999, ®™ark collaborated with satirist Zack Exley on a spoof of George W. Bush's first presidential campaign website, gwbush.com, that parodied and criticized Bush's claims and positions. The spoof site, which looked authentic to many visitors, so outraged the Bush staff that they lobbied the U.S. Federal Elections Commission to shut it down on the grounds that the site should be considered a political organization that had not properly disclosed its funding sources under FEC rules. In comments to a reporter from the *Dallas Times-Herald*, Bush famously stated that in cases like gwbush.com, "there ought to be limits to freedom" (the *Times-Herald* story is linked at http://rtmark. com/bush.html). Subsequent media coverage of Bush's quote, and the spoof site, was immediate and international. Another ®™ark project, voteauction.com, invited American voters to sell their votes to the biggest corporate bidders in the 2000 presidential election; it was abruptly shut down after the Chicago Board of Elections and the New York Board of Elections threatened the developers with legal action, whereupon the site was sold to Austrian net artist Hans Bernhard and his site ubermorgen.com, beyond U.S. legal jurisdiction (Guerrero, Myerson & Jain, 2003; Ludovico, 2009; see also http://www.vote-auction.net/).

®™ark also figured in a high-profile case involving a parody website created by the Yes Men. In December 2002 the collective created a spoof of the Dow Chemical Company website and posted it on the eighteenth anniversary of the toxic gas leak at Dow's Union Carbide plant in Bhopal, India, with links to ®™ark's home site (Delio, 2002; Yes Men, n.d.). Attorneys for Dow alleged that the parody violated its copyrights under the U.S. Digital Millennium Copyright Act (DMCA), but rather than suing the Yes Men and pursuing the case through the courts, Dow complained to NTT/Verio, the telecommunications operator for ®™ark's internet service provider (ISP) in New York City, "The Thing" (http://thing.net). The Thing also served many other prominent arts organizations in New York, including P.S. 1/ Museum of Modern Art, Mabou Mines, *Artforum*, and Nettime.

NTT/Verio's response was to demand that the Yes Men remove the site, which they did. Nonetheless, NTT/Verio terminated The Thing's service permanently at the end of February 2003, interrupting internet access for all their clients. Dow thus succeeded in suppressing what would normally have been considered commentary or parody, and therefore speech protected under the First Amendment to the U.S. Constitution – without the bother of actually airing the matter in court. Later, The Thing's owner, Wolfgang Staehle, told the *Village Voice* that he was considering relocating his service to Europe, beyond the reach of the DMCA (Carr, 2003).[5]

More recently, a founding member of the Critical Art Ensemble and professor of art at the State University of New York (SUNY) Buffalo, Steven Kurz, has been vindicated after a protracted legal struggle with the U.S. Department of Justice (DOJ). He was prosecuted in 2004 after emergency personnel – responding to Kurz's 911 call when his wife and artistic partner Hope Kurz suddenly died of heart failure – decided that the apparatus Kurz used in his artwork was suspicious and that he might be a "bioterrorist." Kurz's work, which employed harmless bacteria and biological testing equipment used in schools to critique genetically modified crops and other organisms, was well known in contemporary art circles and had been exhibited in a number of shows internationally. Nonetheless, he was detained on the way to his wife's funeral by the FBI and the Joint Terrorism Task Force, and questioned for nearly twenty-four hours while his house and studio were raided and his installations, books, car, writings, and even cat were confiscated. His wife's body was taken from the funeral home to be tested, and his house condemned as a health hazard.

Although no evidence of pathogens or public risk was found, Hope Kurz's body was returned, and the house declared habitable in a few days, the U.S. District Attorney continued to pursue the case under the U.S. Patriot Act on the grounds that Kurz had violated a materials transfer agreement and thus committed mail fraud when he obtained the bacteria from a scientist he was collaborating with at the University of Pittsburgh. The reaction from the art world was global and resounding, including high-profile fundraisers for Kurz's legal defense fund, donations from some of the most acclaimed contemporary artists and writers, and condemnations of the DOJ's actions by educators, cultural organizations, and the art press throughout the world. Finally, in June 2008 (over four years after Hope Kurz's death), a Federal judge dismissed the government's indictment out of hand, describing it as "insufficient on its face" – that is, the allegations, even if true, did not in any way constitute a crime. The Justice Department declined to appeal what was clearly an extraordinarily weak case. However, to date none of Kurz's property or written work has been returned by the authorities (see http://caedefensefund.org/index.html).

Despite such difficulties, ®™ark considers controversy to be an ally in raising the visibility of the projects and causes it supports, as in the gwbush.com case and the Steven Kurz prosecution. ®™ark's activities and projects have been covered extensively by the mainstream media as well as the cultural and art press throughout the world (a sampling of coverage is posted on the ®™ark website). The collective has received a number of awards and recognitions, including the $50,000 CalArts Alpert Award in the Arts in 2002 (http://alpertawards.org/archive/winner02/rtmark.html). In 2000 ®™ark was selected for the prestigious Whitney Biennial show – whereupon the group promptly auctioned off its invitations to the preview reception on eBay, netting $4,000 for the mutual funds. ®™ark also altered its part of the Whitney website, so that instead of being directed to ®™ark, visitors would see random rotations of web pages submitted by members of the public (Mirapaul, 2000). Although ®™ark as an organization has been somewhat less active in recent years, its "envoys," such as the Yes Men and the Critical Art Ensemble, continue to exhibit work and stage provocations world-wide (Cudmore, 2009), and ®™ark itself continues to be cited by media and cultural scholars as a leading influence on culture jamming and media activism.

Summary: culture jamming as a genre

As the preceding discussion suggests, culture jamming is a mode of media activism that extends well beyond the boundaries of the internet. As a genre of alternative and activist new media, however – and considering ®™ark as a prime case study or "synecdoche" (Allen, 2003, p. 7) – it exemplifies many of the key features outlined in Chapter 2.

The first feature, and one that is clearly fundamental to ®™ark's continuing effectiveness, is its consistently ironic take on the issues and activities it criticizes. Its public communications are presented with a deadpan, even cartoonish, seriousness that belies the rich irony and playfulness at work throughout the ®™ark "organization" and its projects. ®™ark's corporate identity is itself an ironic move that subverts the purposes and objectives of corporate capitalism and consumerism. As the abstract for the 2000 Whitney Biennial puts it, "Although this site may appear to be just another corporate presence on the Web, ®™ark's purposes are diametrically opposed to those of the corporate world it imitates" (see http://artport.whitney. org/exhibitions/biennial2000/rtmark.shtml). The philanthropic organization Creative Capital, which funds innovative artists and art works, notes that the list of ®™ark's projects 'reads like an insider's guide to the most critical – and often most hilarious – attacks wrought by artists against creeping corporate power over the last decade' (see http://channel.creative-capital.org/ project_83.html). This playful sensibility "imbues all ®™ark projects with the same sense of calculated mischief" (Khamis, 2003).

A second prominent feature of culture jamming as a genre, and of ®™ark in particular, is its small scale. Despite the grandiose corporate shell, ®™ark includes only about five principal members, and no more than a dozen regular participants in all. It provides a simple platform for connecting other small-scale artists and "investors." For example, in a 2001 interview, ®™ark spokesperson Ray Thomas (the only consistently identified person in press accounts of the project) said that the largest "throughput" of any ®™ark fund up to that time occurred in 2000, when the Frontier Fund channeled about $8,500 from investors to artist-workers. "That's an unusual amount for one of our funds, and of course it's not very much at all" (Helfand, 2001). Most ®™ark-supported projects have budgets of only a few hundred dollars, and the respective funds typically handle a few thousand dollars at most at any time. The other projects discussed in this chapter – from the Peretti–Nike case to the Surveillance Camera Players – are all similarly small-scale, low-budget efforts.

®™ark is also a prime example of the interventionist quality of culture jamming. Whether it is the Yes Men sending an impostor "delegate" to a World Trade Organization meeting or the Copenhagen climate conference in 2009, the posting of a parody campaign website that prompts U.S. presidential candidate George Bush to make intemperate remarks to the press about limiting speech rights, or the production of a CD lampooning the intellectual property claims of artists who themselves profit from derivative works, culture jammers intervene in cultural and political practices and representations to point out contradictions and hypocrisy. Indeed, the interventions can be effective enough (at least in the view of their targets) to provoke real, and serious, consequences for the activist-perpetrators and their supporters, as in the shutdown of The Thing ISP in New York, the legal threats of the Bush campaign team, or the arrest of Robbie Conal's guerrilla postering crews.

Some writers – particularly those taking a traditional progressive-left political perspective – have criticized ®™ark and similar projects for their lack of clear political objectives or results. For example, regarding an ®™ark project satirizing third-world sweatshops, one critic notes that

> what is striking from an Old Left point of view is that the project does not attempt to organize the employees of Nike or Kathie Lee to demand better working conditions or higher salaries. Nor does it even try to induce American consumers to act in solidarity with such demands. . . . it is sometimes difficult to see what good Rtmark's actions do. . . . a complete survey of Rtmark's website suggests that, in terms of traditional politics, their aims seem incoherent. (Allen, 2003, p. 8)

In a discussion of ®™ark's Intellectual Property Fund, another writer contends that "in the end, ®™ark seems divided against itself. . . . the ®™ark agenda in effect leaves in place the intellectual property relations on which it poaches" (Irr, 2003, p. 201).

Nonetheless, even some of these critics concede that ®™ark and other online culture jamming efforts may constitute one of the few effective avenues of protest, cultivation of outrage, and intervention in an increasingly "dematerialized" cultural context, where the territory being contested is fundamentally informational and representational (as Debord might suggest). "Rtmark and the subculture that it represents exemplify the form political activism may have to take under postindustrial global capitalism" (Allen, 2003, pp. 7, 11). In terms of activist art, "®™ark demonstrates one model of radical politics and cultural activism coming into synthesis. They pursue political ends through cultural means" (Stallabrass, 2003, p. 12), a strategy with important implications given "the emergence of a collaborative, participatory and unownable culture" (p. 15).

Subcultural literacy is another hallmark of ®™ark and other culture jamming projects, both online and off. From its corporate incarnation to the myriad "funds" and project pitches, ®™ark depends on its visitors' and participants' familiarity with the conventions and clichés of market economics and corporate capitalism. "[A] certain cultural literacy is inevitably called for, an intimate knowledge of symbol and significance, logo and logic. . . . [®™ark's] type of protest relies on a distinct degree of media and cultural literacy" (Khamis, 2003). The project's "activism is underpinned by a theoretical model describing the character of corporations and the mass media. . . . it is ironic that this view of corporate power buys into the conservative view of the market and its creatures as natural forces" (Stallabrass, 2003, p. 13).

In many ways these four features – irony, small scale, interventionism, and subcultural literacy – read like a précis of what makes culture jamming compelling and effective (and fun). While they can be seen as "core" features of the culture jamming genre, the other three features are also evident to varying extents. For example, ®™ark is clearly collaborative: not only is it a joint effort among its creators, it also serves as an organizational mechanism for fostering collaboration among other like-minded artists and patrons – what might be called a structure for "meta-collaboration." As a genre, culture jamming is also heterotopic, in the sense that it creates alternative spaces and opportunities for new ways of seeing culture-as-usual from a different point of view.

®™ark may not seem to be the best example of perishability: it has enjoyed a relatively long life (in internet art-project terms). Indeed it has become somewhat institutionalized as a result of its inclusion in the Whitney Biennial, Ars Electronica in Linz (Austria), and a host of other contemporary arts exhibitions, and as it has become the subject of a growing scholarly literature. However, ®™ark has supported or actually created a host of projects that have been designed to be short-lived or ephemeral, in response to temporary situations or events (e.g., WTO meetings, the Bush presidential campaign), along the lines of conceptual art projects. As noted at the beginning of this chapter, ®™ark, like culture jamming more broadly, is often associated with tactical media, a strategy which emphasizes rapid response and intervention, mobility, and flexibility (Braman, 2002; Cubitt, 2006; Garcia & Lovink, 1977; Richardson, 2003). "[T]he practice of 'tactical media' stresses mobility in the face of fast-moving technological and social change. Action taken to alter them must take account of their mobile nature, and must respond to the minutiae of the current situation" (Stallabrass, 2003, p. 13).

The aim of this chapter has been to show that culture jamming, as a genre of alternative/activist new media, is the latest incarnation in a long line of parodies, media hoaxes, and cultural pranks that precedes the internet era. It is a tactic of cultural resistance and protest aimed at exposing the injustices and absurdities of mainstream society by subverting the imagery and practices of popular culture – especially the pervasive commercialism, consumerism, and corporate power of contemporary market-based society. Among the genres discussed in this book, it is notable for its subcultural acuity, its sense of humor, and its readiness to play pranks on or intervene in any aspect of mainstream culture that takes itself too seriously.

Culture jamming, as its name implies, is also the most aesthetically sophisticated of the genres. The rupture and derangement of ideological spectacles and taken-for-granted assumptions are its stock in trade, and fragmentation, mimicry, juxtaposition, bricolage, appropriation, détournement and dérive are all in its toolbox. Culture jamming is a worthy heir of Dada and the Situationist International. By exposing and recontextualizing the mechanisms and elements of popular culture, it attempts to open new perspectives on the everyday and reveal unexpected ways to "speak truth to power."

However, as the discussion about reverse jamming suggests,

culture jamming runs the risk of becoming a victim of its own success, to the extent that its approach, tactics, and objectives are absorbed and applied in mainstream and alternative culture alike. In an increasingly complex media landscape of always-on ideas, images, and expressions streaming from every possible source, quarter, and point of view, even the most incisive and skillful culture jamming projects may simply be unable to "cut through the clutter." Of course, part of the appeal of culture jamming is its insider quality, its power to reach just those groups who are most in tune with, and prepared to act on, its oppositional or subversive purposes and messages. Networked new media technologies are surely better-suited to this selective, participatory mode of media engagement than are traditional mass media "pipelines." But as some of the critics cited in this chapter point out, a question remains regarding the effectiveness of culture jamming projects as mechanisms of social and cultural change. Is it enough to raise awareness, shape an attitude, or cultivate an ironic stance, if such awareness, attitudes, or stances do not translate into action and a change of a repressive status quo?

In the next chapter, we turn to a genre where action takes center stage and "monkeywrenching the media machine" is taken a bit more literally: alternative computing.

CHAPTER 4

Hacking the New Out of the Old

Alternative Computing

A second genre of alternative/activist new media involves the material infrastructure of information technologies and media. Where culture jamming adopts the forms, styles, and conventions of popular culture and commerce – entertainment, advertising, marketing, fashion, corporate branding – with the purpose of subverting and critiquing them, in alternative computing, activist technologists design, build, and "hack" or reconfigure systems with the purpose of resisting political, commercial, and state restraints on open access to information and the use of information technologies.

The notions of "hackers" and "hacking" have been subjects of intense interest among both academic specialists and the general public for nearly two decades, especially as these terms have been co-opted by law enforcement and popular media as synonyms for malicious, destructive, criminal, or even terroristic activities using computers. As several observers have noted, this rhetorical move is actually an inversion of the original meaning of the words that developed and still prevails within the computing community. Some have argued that this inversion has been a deliberate strategy intended to shift popular perceptions of computing expertise and help lock down or stabilize technical innovation (and rein in innovators), in the name of security and safety (Nissenbaum, 2004; Thomas, 2002) – to "contain the effects of the new information technologies" (Goodrum & Manion, 2000, p. 56). Many writers on online activism also use these terms, and the variation "hacktivism," to refer to a wide variety of projects that use computing technologies for political and cultural protest and resistance.

However, I have chosen the broader term *alternative computing*[1] to describe a range of activities, including but not restricted to hacking, that are united by a shared ethical and political commitment to information access, open systems, and control over one's personal information and communications as fundamental rights and as a necessary condition for emancipatory politics and equitable social participation.[2] This chapter focuses on projects with explicitly constructive political, social, and cultural purposes, rather than those that are primarily criminal, terroristic, or exploitative enterprises. This approach aligns, for example, with the longstanding distinction within the computing community between "white-hat" hackers, who deliberately seek out and expose systems and software vulnerabilities as a way to identify problems and solve them, and destructive "black-hat" hackers or "crackers," who launch computer viruses, break into computers to destroy or steal financial data, wage botnet attacks against financial or political rivals, and so on (Leibowitz, 2003). Although hacktivism, electronic civil disobedience, and other forms of intervention in the computing infrastructure that challenge powerful interests are often characterized as anarchistic or terroristic, especially by those interests, and although some radical projects may engage in illegal activities, the principal focus here is on projects with affirmative aims.

This framing contrasts with that of other authors who have tended to focus on just one type of activity or another (e.g., free/libre/open-source software [FLOSS], hacktivism, electronic civil disobedience, etc.). Second, the term situates hacking and hacktivism, whether in the mastery sense used by computer technologists or in the criminal sense favored by sensationalist media and national security/law enforcement professionals, as just one element among others in a larger socio-technical domain (Jordan & Taylor, 2004). Anthropologist Chris Kelty has characterized this domain and its denizens as a 'recursive public':

> ... geeks argue *about* technology but also argue *with* and *through* it, by building, modifying, and maintaining the very software, networks, and legal tools within which and by which they associate with one another. [This is] why certain arrangements

of technology, organization, and law – specifically that of the Internet and Free Software – are so vitally important to these geeks. (Kelty, 2008, p. 5, emphasis added)

That is, in alternative computing, the technological infrastructure itself becomes the arena for expression and social change – not just a means to a social end, but an expression and manifestation of social and political participation in itself. It is a crucial example of what Pablo Boczkowski and I have called the "double materiality" of media and information technologies: they are both the means of cultural/political expression and cultural/political expressions in themselves, simultaneously "cultural material and material culture" (Boczkowski & Lievrouw, 2008, p. 955). Activist technologists consider systems as a sort of meritocratic canvas or stage for trying out ideas and expressing themselves, which in principle should be limited only by the ability or skill of the user, just as in painting, music, writing, or other forms of creative work.

In this chapter we explore the cultural and ethical foundations of this activist genre, including its relationship to hacking, "hacktivism," and other forms of online political action. The case of Eric Corley, the pseudonymous publisher of the online magazine *2600: The Hacker Quarterly*, and the publication's involvement in the circulation of the Decrypt Content Scrambling System (DeCSS) program, is examined to illustrate how the political and ethical commitments of alternative computing, combined with the technological savvy of its practitioners, make it at once a powerful activist strategy and a high-profile target for government and commercial interests intent on controlling access to information and information technology. The chapter closes with a brief review of the key features of alternative computing as an alternative/activist new media genre.

The domain of alternative computing

The tactics and techniques of alternative computing vary widely. They range from the design and distribution of "open source" or "free" software whose licensing terms undermine the intellectual-property-driven business models of mainstream software and media firms, to the planting of "Easter eggs" (small bits of hidden code) in software programs that may unexpectedly "roll the credits" (to acknowledge the contributions of the program's otherwise uncredited and anonymous programmers) or suddenly redirect users to a game, video, or other activity hidden in the program.[3] Some projects publicly demonstrate the susceptibility of critical systems to security breaches, breakdowns, or sabotage – often over the vendor's objections. Activists may also engage in more disruptive actions, such as the development and circulation of data encryption programs that elude state and commercial surveillance; disabling or sabotaging digital copy protection schemes (so-called "digital rights management," or DRM) or surveillance cameras (e.g., the Institute for Applied Autonomy; see Chapter 3); or mapping and posting locations where users can piggyback on unsecured wireless broadband access. In some controversial cases, activists have designed and launched software that generates denial-of-service (DOS), spam, or "ping-storm" attacks that flood and overwhelm the systems of organizations that activists believe are engaged in exploitative, unjust, or corrupt activities (e.g., the Electronic Disturbance Theater's FloodNet application, used by the Zapatista insurgents in Mexico; see Chapter 3). Activist programmers also built the original open-journalism web platform for the first Independent Media Center (IMC) at the World Trade Organization protests in Seattle in 1999, which has been adopted and refined by IMCs around the world (see Chapter 5).

These diverse activities and tactics are tied together by their deliberately interventionist nature. In one way or another, alternative computing projects implement, manipulate, or modify the technology itself, to make a social, political, or economic point. Activists engaged in alternative computing (whether professional engineers or amateur "geeks") have a high degree of technical mastery and tend to share the belief that in the right hands, computing technology is a force for good. As we will see in the next section, the roots of this broadly libertarian, meritocratic worldview are attributable to the "hacker ethic" that developed among highly skilled programmers and engineers in the 1960s and 1970s. This perspective, which combined technical elitism with counterculture visions of a more just, open society, has been a key influence in the development of several major activist organizations, including the Electronic Frontier Foundation (http://www.eff.org) and Computer Professionals for Social Responsibility (http://www.cpsr.org), as well as in more *ad hoc* activist projects. It considers any constraint on the ability to generate and share knowledge, including technical knowledge, as contrary to the goals and realization of a good society.

Of course, as illustrated by the culture jamming example in the previous chapter (and, indeed, this entire volume), many forms of activism today employ computing in one way or another. Political campaigns and protest movements use email to raise money, organize events, and communicate with supporters. Bloggers report news items, share opinions, and generate debates with their readers. Culture jammers create spoof websites and banner advertisements. However, in these other forms, the technology itself is usually treated as a channel for communication, rather than a site for intervention in itself. Stefan Wray (1998) points out that different types of online activism can be viewed along a continuum from "all word" to "all deed" – that is, from projects that are primarily communicative to those that are more like direct action or "electronic civil disobedience," as strikes or street demonstrations are for more traditional social movements. As conceptualized here, alternative computing lies closer to the "all deed" end of the spectrum. And because it targets high-value systems that reach into all aspects of commerce, government, law enforcement, and culture, it is also one of the most high-risk – and potentially transformational – genres of new media activism. Many of the characteristics that make alternative computing effective (and risky) come from its historical relationship to a creative, high-stakes form of demonstrating technological expertise within the culture of computing and high tech: *hacking*.

The origins of alternative computing: the hacker ethic

In 1996, an informal student handbook circulated on the campus of the Massachusetts Institute of Technology (MIT) in Cambridge, entitled *HowToGAMIT (Get Around MIT)*. MIT is among the most prestigious American engineering schools, and its students have a long history of staging elaborate technical pranks, or "hacks," in which the Institute's facilities, equipment, and services are all resources (and fair game) for highly skilled engineering students wanting to show off their ingenuity and to blow off a little steam. The *HowToGAMIT* handbook includes a "hacker's code," an honor system devised by students over the years to govern pranking projects. Among its precepts, would-be hackers are admonished to:

> Be *safe*. Your safety, the safety of your fellow hackers, and the safety of anyone you hack should never be compromised. . . . Be *subtle*. Leave no evidence that you were ever there. . . . Leave no damage. . . . Do not steal anything. . . . Brute force is the last resort of the incompetent. . . . Do not hack alone (just like swimming). (Quoted in Peterson, 2003, p. 10, emphasis in original)

The term *hacker* was adopted within the computing/software community in the early days of the field[4] to describe exceptionally skilled programmers who were adept at creating counterintuitive, elegant solutions, or "hacks," for difficult or intractable programming problems (Levy, 1984; Nissenbaum, 2004; Peterson, 2003; Thomas, 2002). Hacks were intended to demonstrate the skill of the programmer/engineer rather than to disrupt or damage a system *per se*. These programmers, who tended to mistrust authority and to be more interested in ingenious, demonstrable solutions than in bureaucratic rules, were drawn to the counterculture values and lifestyles that flourished in affluent, technologically advanced societies in the 1960s and 1970s. Within this elite community a sort of "digital utopianism" developed that viewed computing not only as a class of technological tools, but as a full-fledged force for positive social transformation as well (Turner, 2006). For these younger technologists and engineers, hacking represented a

> commitment to total and free access to computers and information, belief in the immense powers of computers to improve people's lives and create art and beauty, mistrust of centralized authority, a disdain for obstacles erected against free access to computing, and an insistence that hackers be evaluated by no other criteria than technical virtuosity and accomplishment (by hacking alone and not "bogus" criteria such as degrees, age, race, or position). (Nissenbaum, 2004, p. 197)

It is interesting to note that such "digital utopianism" arose at around the same countercultural moment as the Situationists in France. However, instead of making art, writing dense theoretical tracts, détourning fashion magazines and comics, shooting experimental films, setting out on *dérives*, and clashing with national police across the barricades, young American technologists stayed up late, wrote and shared code, left friendly code "calling cards" or Easter eggs in presumably secure systems, experimented with hallucinogenics and communal living, invented and played games using massive, expensive computer networks, read "speculative fiction," and imagined a future where computers would "change your life for the better" (Levy, 1984, p. 33). The fundamental anti-authoritarianism of these first-generation hackers motivated them to adapt and scale down massive military technology to build their own homemade, hobbyist "microcomputers," which became the prototype for the personal computer – and may still be the most significant and enduring hacker legacy. "Without the hackers of the 1960s, there never would have been a PC; without the PC, there would have never been a PC industry; without a PC industry, there would never have been the hackers of the 1980s and 1990s" (Thomas, 2002, p. 18). As Fred Turner's analysis (2006) suggests, the blending of counterculture aesthetics and lifestyles, left-libertarian politics, and the techno-idealism of young, creative, and highly motivated engineers and computer hobbyists might well be summed up in the subtitle of the original *Whole*

Earth Catalog, the early bible of counterculture living: *access to tools.*

Like the Situationists, hackers and hacker culture have always been attracted to the manifesto form, commensurate with their social and political ambitions. The sample of manifestos in the box below were written by some of the most renowned hackers and influential advocates of the digital revolution, including Richard Stallman, founder of the Free Software movement and a progenitor of open source; John Perry Barlow, lyricist for the Grateful Dead and co-founder of the Electronic Frontier Foundation; McKenzie Wark, founding member of the influential Nettime listserv and a professor of media and cultural studies at New York University; and hackers Timothy May, Anarchy and the AoC, and The Mentor. Their statements illustrate the writers' sense of the dramatic, almost apocalyptic, importance of computing technology and practice for the transformation of society, culture, and politics.

The last passage, by McKenzie Wark, which was written as a deliberate variation on the *Communist Manifesto* (as was May's *Crypto Anarchist Manifesto*), links creative work – hacking – and social change in a way that Alain Touraine would surely recognize. In economies where information is the prime commodity, and information technologies the key means of production, a society's ability to "act on itself" depends on those with the ability to "hack" – i.e., to manipulate, redesign, reconfigure, play with – the information infrastructure and its products in novel and creative ways.

Aside from the occasional indulgence in juvenile, grandiose, or siege-mentality rhetoric, the excerpts suggest several core themes or concerns that continue to animate alternative computing as a form of online activism. Perhaps none are as important as the preservation of open access to information and information/media technology, to anyone for any constructive purpose; a corresponding opposition to any barrier to access, whether technological, institutional, cultural, or philosophical; and the right to control one's own information and communications. Thus,

I consider that the golden rule required that if I like a program I must share it with other people who like it. Software sellers want to divide the users and conquer them, making each user agree not to share with others. I refuse to break solidarity with other users in this way.

Richard Stallman, *The GNU Manifesto*, 1985 (from Stallman, 2002 [1985], p. 32)

This is our world now . . . the world of the electron and the switch, the beauty of the baud. We make use of a service already existing without paying for what could be dirt-cheap if it wasn't run by profiteering gluttons, and you call us criminals. We explore . . . and you call us criminals. We seek after knowledge . . . and you call us criminals. We exist without skin color, without nationality, without religious bias . . . and you call us criminals. You build atomic bombs, you wage wars, you murder, cheat, and lie to us and try to make us believe it's for our own good, yet we're the criminals.

Yes, I am a criminal. My crime is that of curiosity. My crime is that of judging people by what they say and think, not what they look like. My crime is that of outsmarting you, something that you will never forgive me for.

I am a hacker, and this is my manifesto. You may stop this individual, but you can't stop us all . . . after all, we're all alike.

The Mentor, *The Conscience of a Hacker/The Hacker Manifesto* (Mentor, 1986)

A specter is haunting the modern world, the specter of crypto anarchy. . . . Just as the technology of printing altered and reduced the power of medieval guilds and the social power structure, so too will cryptologic methods fundamentally alter the nature of corporations and of government interference in economic transactions. . . . just as a seemingly minor invention like barbed wire [altered] forever the concepts of land and property rights in the frontier west, so too will the seemingly minor discovery out of an arcane branch of mathematics come to be the wire clippers which dismantle the barbed wire around intellectual property.

Timothy May, *The Crypto Anarchist Manifesto*, 1992 (quoted in Ludlow, 2001, pp. 61–3)

*We, the computer-literate and technologically superior, in
order to break the ignorant chains of those who hold us back,
do hereby declare our freedom from those who control what
they do not understand. . . . We reject the repulsive nonsense
shoved down our throats by all forms of media telling of the
dangers of piracy, pornography, and in general, free thought.
. . . The internet (NOT info-superhighway, or i-way, as those
terms are simply insulting and degrading, made up by the
ignorant) cannot and SHOULD NOT be regulated. It should
be allowed to make it's [sic] own rules. It is bigger than any
world you can and can't imagine, and it will not be controlled.
It is the embodiment of all that is free; free information,
friendship, alliances, materials, ideas, suggestions, news, and
more. . . . those of us who see clearly know that the internet is
the greatest invention ever, topping the telephone and electricity.
It is a gathering of the mental body of billions of people, and
we will not be stopped. . . . It is a technological revolution,
and a revolution of ideas. We will fight in battles for our
freedom to think, should there be any, but we will not start
any. We are not a violent group, but our opposition believes
ideas should not be let loose to grow, and they will begin the
battle. They have no honor, stealing from us our rights, our
liberty, and our freedom of thought. And for this, we label them
unforgiven . . . .*

    Anarchy and the AoC, *Declaration of Digital Independence*
                                    (Anarchy and the AoC, 1993)

*Governments of the Industrial World, you weary giants of flesh
and steel, I come from Cyberspace, the new home of Mind. . . .
You have not engaged in our great and gathering conversation,
nor did you create the wealth of our marketplaces. . . . We
are creating a world that all may enter without privilege or
prejudice. . . . We are creating a world where anyone, anywhere
may express his or her beliefs, no matter how singular, without
fear of being coerced into silence or conformity. Your legal
concepts of property, expression, identity, movement, and
context do not apply to us. They are based on matter. There is
no matter here.*

        John Perry Barlow, *A Declaration of the Independence of
        Cyberspace*, 1996 (quoted in Ludlow, 2001, pp. 28–9)

> *Hackers create the possibility of new things entering the world.*
> *Not always great things, or even good things, but new things.*
> *In art, in science, in philosophy and culture, in any production*
> *of knowledge where data can be gathered, where information*
> *can be extracted from it, and where in that information new*
> *possibilities for the world produced, there are hackers hacking*
> *the new out of the old.*
> McKenzie Wark, *A Hacker Manifesto* (Wark, 2004, § 004)

the major targets of alternative computing projects include censorship; restrictions on free speech and interaction; technical or price constraints on internet use (such as challenges to the "network neutrality" principle established in the early days of ARPANET; see Sandvig, 2007); state and corporate secrecy; the surveillance, profiling, and collection of dossiers on individuals; intellectual and academic freedom; and, especially, restrictive or coercive intellectual property laws.

Indeed, struggles over copyright have become a core rallying point for alternative computing, particularly the implementation of technological "hobbles," gateways or lock-outs (DRM technologies) intended to prevent people from retrieving, sharing, or circulating information in ways unauthorized by rights owners or government authorities. Peer-to-peer (P2P) file sharing systems, for example, have been a particular target of law enforcement and media industries for over a decade. There is nothing inherently illicit or oppositional about P2P systems; they are distributed computing architectures that allow users to locate and retrieve files from each other's computers. As its name suggests, P2P architecture is based on the idea that people seek and give advice, and make recommendations, within networks of other people with similar interests. P2P systems are social and cooperative environments by definition, providing opportunities for people to share what they know and for "social authorship" (Atton, 2004, p. 103).

In 1999 Shawn Fanning created the first "off the shelf" P2P system, Napster. Fanning was no intellectual property crusader;

he was a college student who wanted to help friends share music files. But Napster became an immediate and immense success, attracting both thousands of enthusiastic file sharing users and a massive legal crackdown from the music industry. Entertainment firms sued Fanning on the grounds that P2P architecture was intended to facilitate illegal file copying, and thus violated the anticircumvention provisions of the U.S. Digital Millennium Copyright Act. Fanning was forced to shut Napster down and to sell his software and patents to the media giant Bertelsmann to meet his legal expenses. (Napster has since been re-established as a corporate paid-subscription service.)

But Napster's success had already spawned a host of similar services with different, internationally distributed structures out of the reach of U.S. copyright restrictions. Over the next decade P2P services like KaZaA, Gnutella, Grokster, Morpheus, the Pirate Bay, LimeWire, and others entered into a legal cat-and-mouse game with the media industries and law enforcement authorities, changing their architectures or geographic locations in response to legal and police actions. Industry rights holders have also attempted – though with little success to date – to cast P2P architecture itself as illegitimate, though universities, libraries, voice-over-IP (VoIP) services like Skype, and other organizations that use P2P systems to share materials legally, as well as the computing industry itself, have opposed moves to sanction particular technological designs.

Over time, P2P file sharing services have lost several major legal cases and have been held liable for the infringing actions of their users, including Napster in 2001, Grokster in 2005, the Pirate Bay in 2009, and, most recently, LimeWire in May 2010. Nonetheless, users and programmers have continued to defend file sharing on social and ethical grounds, seeing P2P as a form of anti-corporate, anti-market economic and cultural resistance against a global corporate oligopoly intent on propping up an exhausted business model and monetizing all forms of information and culture. Indeed, the Pirate Bay conviction in Sweden sparked an upsurge of recruitment for the Pirate Party, whose platform includes reform of punitive intellectual property laws. The Pirate Party quickly grew to become one of the largest political parties in Sweden and in 2009 gained enough votes to take two seats in the European Parliament.

Taking another approach, the "Defective by Design" campaign of the Free Software Foundation (http://www.defectivebydesign. org) opposes digital rights management (DRM) technologies that prevent the copying or distribution of information, or that limit the ways that users may employ the products they buy, such as mobile telephone lock-out mechanisms that restrict customers' choices of service providers, software interoperability, or content. (Several recent examples involve Apple's iPhone, including its exclusive arrangement with AT&T as its service provider in the U.S. market; Apple's refusal to support iPhone applications, or "apps," that employ Adobe's Flash software; and its apparently arbitrary and opaque standards for which apps will be supported for the device; Stelter, 2010). Not only do such mechanisms artificially enclose users in proprietary "walled gardens" that block access and interactions to just those services allowed (and charged for) by the provider, says Defective by Design; they are deliberately built to be sub-optimal or "defective" technologies that retard innovation and inhibit new uses and markets. The campaign encourages software developers to invent workarounds or "repairs" for the defects that will enable them to be used in other ways than those stipulated by vendors.

Obviously, alternative computing projects have their strident critics, especially among those who see all such efforts as thinly veiled criminal activities intended to subvert copyright, steal corporate and state secrets, infringe patents, violate company and individual privacy, sabotage private property and market-based business models, undermine national security, and so on. The objections are understandable: where information is the prime commodity, an ethos that insists that "information wants to be free" poses a fundamental challenge to the very basis of the dominant economic system. Hacktivism, electronic civil

disobedience, and related activities are seen as naïve at best, terroristic at worst.

On the other hand, some analysts have pointed out that many
alternative computing projects, like older forms of political protest, use blockade, trespass, boycott, and other non-violent tactics
to resist laws they consider unjust or unwarranted. These writers
contend that, to the extent that activists articulate their ethical
and political motivations and goals, and accept the consequences
of breaking the laws as a means to change them, such projects
should be considered fully legitimate forms of political protest
and not subjected to disproportionate or punitive punishment
merely because the action occurs online (Goodrum & Manion,
2000). For these observers, the harsh sentences handed out
to hacktivists and programmers under the guise of national or
economic security, or in the name of global copyright regimes
engineered by U.S. entertainment firms, do not reflect whatever
real threat such projects may pose to the infrastructure or social
order. Rather, they are a product of the moral panic that has been
carefully cultivated around hacking, and indeed any type of "off-
label" computer use, by law enforcement and the media.

In the next section, we turn to a case study that amply
illustrates these countervailing interests and tensions – the publication of the DeCSS code in *The Hacker Quarterly* and its legal
and technical consequences.

DeCSS and *The Hacker Quarterly*

As suggested above, in recent years the label *hacker* has been
taken up by law enforcement agencies, government, and the
private sector, and frequently repeated in the popular media,
as a synonym for vandal, thief, or terrorist. There has been an
effort to cast independent technological skill and creativity as a
dangerous or criminal activity, often by associating hacking with
infringement of intellectual property rights – which itself has
been increasingly reframed in terms of "piracy" and "trafficking"
(Nissenbaum, 2004; Thomas, 2002). This shift came to the fore

in a landmark case involving the online journalist Eric Corley and his magazine *2600: The Hacker Quarterly* (http://www.2600. com).[5]

2600: The Hacker Quarterly began publication in 1995, first as a print periodical and then also online (it publishes today in both formats). Its name is a reference to the audio frequency used in "blue boxes," devices built by self-styled "phone phreaks" in the 1970s and 1980s to gain free access to AT&T's long-distance telephone system in the U.S. The publication covers topics and issues that are mainly of interest to software and hardware engineers and computer hobbyists.

In late 1999 Corley published a story about a short program, the Decrypt Content Scrambling System (DeCSS), which had been written and posted online by a 16-year-old Norwegian programmer named Jon Lech Johansen. DeCSS unlocked the Content Scrambling System (CSS), a DRM technology that prevented users from playing DVDs (including those they had legally purchased) on computers running non-Microsoft or -Apple operating systems, especially open-source systems like Linux favored among professional and amateur programmers. Johansen had discovered how to unlock CSS by reverse-engineering it – that is, he took the original program apart to learn how it was built and how it might be modified. Johansen posted his code online, and it was soon circulating widely on the Web. Corley reported on the discovery in *2600*, including the code itself and links to other sites online where it was available.

After DeCSS appeared in *2600*, it came to the attention of DVD producers in the entertainment industry and their attorneys, who took immediate legal action. They argued that by revealing weaknesses in the CSS system, DeCSS violated a trade secret. In the process of decryption, DeCSS also created an unlocked copy of the DVD contents on the user's computer drive; industry representatives alleged that this feature facilitated the illegal copying and distribution of their works and thus (echoing the argument used against P2P file sharing) violated the anticircumvention provision of the U.S. Digital Millennium Copyright

Act (DMCA). A coalition comprising essentially all of the major U.S. film studios (Universal Studios, Paramount, MGM, Time-Warner, Tristar, Disney, and 20th Century Fox) sued Corley and several other websites that had posted the code, seeking an order to have it removed from those sites. Corley invoked his First Amendment speech and press rights as a defense, arguing that *2600* should have as much right to cover and describe DeCSS as, for example, the *New York Times*, which had also published stories about DeCSS and its sources but was not prosecuted by the studios.

Initially, in late December 1999, there was an outpouring of protest from Corley's and Johansen's supporters in the computing community around the world, and California Superior Court Judge William Elfving temporarily denied the industry's request for a restraining order. However, in January 2000, U.S. District Judge Lewis Kaplan, in the Southern District of New York, did issue a preliminary injunction that directed Corley to remove the program from the *2600* website. In February, he issued a further memorandum declaring that executable computer code is not protected speech under the First Amendment of the U.S. Constitution. On January 14, the Motion Picture Association of America (MPAA) filed two more lawsuits against *2600* and Corley in the Southern District of New York and in Connecticut, alleging violation of the DMCA. On January 25, both Jon Johansen and his father were arrested at their home in Norway (the website where DeCSS was posted was in the father's name). Corley complied with Judge Kaplan's take-down order, but in what he called an act of electronic civil disobedience, he maintained links from *2600* to other sites where DeCSS was still available.

However, in August the court ruled that not only was Corley not allowed to post the text of the DeCSS code itself, he was also prohibited from posting links to any other site or source for DeCSS, even those in jurisdictions where the program was legal (as in Europe and other parts of the world). On appeal in 2002, the U.S. Second Circuit Court of Appeals upheld the original ruling. With his resources and options depleted, and his co-defendants having settled with the industry plaintiffs, Corley chose not to appeal the decision to the U.S. Supreme Court.

Nonetheless, neither the 2002 judgment against Corley, nor the subsequent obsolescence and replacement of DeCSS by a myriad of other decryption programs have interrupted the posting or linking online to executable forms of the original DeCSS by other activists. In what has amounted to an electronic civil disobedience movement protesting the DMCA and the censorship of 2600, activists from the U.S. and around the world have continued to post the code in defiance of the court's action (electronic civil disobedience is discussed at more length in Chapter 6). Some activists converted the code into artworks, on the principle that works of art are still unambiguously protected as free speech by the First Amendment to the U.S. Constitution. Dr. David Touretzky, a research professor of computer science and neuroscience at Carnegie-Mellon University in Pittsburgh, PA, created the *Gallery of CSS Descramblers* to make the point that executable computer code is in fact speech and should be protected as such (http://www.cs.cmu.edu/~dst/DeCSS/Gallery/index.html). The Gallery includes dramatic readings of the code, renderings on clothing, musical transcriptions, two short films (*DeCSS the Movie* and *Stairs of Freedom*) containing animations of the code, and, notably, the 2002 *DeCSS Haiku* by Seth Schoen, which Touretzky describes as "both a commentary on the DeCSS situation and a correct and complete description of the descrambling algorithm. Truly inspired." The *DeCSS Haiku* was later featured in stories in the *Wall Street Journal, San Francisco Chronicle, Wired,* and the *New York Times Magazine.* (Schoen also discusses the haiku at http://www.loyalty.org/~schoen/haiku.html.) To this day, however, Corley and 2600 are still enjoined from posting either the code or links to it.

Interestingly, DeCSS endures as a rallying point for activist technologists concerned about the consequences of restrictive intellectual property regimes like the DMCA for both technology development and speech rights. Using large-scale content analyses of the web, Eschenfelder and Desai (2004) found that there was almost no decline in the number of sites, including U.S.-hosted websites, where DeCSS itself was posted or that linked to other sites where executable versions were available, between the time of the original injunction and 2003. By early 2004, DeCSS was still being posted on numerous sites around the world, particularly in the Netherlands, Germany, France, and the United Kingdom (Eschenfelder, 2005), as well as in the U.S., where such posting was still prosecutable under the DMCA – even though DeCSS had long since become obsolete.

And in a more recent turn, Jon Johansen, the programmer who began it all (and who, since the 2600 case, has become something of a celebrity among programmers, known as "DVD Jon"), created one of the first hacks for unlocking the original iPhone in 2007. Under the headline "iPhone Independence Day," Johansen published the hack on his blog (http://nanocr. eu/2007/07/03/iphone-without-att/). It allows owners to activate the phone using Windows, without subscribing to the AT&T wireless plan mandated by Apple (Vamosi, 2007).

Summary: alternative computing as a genre

At first glance, the 2600/DeCSS case would not seem to have much in common with more explicitly "political" activist projects, such as those related to antiwar, environmental, or anti-globalization movements. Ultimately, DeCSS is a tool that makes it easier for consumers to enjoy popular entertainment programs, and was invented by a teenager who wanted to watch movies on a Linux-equipped computer. However, in many ways the 2600/DeCSS case crystallizes the myriad interests and stakes that come into play in activist computing.

On one hand, state and legal authorities and industry representatives take the view that the internet and computing infrastructure are so vital to the economy and security that a "zero tolerance" approach is essential to prevent serious harm whenever technologies are used for anything but government- or corporate-authorized purposes. This perspective has tended to dominate most discussions about internet policy and is largely responsible for the prosecutorial zeal evidenced in recent criminal cases involving computer hacking or breaches. On the other hand, critics of this view contend that such a heavy-handed approach has propped up an unsustainable intellectual property regime that stifles invention and innovation, legal sanctions that are wildly disproportionate to the actual risks and losses involved, and the criminalization of the very exploratory tinkering techniques that lie at the heart of software engineering and computing culture. The net effect may be a more stable, reliable, and "safe" internet, but it is also one that is increasingly closed to the sort of transformative innovativeness that created and sustained networked computing in the first place – one that is, as some writers have put it, "slouching toward the ordinary" (Herring, 2004) or "wired shut" (Gillespie, 2007).

In addition, many believe that one of the most significant outcomes of the 2600/DeCSS case is that it has helped accelerate moves toward an unprecedented shift in the legal balance between speech and property rights in American law (e.g., Cohen, 2003, 2006; Gillespie, 2007; Lessig, 2001; Litman, 2001; McLeod, 2005). By giving priority to the property rights of copyright holders – even in a case that did not in fact involve infringement *per se*, but only the dissemination of information that could conceivably be used to infringe – the legal decision against Corley allows the "anticircumvention" provisions of the DMCA to take precedence over the First Amendment rights of speech and press. The decision also suggests that internet-based journalists are not entitled to the same speech and press protections and privileges that print and broadcast journalists take for granted. This a troubling consequence given the recent economic crisis among mainstream news organizations and the closure or radical staffing cuts in ostensibly "legitimate," traditional newsrooms protected by the First Amendment. Online publications may be subject to prior restraint, or censored after publication, in ways that would be unthinkable for print and broadcast news. (We will revisit this issue in the next chapter on Indymedia and the blogosphere.) As Corley put it in his announcement that 2600 would not appeal the decision to the Supreme Court, both news about and links to DeCSS had been published by the *New York Times,* the *Village Voice,* and the *San Jose Mercury-News,* yet only 2600 and other small online outlets were targeted in the original lawsuit (http://www.2600. com/news/view/article/1233). In addition, by explicitly excluding executable computer code as speech, the ruling can be seen as a direct repudiation of the values of experimentation, innovativeness, and publicness that are central to high-tech culture.

It can be argued that three features of alternative computing, as a genre of new media activism, have made it the central focus of these debates. The first, alluded to earlier in this chapter, is that it is interventionist by definition. For computer professionals and hobbyists, it is not enough to hypothesize, criticize, or debate technology as a force in society; activist technologists wield that force directly by reconfiguring the infrastructure itself. This is a primary reason why computing expertise continues to be simultaneously celebrated and feared in popular culture portrayals (Kelty, 2007; Nissenbaum, 2004; Thomas, 2002). Like culture jamming, alternative computing may be one more "form political activism may have to take" (Allen, 2003, pp. 7, 11) in a society where all aspects of expression and interaction are pervasively mediated by extensive computing networks, and where legacy technologies like print and broadcasting play an increasingly ancillary role, serving educated elites at one extreme and marginalized underclasses at the other.

Second, alternative computing is profoundly heterotopic in its worldview, practice, and ethical commitments. This may be attributable to the historically libertarian or countercultural perspectives within the computing community documented by a number of writers (e.g., Barbrook, 2001; Turner, 2006). The manifestos of hackers, geeks, and cypherpunks, aphorisms like "information wants to be free," fears about "jackboots on the

Infobahn," and the policy proposals of organizations like the Electronic Frontier Foundation and Computer Professionals for Social Responsibility reveal a deep distrust of centralized authority, mainstream social conventions, and privilege gained through anything except intellectual prowess, technical skill, resourcefulness, and creativity, as well as a desire to create and preserve (possibly utopian) spaces where people who feel like "outsiders" in most social contexts can live, work, and play with their peers.[6]

Finally, and consistent with the heterotopic nature of this activist genre, alternative computing projects are almost always small scale in conception and execution – although, as the DeCSS and other cases reviewed here attest, they can have far-reaching technological and social consequences. For example, when undergraduate student Shawn Fanning devised the peer-to-peer file sharing system he called Napster (after his own nickname) in 1999, he may have intended only to create an easy way for a few like-minded friends to search for and share music online. It seems unlikely that he could have foreseen how quickly his innovation would proliferate across college campuses and around the world, that in less than a decade peer-to-peer would transform the consumption of traditional media content for an entire generation, that he would first make a fortune and then end up in bankruptcy, or that Napster would touch off a vast legal and economic struggle over how media content of all kinds should be distributed and sold, including recent efforts by music and movie studios to outlaw peer-to-peer technology itself. Likewise, Eric Corley may not have anticipated that publishing a few lines of code that were already circulating online would incur the wrath (and the full legal and financial force) of the U.S. entertainment industry, or that his loss in court would change the definition of "freedom of the press."

Ironically, perhaps, the manifesto writers' intuitions about the transformational power of computing, in the right hands, may have been right all along.

CHAPTER 5

Breaking Through the Information Blockade

Participatory Journalism and Indymedia

It is the year 2015, and the institutional foundations of American journalism and the news industry are in the last stages of collapse. Google and Amazon have already merged to form Googlezon, a protean force that dominates all aspects of entertainment and culture by harvesting content from traditional media outlets and serving it back to individual consumers in algorithmically selected packages minutely tailored to their tastes and interests. As the narrator recalls,

> Twentieth-century news organizations are an afterthought, a lonely remnant of a not-too-distant past. . . . The News Wars of 2010 are notable for the fact that no actual news organizations take part. . . . in 2011 the slumbering fourth estate finally awakes to make its first, and final, stand. The *New York Times* sues Googlezon, claiming that the company's fact-stripping robots are a violation of copyright law.
>
> . . . On Sunday, March 9, 2014, Googlezon unleashes EPIC, the Evolving Personalized Information Construct. . . . Everyone contributes, and many people get paid a tiny cut of Googlezon's immense advertising revenue, proportional to the popularity of their contributions. . . . In 2014 the *New York Times* goes offline [and] becomes a print-only newsletter for the elite and the elderly.
>
> . . . 2015: Pinky Nankani, a refugee from the defunct *New York Times* digital edition, finds a new journalistic calling. She begins to collect photo-GPS-tagged neighborhood broadcasts. Soon Pinky's feed is a local lodestar, and more and more of her neighbors tag their broadcasts with GPS data, as they realize they too could be a part of it. (*EPIC 2015*; http://www.albinoblacksheep. com/flash/epic)

EPIC 2015, a mock-documentary by Robin Sloan and Matt Thompson, is a parody (Thompson, 2005). Nonetheless, its vision of journalism's future as an *ad hoc*, hyperlocal, freelance pursuit of a few amateurs with time on their hands, and its nightmare prognosis for the news industry and media institutions, seem remarkably prescient today, as the fortunes of major print and broadcast news organizations have plummeted and online journalism projects using social media proliferate.

To date, *EPIC 2015*'s dystopian vision of the "daily me" (Negroponte, 1995) has not been realized – at least, not entirely. But the industry's situation is unquestionably dire, a mixture of declining advertising revenues, shrinking audiences, and the challenge of new media technologies that extend their newsgathering and editorial powers, and simultaneously break down their privileged positions as information gatekeepers and agenda-setters. The current economic downturn has only accelerated the downward spiral, as newspapers in cities across the U.S. and Europe lay off legions of professional reporters or are forced to close entirely. David Carr, who covers the media industry for the *New York Times*, put it recently as follows: "Clearly, the sky is falling. The question is how many people will be left to cover it" (Carr, 2008).

A fourth genre of alternative and activist new media offers at least a partial answer to Carr's question: more people than we might think. The rise of *participatory journalism* – including citizen, grassroots, or open-source journalism projects, independent news and opinion blogs, and activist Indymedia sites – provides rich examples of local and special-interest reporting, editing, and opinion that simultaneously uphold and critique the traditional values and practices of journalism and the press. Like their forebears in the alternative, underground, and radical press, these projects provide coverage of under-reported news stories, commentary, and information sources from an alternative or oppositional perspective, as well as a running critique and deconstruction of mainstream media and news coverage. However, in contrast to the "vanguardism" of their radical forebears, most alternative journalism projects do not exist as mouthpieces or house organs for transmitting a centrally approved political line or message (Atton, 2003; Downing et al., 2001).

Instead, the goal is to create a diverse media space in which any and all voices can be heard, and where anyone may contribute reporting or opinion with a minimum of prior editorial gatekeeping, reflecting a commitment to speech and participation as the cornerstone of "radical democracy" (Pickard, 2006a, 2006b, 2008). The practice of journalism is adopted as a method of participation; thus these projects explicitly separate the practice of journalism from the institutional role and interests of traditional news and media industries. Such sites are often staffed by amateur or volunteer contributors, sometimes in collaboration with paid reporters and editors. Instead of the traditional advertising-based business model, some projects have adopted alternative support models, including collectives, cooperatives, not-for-profit foundations, and "crowdfunding" or community-funded journalism, to support their activities (Kershaw, 2008).

New forms of participatory journalism consider connectivity, interactivity, and community as essential to the practice of journalism and the production of news, and stress the fading distinctions among information providers, reporters, editors, and readers made possible by internet technologies (Deuze, 2003; Ryfe & Mensing, 2008).[1] *Indymedia,* in particular – the movement launched by media activists at the World Trade Organization protests in 1999, and which today includes about 175 Independent Media Centers (IMCs) worldwide – aims to create a "communications commons" whose watchword over the last decade has been "Don't hate the media – become the media" (Kidd, 2003).[2]

The remainder of this chapter begins with a brief overview of the current crisis in the news industry and the economic and technological challenges it faces. With this as context, we consider the concomitant rise of new forms of alternative or activist reporting, editing, opinion, and commentary online that comprise participatory journalism, and review some of the criticisms of these emergent forms. The latter part of the chapter focuses on the Indymedia movement as a central example and case study. In addition to being one of the most widespread forms of online media activism, Indymedia has been one of the most-studied activist media projects in recent years. As we will see, the successes – and pitfalls – of the Indymedia movement in its first decade suggest the kinds of challenges that lie ahead for journalism and the news, especially with respect to their changing roles within democratic political systems.

The press "crisis" in a new media context

Of the myriad recent accounts of impending collapse in the news business, perhaps none has better captured the industry's pervasive gloom and dismay than an *Economist* cover story in 2006: "Who Killed the Newspaper?" The special report enumerates all the usual suspects: advertisers defecting to other media; shareholders' relentless, ever-expanding demands for profit; acquiescent managers too ready to discard editorial talent to mollify shareholders; shifts away from straight news and analysis to entertainment and lifestyle coverage in attempts to woo younger audiences; the rise of competing free dailies with little interest in incisive investigative stories or more complex "watchdog" political reporting. And, of course, "the Internet" (*Economist*, 2006b).

The report concludes, however, that the decline of print dailies probably has had more to do with the complacency and defensiveness of an industry intent on propping up its traditional ways of doing business, and that has resisted technological change and engagement with its readers (in much the same way as other sectors of the media industry, including book publishing, television, motion pictures, and recorded music, have tended to resist new media technologies and their audiences' changing expectations). "In the past, newspaper companies saw little need to experiment or to change and spent little or nothing on research and development" (*Economist*, 2006c, p. 52).

Indeed, papers with websites have often treated them as

distractions from their core business of manufacturing and distributing newspapers, saving their best journalists and content for the print editions. Some major print and broadcast news organizations have ordered staff reporters and editors to stop posting reports to their own blogs, including first-hand accounts from the war in Iraq and conflicts in Kurdistan. The papers and networks demanded that the reporters stop blogging on the grounds that such "off the clock" postings would either expose the firms to liability lawsuits or "draw eyeballs away" from their traditional content and advertisers (Bowman & Willis, 2003). Increasingly, however, those in the print media are realizing the importance of their web presence. Edward Roussel, online editorial director of the *Telegraph* Group in Britain, observes, "Before, newspapers used their second- and third-rate journalists for the internet, but now we know we've got to use our very best" (*Economist*, 2006c, p. 53). *New Yorker* writer Nicholas Lemann agrees: "As journalism moves to the Internet, the main project ought to be moving reporters there, not stripping them away" (Lemann, 2006, p. 49).

The sense of crisis among industry leaders is paralleled by deep anxieties among working journalists themselves, who see their carefully nurtured professional practices and prerogatives being threatened by a rising tide of online dilettantes and a distrustful public. "Journalism schools and think-tanks, especially in America, are worried about the effect of a crumbling Fourth Estate" (*Economist*, 2006b, p. 9). The new entrants have been called everything from "barbarians at the gates" to "garage-band" amateurs ("What's Next?", 1999). But longstanding worries about the judgment and accountability of professional journalists, and declining public trust in the mainstream media in general, have also taken their toll. According to George Brock, International Editor of the *Times* of London,

> Taken together they mean that journalism is in trouble as an idea. Does this matter? The fourth estate cannot, thank goodness, be managed, reformed or even considered as a coherently organized profession. But journalists could think more clearly

than they do about how to improve the level of trust in their work. The case for the profession needs making all over again. (Brock, 2008, p. 23)

Pablo Boczkowski (2004) analyzes newspapers' adoption of digital technologies and online publishing over the last three decades. Although he avoids simple causal explanations, he draws many of the same conclusions about the news industry and journalism as the critics do. He finds that most papers have focused on "protecting the print franchise," drawing clear organizational and operational boundaries between their print and online editions, and favoring short-term gains instead of long-term investments in technology and innovation. They have reproduced a traditional, gatekeeping editorial model ("we publish, you read") in their online editions rather than develop new models "geared to the facilitation and management of user-authored content" (p. 177). Readers are seen as technically unsophisticated consumers rather than tech-savvy producers of information.

Whether news organizations have clung to their traditional models and prerogatives, or have been more willing to experiment, Boczkowski argues that the ways that newspapers produce and distribute news, and the professional and organizational culture of journalism, have changed dramatically in recent decades in the wake of the changing technologies of news gathering, editing, and publishing. However, he also notes that the concept of *convergence* (something of a cliché among industry analysts and new media academics) offers little help in understanding the changes buffeting the news business. Framing change in terms of convergence tends to focus on the end products of change rather than the processes that produce them, overemphasize the novelty of digital technologies and the social changes associated with them, and overlook the ongoing recombination of old and new. By definition, the convergence perspective also elides existing distinctions among media systems and forms, and thus obscures new boundaries that develop among technologies, institutions, and practices over time. Boczkowski suggests that it is more useful to think of the changes associated with media and information technologies as emergent rather than convergent, the result of a continuous process of reshaping and reconfiguration that does not necessarily lead to a fixed or stable end state that departs completely from what went before.

Participatory journalism: definitions

So, how to frame this new, emergent situation for journalism and the press in the context of the internet and social media? As some of the preceding remarks suggest, perhaps the single most striking feature is the growing involvement of amateurs and "ordinary people" – what media scholar and journalist Jay Rosen (2006) calls "the people formerly known as the audience" – in the production of news and commentary online. These novice correspondents write about their local communities, or about political, cultural, or economic issues that are overlooked or marginalized by the mainstream press. According to journalism researcher Robert Huesca, they "are typically excluded from or misrepresented by local television news: low-income women, minorities and youth – the very demographic and lifestyle groups who have little access to the media and that advertisers don't want" (see http://en.wikipedia.org/wiki/Citizen_journalism).

Even professional journalists who have reservations about their fledgling colleagues acknowledge that amateurs can be competent and even compelling reporters. J.D. Lasica, senior editor of the *Online Journalism Review*, concedes that "When small independent online publications and collaborative news sites with an amateur staff perform original reporting on community affairs, few would contest that they're engaged in journalism" (Lasica, 2003). Bloggers and other amateur journalists have broken important stories outright (e.g., political purges of U.S. attorneys by the Bush administration, reported by Talking Points Memo [Niles, 2007]), provided critical fact-checking neglected by mainstream news organizations (e.g., independent tabulations of deaths and casualties by the Iraq Body Count and Iraq Coalition Casualty Count sites: http://www.iraqbodycount.org, http://www.icasualties.org), or contributed additional reporting that decisively changed the impact of certain stories.

In an interview with the OpenBusiness blog, *Economist* technology reporter Kenneth Neil Cukier is enthusiastic about the rise of amateur journalism. The internet, he says, is helping to promote a "reformation" in journalism comparable to the challenge to the medieval Church posed by the printing press, enabling people to participate more directly in making and reporting news on their own terms. Cukier also likens today's "amateur journalists" to the "gentleman scientists" of the eighteenth century, another group of influential amateurs who laid the groundwork for modern science (OpenBusiness, 2006).

If traditional news organizations faced with financial and operational upheaval have tended to view the new contenders with distrust or outright disdain, the "garage-band" amateurs themselves – and, increasingly, trained journalists sidelined or laid off by their mainstream employers – have moved ahead with new, improvisational, or hybrid approaches to news gathering, reporting, editing, and publishing online. The shifting boundaries and tensions between mainstream and online media, and between professional and amateur journalism, are suggested by the proliferation of different names for these activities and the range of views about what counts as "real" journalism online.

Citizen journalism, for example, has been defined as "people without professional journalism training [using] the tools of modern technology and the global distribution of the Internet to create, augment or fact-check media on their own or in collaboration with others" (Glazer, 2006). Citizen journalism "harness[es] the power of an audience permitted for the first time to truly participate in the news media"; participation can range from public commentary on published pieces to full "wiki journalism" with readers as editors (Outing, 2005). *Wired* editor Chris Anderson (2006) offers a simple typology of "actually existing" citizen journalism projects, including personal home pages, Indymedia, and blogs. He notes that since 9/11, the dramatic growth of blogging has led to it becoming a "shorthand term for much of the grassroots media and journalism work that has occurred, and increasing acceptance of the practice as journalism."

Other observers prefer the term *open-source journalism*, which was first attributed to a story by Andrew Leonard appearing in *Salon* in 1999. The piece described how *Jane's Intelligence Review* had invited the readers of the tech news website Slashdot to critique and correct the technical facts in an article on cyberterrorism that *Jane's* was preparing for publication. The response was swift and decisive: "Slashdot members sliced and diced Jane's story into tiny little pieces" and the story was subsequently withdrawn (Leonard, 1999). Over time, the original emphasis on open, public fact-checking in open-source journalism projects has shifted toward the current understanding, which is drawn from open-source software development – that is, the dynamic reporting and revision of news in an ongoing peer-review process, "a new kind of journalism . . . [that] provides great value simply by concentrating so much expertise" (Leonard, 1999). This framing of open-source journalism was named one of the "Top Ten Ideas of 2004" by Jay Rosen's PressThink blog (Rosen, 2004). (We revisit contemporary tagging and folksonomic projects in Chapter 7.)

A host of other labels are also used to describe the variety of emerging forms of online journalism. Mark Glazer, in his MediaShift weblog for PBS in the U.S., notes that grassroots, citizen, open-source, networked, bottom-up, hyperlocal, civic, and distributed journalism are often used as more or less equivalent terms. But whatever it is called, journalism values and practices are at its heart: Glazer (2006) quotes a BuzzMetrics executive who insists, "why not just call journalism 'journalism' . . . [it] can be 'practiced' in all sorts of ways."

For the purposes of the present discussion, a more general term, participatory journalism, is most useful. It suggests that readers, writers, and editors participate jointly in the ongoing process of news production and circulation via online and social media – indeed, that they share and trade these various roles in the process. One "working definition" of participatory journalism calls it:

> The act of a citizen, or group of citizens, playing an active role in the process of collecting, reporting, analyzing and disseminating news and information. The intent of this participation is to provide independent, reliable, accurate, wide-ranging and relevant information that a democracy requires.
>
> Participatory journalism is a bottom-up, emergent phenomenon in which there is little or no editorial oversight or formal journalistic workflow dictating the decisions of a staff. Instead, it is the result of many simultaneous, distributed conversations that either blossom or quickly atrophy in the Web's social network. (Bowman & Willis, 2003, p. 9)

David Ryfe and Donica Mensing (2008) note that at first glance, participatory journalists espouse the same values and aims as professional mainstream journalists, i.e., informing citizens by "providing information that is, to the extent possible, non-biased, non-partisan, and fair" (p. 12). Based on discourse analyses of website content and interviews with participant journalists at twenty-one websites, the authors find that participatory journalists

> feel compelled to practice journalism not because they see the ethos of professional journalism as illegitimate, or because they wish to invent a new form of journalism. Rather, they feel compelled to do journalism because they believe that professional journalists are not doing their jobs. . . . conventional journalists too often focus on the wrong topics or are too biased, and this makes it difficult for citizens to form common judgements. (pp. 14–15)

However, Ryfe and Mensing also find that participatory journalists differ from conventional journalists in one crucial respect: their insistence that journalism should foster interaction and the participation of readers, reporters, editors, and indeed the whole community, in the generation of news. '[C]itizens become informed not by consuming information, but by interacting with others around information. It is the process of mutually influencing one another – interaction – that creates the condition of being informed' (p. 17). From the participatory perspective, news is less a matter of content manufactured by professional experts and delivered to consumers than it is the outcome of continuous rounds of posting, counter-posting, commentary, and debate, a process that has been vastly facilitated by the proliferation and adoption of new media technologies.

Ryfe and Mensing contend that this shift in focus is best understood by taking a longer historical view of the purposes of journalism over time. Most professional journalists and mainstream news organizations have adopted a modernist, progressive, "informational" model of journalism that is historically specific to the early twentieth century. The gathering and transmission of verified, objective, and truthful facts to the general public are seen as the best means of creating an "informed," self-governing citizenry in a democracy. Professional journalists and educators often claim that this model has always been the foundation of good journalistic practice.

However, the authors disagree, and show that journalism's purposes have changed dramatically throughout American history, only becoming a "journalism of information" in the twentieth century. They recall a debate between Walter Lippmann and John Dewey in the 1920s, in which Lippmann insisted that in a complex, modern society, the public needs experts and professional journalists to frame the issues for them and to guide their decision-making. Dewey held that knowledge was a social phenomenon, emerging from people's interactions with one another and with powerful institutions, rather than the understanding of particular facts. "As is well known, Lippman 'won' this debate, if by winning we mean that in the twentieth century professional journalism aligned itself more with his views than with those of Dewey" (Ryfe & Mensing, 2008, p. 19). Journalism, the authors say, may be undergoing a philosophical realignment away from Lippmann's and toward Dewey's view, i.e., away from "journalism-as-transmission-of-information" and toward "journalism-as-participation," with the potential to transform journalism as a practice and of the press as an institution.

Participatory journalism: critiques

Whether participatory journalism actually marks a significant change for journalism and the press remains open to dispute. Critics of new forms of online journalism warn that the declining institutional power of the fourth estate will have far-reaching and ruinous consequences for democracy itself. They insist that the traditional press still has an indispensable role to play as the key gatekeeper, agenda-setter, and mediator between the people and their governments and other powerful institutions, and that this role is distinct from that of the traditional "audience." J.D. Lasica (2003) points out that participatory journalism is supposed to be a process

> in which a news organization works with its audience to have that "conversation" that is news . . . [but] a conversation is not 1,000 people shouting at once. Good conversation is two-way, among a few people. If viewers are allowed to post anything they want on the message board I host, it invites all sorts of dangers, not the least of which is a defamation lawsuit.

Mike Godwin (1999) enumerates four typical objections from the trade:

> *How can they be journalists if they've got no editors?* . . . It will be harder to tell truth from fiction and rumor. Once it's possible for anyone to write and publish something that has the appearance of being "real" journalism, the public is likely to be fooled by frauds and phonies . . . *won't there be a Gresham's law effect in which all the bad, phony journalism drives out the good, true stuff?* . . . These little guys will never be able to do what the big boys do. No Web-based one-man-show journalist has the resources to do the important stories. . . . *What about fairness and accuracy? What happens when there's a sudden influx of amateur journalists who haven't served the kind of ethical apprenticeship that those of us who came up through traditional media organizations have served?* (Godwin, 1999, pp. 39–41, emphasis added)

He responds that a journalism degree and apprenticeship in mainstream news organizations are not the only paths to journalistic competence, and that the immediate cycle of feedback and criticism online can be just as effective a means of reinforcing quality as the institutional, editorial gatekeeping that shelters most mainstream journalists from much direct contact with the public. The idea that only big institutions can produce quality journalism or handle the "important" stories that are central to a democracy is arrogant, he says, and rejects the assumption that the public at large is an "unthinking, unreflective, uncritical consumer of news" (Godwin, 1999, p. 40). While major news organizations – "heavyweights" – certainly have the resources and institutional gravitas to take journalistic risks and resist intimidation, institutional inertia and interests can also discourage "journalistic entrepreneurship" and neglect complex, narrowly focused, or long-term stories that require sustained attention and development. By embracing and collaborating with the new amateurs, mainstream journalists can provide ethical guidance that will raise journalistic standards across media forms and outlets.

Another critic, Vincent Maher (2005), summarizes his objections to amateur efforts as what he calls the "three deadly E's": ethics, economics, and epistemology. In terms of ethics, Maher argues that professional journalists are governed by established institutional codes and standards, professional training, and accountability to their employers. Citizen journalists, in contrast, are "self-taught," governed only by "uncoordinated individual self-interest and fear of litigation," their own subjectivity, and commentary by readers.

Regarding economics, Maher claims that in traditional news organizations, professional journalists are protected from the economic demands and priorities of advertisers (traditionally called "the wall" between advertising and editorial content). In addition, advertising in traditional media is non-contextual, that is, unrelated to the editorial content it appears with. Both of these factors tend to insulate journalists from undue economic influence on their news judgment and coverage. In contrast, citizen journalists' editorial decisions are directly influenced by "what sells," and the advertising on their sites is contextual, that is, closely related to the content being presented.

Finally, with respect to epistemology, Maher says, "the blogosphere . . . is a mess." He asserts that where traditional journalism and "old media" are tools for "reflection and crystallization of truths," citizen journalism is merely a "tool for activism [and] contesting truths." That is, traditional media produce "real" knowledge, while online projects, dependent on participatory peer production, can make no such authoritative knowledge claims: "The process of publishing a story is a localized and controlled attempt to create a *piece of knowledge as a finished and stand-alone object* for others to interact with" (Maher, 2005, emphasis added).

Certainly, the critics raise crucial issues about the credibility, reliability, and consistency of new forms of journalism and the role they might play in a democracy. The question of editing, in particular, is so often cited that it might be added as a fourth "deadly E." Both advocates and detractors of new forms of journalism online worry that no amount of participatory posting, updating, commentary, fact-checking, and annotation can substitute for the eyes and judgment of experienced editors who can spot problems or inconsistencies in a story that writers may overlook, or who can help fit a story into a particular community context or larger pattern of events. As William Dutton (2009) has observed, even the simplest listserv, chatroom, or blog requires moderation, if only to sort through the incessant "noise" of spam, off-topic posting, and other "contributions" that can quickly reduce an otherwise valuable site to a frustrating and disorganized hodgepodge. Editing, from this perspective, separates journalism from commonplace chatter and rumor.

In sum, participatory journalism, like any emerging practice, has its strengths and weaknesses. To put these various factors into perspective, we turn to the example of Indymedia, one of the earliest and most successful forms of participatory journalism online.

"Be the media": Indymedia's first decade

The Independent Media Center, or Indymedia, movement enjoys the distinction of being one of the most-studied cases in the research literature on new media activism.[3] Indymedia has been celebrated as "an institutional exemplar of contemporary internet-based activism" (Pickard, 2006b, p. 317), "the most thorough working-out on the Internet of the conditions and processes of radical media projects" (Atton, 2003, p. 9), and as being "at the forefront of creating new multifaceted, decentralized virtual public spheres that advance democratic discourses and global-justice projects" (Morris, 2004, p. 348). Not only has it been among the fastest-growing online journalism projects (see Figure 5.1), it is also one of the most politically activist forms, hewing to a strict left-liberal (indeed, radical) political philosophy that has shaped its coverage and content as well as its methods of news-production and -distribution.

For many observers, the innovation that sets Indymedia apart from other grass-roots journalism projects, and the pivotal element in the "Indymedia news model" (Platon & Deuze, 2003), is the open-publishing platform built into every IMC site. Open publishing permits anyone with Internet access to post reports, images, audio, or video on any Indymedia site without prior clearance by editors. IMCs have editorial teams and policies, but their activities are restricted to choosing items to feature on the main IMC newswire pages, and moderating items that do not fit broad IMC guidelines for inclusion in the newswire, e.g., advertising, pieces that are discriminatory, inaccurate, or libelous, personal attacks, re-postings from other sources, non-news ("purely comment, opinion, or rants"), and so on.[4] With very few exceptions (e.g., pornography), no posts are actually removed from Indymedia sites, even if they violate the guidelines; these items are relegated to pages that are "hidden" from routine page views but remain accessible. In principle, Indymedia newswires are open to any contributions that fit the guidelines and the broader Indymedia mission, stated on the indymedia.

org home page, of creating "radical, accurate, and passionate tellings of truth." In practice, Indymedia contributions take an almost exclusively left-radical, anti-globalist, anti-capitalist political viewpoint.

The first Independent Media Center was launched in Seattle, Washington, in late 1999, in advance of a meeting of the World Trade Organization held there in November that year. Numerous organizations with broadly progressive, liberal, or social- or global-justice aims had planned protests and demonstrations in response to the meeting. Local media activists wanted to produce a news service that would provide a counterpoint to the mainstream coverage of most global summits: the deferential, celebrity-style treatment of national leaders, the unquestioning acceptance of the WTO and its aims, and the marginalization of protesters' objections. They hoped to present an "inside" or "street" view of the meetings and protests for a global audience, and to cover summit-related events (such as press conferences, panel discussions, or debates) that the mainstream press usually ignored. They also understood that by going online, they would be free from the usual deadlines and cutoffs of the mass media news cycle, and could provide continuous, real-time coverage to anyone with Internet access. Several months in advance, they began to organize an alternative "multimedia people's newsroom" as a base of operations (Kidd, 2003; Morris, 2004; Paton, 1999).

Local housing activists donated a space for the Seattle IMC. Equipment, expertise, and technical support were donated by a cadre of self-styled hackers and "tech geeks" from the local high-tech industry, many of whom had experience with the free software movement and open-source software development (see Chapter 4). Rob Glaser, one of the city's renowned "Microsoft millionaires" and the chief executive officer of Real Networks, contributed state-of-the-art multimedia streaming technology and financial support through his foundation (Paton, 1999). Volunteer programmers built the original IMC website, incorporating a multimedia open-publishing platform that had been created by activist programmers in Sydney, Australia, earlier that summer.

When it went online in November, the system far exceeded organizers' expectations. Between 300 and 400 activists and correspondents were officially registered with the local IMC and the website, with access to sophisticated video and audio editing suites at the Center. Technical support staff in Seattle, assisted long-distance by techs in Sydney, kept the website running, upgraded, and repaired as traffic to the site soared (later estimates varied from one million to over two million hits or page views during the course of the meeting and protests). A local organizer was quoted in the *Christian Science Monitor*: "From the standpoint of all these independent media, the WTO couldn't have picked a worse place to hold their meeting. . . . I mean, it's Seattle – we've got all the techies you'd ever want and all these companies specializing in everything they need to stream these stories all over the world. It's perfect that the WTO came here. Perfect" (Paton, 1999).

The reporting on the IMC site, particularly the constantly updated streaming video and audio reports, diverged dramatically from mainstream television and print coverage, where the "Battle in Seattle" was quickly reduced to little more than a violent street fight between a mob of anarchists and beleaguered riot police. Still, several major news organizations, including CNN, picked up material from the IMC site and provided links to its coverage.

Indymedia was on its way. Activist groups in other cities lined up to start their own Centers; following the Seattle model, IMCs were often organized to coincide with high-profile political and economic protests. The Seattle IMC's web technology, designed around an open-source software platform, the open publishing system, and the programmers' own rigorous interpretation of the free-software ethic, was easily exported and adapted by emerging Indymedia "locals" and their homegrown "tech geeks." In less than a year, twenty-eight IMCs were operating as a loosely affiliated network. By mid-2001 the number had risen to nearly sixty;

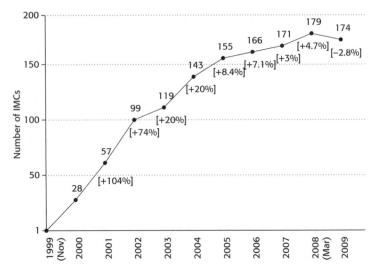

Sources: http://www.indymedia.org, historical data accessed via The Wayback Machine, http://www.archive.org. All counts in July except as noted.

Figure 5.1. Number and annual percent change of Independent Media Centers (IMCs) worldwide, 1999–2009

by mid-2002, after the terror attacks of 9/11, the network had expanded to about a hundred sites, with roughly sixty of these located and operating outside the U.S. (see Figure 5.1).

This astonishing trajectory was bound to create stresses and tensions within the network, especially given the members' "radical egalitarianism" and strict adherence to consensus decision processes (Pickard, 2006b). Whereas radical media of an earlier era tended to rely on hierarchical organization and the leadership of a "vanguard" of thinkers and activists to shape the issues and messages for the rank and file and to set the agenda for action, the new networked, "leaderless" form of organizing, supported by the new media infrastructure, made such hierarchical organizational forms unnecessary (Bennett, 2003). IMCs were adamantly independent, insisting that no single IMC had any priority over any others. Yet they needed some kind of process that would allow them to share information and resources, manage the polyglot tide of reporting and opinion flooding onto the Indymedia sites, and coordinate globally dispersed mobilization and activism activities.

Thus the next milestone in the Indymedia story was a sort of collective "time out" that allowed network members to formulate basic principles and operating policies. Only a year after the WTO protests, network techs called a temporary moratorium on the addition of new IMCs, to deal with the deluge of requests for assistance with setting up new sites (Morris, 2004). The techs felt that the admission of new IMCs should be determined by a more deliberative, open process governed by standardized principles, rather than on an *ad hoc*, first-come, first-served basis in which technical staff acted as *de facto* gatekeepers.

Meanwhile, network activists hammered out basic membership criteria for new IMCs in early 2001, as well as the Principles of Unity (POU), a ten-point summary of the movement's core values (see box below). The Principles were proposed and discussed in April 2001 by about seventy IMC members from around the world, at a meeting held in conjunction with the Project Censored Conference in San Francisco. A draft document was subsequently circulated to all local IMCs to solicit their feedback.

The POU document is called "the glue that defines the IMC network," and acceptance into the network now requires a new IMC to endorse the Principles. Nonetheless, the process of formulating and approving the Principles has been cited by some analysts as an illustration of the limitations of strict consensus governance in such a loosely confederated network organization (e.g., Morris, 2004; Pickard, 2006a, 2006b, 2008). IMCs continue to debate key elements of the Principles, and a final document has still not been formally adopted network-wide. Indeed, about thirty to forty "legacy IMCs" (those established before the Principles were drafted) were originally exempted from having to endorse them at all, though many of those collectives have since done so (Pickard, 2006b).

INDYMEDIA PRINCIPLES OF UNITY

(Source: http://docs.indymedia.org/Global/PrinciplesOfUnity)

This document is a work in progress and an attempt to state the basic principles for which we all stand. As such, please take time in your local meeting to read, debate and discuss it. All bracketed items are part of the priciples of unity but have been specifically identified as in need of further definition, clarification and "wordsmithing." Please feel free to contact the working group with any questions. We welcome and look forward to your input.

1. The Independent Media Center Network (IMCN) is based upon principles of equality, decentralization and local autonomy. The IMCN is not derived from a centralized bureaucratic process, but from the self-organization of autonomous collectives that recognize the importance in developing a union of networks.

2. All IMC's consider open exchange of and open access to information a prerequisite to the building of a more free and just society.

3. [All IMC's respect the right of activists who choose not to be photographed or filmed.]

4. All IMC's, based upon the trust of their contributors and readers, shall utilize open web based publishing, allowing individuals, groups and organizations to express their views, anonymously if desired.
   **see appendix: Open Publishing document → still in proposal phase, at this address: http://lists.indymedia.org/mailman/public/imc-communication/2001-April/001707.html
   http://lists.indymedia.org/mailman/public/imc-communication/2001-April/000874.html

5. The IMC Network and all local IMC collectives shall be not-for-profit.

6. All IMC's recognize the importance of process to social change and are committed to the development of non-hierarchical and anti-authoritarian relationships, from interpersonal relationships to group dynamics. Therefore, shall organize themselves collectively and be committed to the principle of consensus decision making and the development of a direct, participatory democratic process that is transparent to its membership.

7. [All IMC's recognize that a prerequisite for participation in the decision making process of each local group is the contribution of an individual's labor to the group.]

8 All IMC's are committed to caring for one another and our respective communities both collectively and as individuals and will promote the sharing of resources including knowledge, skills and equipment.
9 All IMC's shall be committed to the use of free source code, whenever possible, in order to develop the digital infrastructure, and to increase the independence of the network by not relying on proprietary software.
10 All IMC's shall be committed to the principle of human equality, and shall not discriminate, including discrimination based upon race, gender, age, class or sexual orientation. Recognizing the vast cultural traditions within the network, we are committed to building [diversity] within our localities.

The moratorium and policy debates scarcely affected the expansion of the Indymedia network, however. It continued to grow at double-digit rates through the middle of the decade. But continued growth also exacerbated the network's persistent problems with resources and sustainability, particularly a near-total reliance on volunteer staffers and contributors (at once passionately committed, and prone to high rates of burnout and turnover) and a lack of reliable funding sources. These problems were the focal point of a funding controversy in late 2002.

Since the network's inception, member IMCs had been responsible for obtaining their own support locally, although member collectives were also expected to contribute a small portion of their funds towards the support of the umbrella organization and website. To facilitate its fundraising efforts, the Urbana-Champaign (Illinois) IMC had reorganized as a 501(c) (3) non-profit organization under U.S. tax law. They had applied successfully for a $50,000.00 grant from the Ford Foundation to support an international conference for all network IMCs, including travel grants so that IMC delegates from around the world could attend.

However, just before the grant was awarded, a small contingent of collectives, led by the Argentina IMC, raised objections owing to the Ford Foundation's legacy of controversial economic and political activities in the developing world. Some felt that accepting money from a foundation with historical ties to corporate capital was the first step down a road toward institutionalization that would betray Indymedia's radical political principles. Although the money was only being awarded to the UC IMC, consensus process dictated that unless all IMCs agreed that the UC IMC could accept the grant, it should be refused. Ultimately, the UC IMC turned it down.

Thus, a handful of IMCs were able to block funding that might have helped build the movement's solidarity and effectiveness as an alternative media organization. The sustainability of the IMC network, and the balance between securing the necessary resources to operate and maintaining the network's radical democratic principles, had been a concern among many Indymedia participants from the earliest days. As a contributor to the imc-process listserv put it in late 2000, "We should keep in mind what happens when a volunteer-run organization gets professionalized – just look at NPR or Pacifica."[5] However, according to another longtime Indymedia volunteer and media scholar, the Ford Foundation incident was particularly ironic because the money "may have gone a long way towards preventing [such a] drift away from radical politics. . . . Such impasses may cast doubt on the IMC network's long-term sustainability – especially as they continue to gain scores of new member organizations each year" (Pickard, 2006b, p. 316).

In one particularly intriguing episode, which came to be called "the Ahimsa Incident" among Indymedia insiders, two of the network's servers (Ahimsa1 and Ahimsa2) were seized without explanation from a web hosting facility in London (UK) in early October 2004. The servers supported over twenty IMC websites in Europe, Central and South America, and the U.S. The operator of the hosting facility, a firm in San Antonio, Texas, would say only that an order "to provide your hardware to the requesting agency" had come from the U.S. District Court for the Western District of Texas, and that the court had prohibited them from discussing the matter. Inquiries by the Electronic

Frontier Foundation on Indymedia's behalf found that the court documents had been sealed; neither the court, the FBI, the U.S. Department of State or Department of Justice, nor the facility's owner, would say who had requested the seizure or why. Lawyers for the EFF filed a motion to unseal the documents.[6]

The court documents, unsealed in July 2005, and further investigations by the EFF revealed that a public prosecutor in Bologna, Italy, who wanted IP address information about users of the Italy IMC website had made the request. Although the reason for the request was unspecified – the files also contained a letter from the Italian government asking that the matter be kept secret – it had been made under the provisions of the Mutual Legal Assistance Treaty (MLAT), which allows nations to ask other signatories for assistance in investigations of high-level international criminal activity such as kidnapping, money laundering, drug trafficking, and terrorism. As it happened, confiscating the servers was futile because they were configured not to capture IP address information about any computer reading or posting to IMC sites, as per Indymedia policy.

However, the EFF also located an Associated Press news story quoting an unidentified FBI agent familiar with the case who said "there were two different [MLAT] requests from two different countries that are in no way connected except that both pertain to Indymedia." FBI agents had in fact contacted both the London facility's owner and a Seattle IMC staff member a few weeks before the October seizure about materials posted on the Nantes (France) IMC website (hosted on the Ahimsa servers). They claimed that the Nantes site contained personally identifying information about two Swiss undercover agents. After reviewing the site, the Ahimsa webmaster found no such information. However, in a photo posted on the site, the administrator did mask the faces of two agents disguised as protesters at an anti-globalization demonstration.

In the end, the Swiss government would not confirm that it had any role in making an MLAT request. The UK government also denied that it had anything to do with the seizure order, and launched an investigation to determine whether the American owner of the London facility had violated UK data protection laws. Indymedia websites across three continents were taken offline for days. The owner of the web hosting facility decided that its employees had mistakenly interpreted the court order, and could have complied by providing copies of specific records from the servers rather than surrendering the servers outright. Without explanation, the servers were returned to the facility and restored to operation just five days after they were confiscated. To date, the reason for the seizures has still not been determined.

Debates over decision-making, shortages of staff and money, and legal challenges to Indymedia's legitimacy and politics continue to preoccupy its activists and to shape network operations. Still, the network has continued to grow, if at a less rapid pace, since the mid-2000s. Indymedia has become something of a "brand" in the world of alternative and activist journalism and media, particularly because of its broadly anti-globalization slant and its own (perhaps ironically) global reach as a news service (Deuze, 2001, 2003; Platon & Deuze, 2003).

Most observers agree that the Indymedia movement has been one of the real success stories of alternative and activist new media, with important implications for media activism, the understanding of grass-roots organizing, critical and political theory, and journalistic practice. Some also think that its energy may dissipate, and the movement may face an uncertain future, unless Indymedia activists find ways to deal with its persistent structural and philosophical contradictions: global vs. local, autonomy vs. collaboration, open publishing vs. editorial selection, radicalism vs. reformism, volunteer vs. paid, consensus vs. leadership, truth vs. ideology, and so on – what the *Columbia Journalism Review* has summed up as Indymedia's "passion vs. pragmatism" (Beckerman, 2003; see also Morris, 2004; Pickard, 2006b, 2008).

Another issue is the relationship of Indymedia to the changing landscape of Web 2.0. In a March 2006 posting on the Media Geographies blog, Trebor Scholz notes that Indymedia, streaming technologies, and the open publishing approach were state of the art in 2000. By 2006, however, IMCs were competing with blogs, tagging sites, and other social media:

> I rarely go to Indymedia for alternative news. And I don't write there either. . . . social web media have largely caught up with the open publishing technology that Indymedia offered in 2000, a few years before blogs started to blossom in 2004. I don't have statistics on Indymedia sites but my guess would be that the numbers of participators [*sic*] are on the decline. (http://mediageographies.blogspot.com/2006/03/trebor-scholz-idc-net-autonomy.html)

Figure 5.1 suggests that Scholz's remarks may have been prescient. Although the number of Indymedia sites was still growing in 2006, the rate of increase had flattened out considerably, after the dramatic rise from 1999 to 2004. Between early 2008 and mid-2009, the number of IMCs listed on the main indymedia.org website declined (if slightly) for the first time.

However, the number of members in the network may be a less important indicator of Indymedia's significance than its pioneering role as a form of grass-roots, participatory journalism practice. We conclude the chapter by considering participatory journalism as a genre of alternative/activist new media.

Summary: participatory journalism as a genre

As with the other types of alternative and activist new media projects, participatory journalism operates as a genre with a distinctive form and purpose, and corresponds to particular practices and institutions in society (in this case, journalism and the press). Just as culture jamming critiques and subverts the popular culture industry by using the forms, conventions, and imagery of popular culture itself, and just as alternative computing resists and overcomes constraints on open access to information and information technology by reconfiguring or hacking those systems, participatory journalism seeks to critique and reform the press as an institution by involving "amateur" or "native" reporters and writers in the practice of journalism. Participatory journalism constitutes a move away from the manufacture of a media "product," and from journalism as an "expert culture and commodity" (Atton, 2004, p. 60), toward an interactive, conversational process which, ideally, involves citizens more fully in public life. Participatory journalism thus adopts the *form* of professional journalistic practices and values, but with the *purpose* of challenging and transforming the press as an institution.

Like other genres, participatory journalism has distinctive features or characteristics, which (as outlined in Chapter 2) can be grouped into three basic categories: scope, stance, and agency/action.

Scope. Alternative/activist new media genres are notable for their small scale and their collaborative quality; it is fair to say that these two characteristics virtually define participatory journalism. Participatory journalism projects are typically kept small to encourage the participation of non-professionals in the coverage of local or specialized issues that large news organizations would ordinarily consider too minor to cover. And as the Indymedia example shows, collaboration is the *sine qua non* of participatory journalism projects, in which an interactive, "conversational" partnership blurs the boundaries between journalists and the communities they cover. Despite its geographic dispersion, the Indymedia network is fundamentally local, insists on the autonomy of the member IMCs, and conceives and generates the newswire entirely as a bottom-up enterprise.

Stance. Three characteristics relate to a genre's position or stance *vis-à-vis* the mainstream institutions to which it corresponds, and society at large. Alternative/activist new media projects are typically heterotopic (i.e., they constitute separate or alternate spaces from the mainstream), exhibit a subcultural sensibility, and may have an ironic or playful quality. Certainly, participatory journalism projects position themselves as outsiders or in opposition to the mainstream press. In the case of organizations with strong radical ideologies like Indymedia, a prevailing discourse of opposition to dominant institutions and interests serves as an effective subcultural "boundary" that demarcates the alternative from the mainstream, and issues and perspectives that are politically acceptable from those that are not.

Nonetheless, participatory journalism also shares many similarities with the mainstream press, particularly practitioners' adoption of the ethos, values, and practices of professional journalism – to "provide independent, reliable, accurate, wide-ranging and relevant information that a democracy requires" (Bowman & Willis, 2003, p. 9). Radical politics notwithstanding, Indymedia and similar outlets "present a hybrid of radical content and news values with mainstream production values, institutional frameworks and professionalized reporting," and although they are interpreted and contextualized through a radical-democratic lens, "mainstream sources are more prominent [in Indymedia] than in most grassroots media projects" (Atton, 2003, pp. 12–13).

Sara Platon and Mark Deuze (2003) also find that Indymedia's "open publishing shows characteristics similar to mainstream media regarding traditional news values" (p. 346) and that its editorial process is characterized by "active negotiation . . . between the ideals of open publishing and enabling participation for all, typical 'journalistic' ideals of maintaining some kind of control over a published story and storytelling in general" (p. 350).

This "aspirational" appropriation of to the values and practices of professional journalism also leaves little room for the playful, ironic, or pranking attitude that we have seen with culture jamming and alternative computing: participatory journalism seems to take itself seriously. On balance, we can say that participatory journalism sets itself apart from the institutions and power of the mainstream press – but not too far apart.

Agency/Action. Genres also differ in terms of the actions they undertake and the agency of their participants. Alternative/ activist new media projects are interventionist, i.e., they aim to interrupt and alter existing conditions and meanings. They are also perishable – short-term, rapid responses to changing circumstances.

On the first count, participatory journalism is clearly interventionist, being activism of both "word" and "deed" (Wray, 1998). It reframes the news as discourse and symbolic content, and constitutes direct action intended to change the material conditions of journalism as a practice and the press as an institution. Both aims reflect participatory journalism's roots in the radical, alternative, and underground press, and in the broader *media activism* movement, which emerged among left-wing media scholars, artists, and activists in the 1960s in response to the diffusion of mass media (particularly television and radio) throughout the world. According to these critics, western (i.e., American) media and entertainment industries, in league with the U.S. government and financial interests, have pursued a relentless strategy of *cultural imperialism* around the globe, promoting an irresistible stream of western images, products, and values, especially in the developing world. Cultural imperialism disseminates American political ideology, ensures open markets for American products, and blocks or marginalizes the perspectives and interests of less powerful nations and communities, especially those without fully developed media industries.[7]

Local and marginalized communities can resist cultural domination and homogenization, first, by taking a critical view of corporate media products and messages, and, second, by creating and supporting their own local, "home-grown" media and content that better represents their interests, viewpoints, and cultures than dominant media sources do. Such projects have ranged from alternative newspapers, underground films, and pirate radio stations in the 1960s, to community-access cable and video in the 1970s, to 'zines in the 1980s, to tactical media projects in the 1990s and beyond (Braman, 2002; Cubitt, 2006; Garcia & Lovink, 1997). Participatory journalism can be seen as a development within this longer activist tradition.

However, participatory journalism differs from the broader

field of media activism in one key respect: perishability. Historically, projects like pirate radio, 'zines, and particularly tactical media have been explicitly short-lived and ephemeral: "Our hybrid forms are always provisional. What counts are the temporary connections you are able to make. Here and now, not some vaporware promised for the future. But what we can do on the spot with the media we have access to" (Garcia & Lovink, 1997). Radio broadcasts, photocopied pamphlets, street art, guerrilla video, impromptu flashmobs, and the work of tactical "nomadic media warriors" are all ephemeral by definition. However, participatory journalism projects – even those like Indymedia that formally disavow any institutional or "professional" aspirations – have nonetheless taken on a documentary, witnessing role that requires sustained commitment and reliable record-keeping in order to function effectively as a credible information source.

Indymedia is a prime example: analyses of postings to their process and technical listservs and interviews with longtime network activists reveal that sustainability of the network has been a perennial worry (Atton, 2003, 2004; Beckerman, 2003; Jankowski & Jansen, 2003; Morris, 2004; Pickard, 2006a, 2006b, 2008; Platon & Deuze, 2003). It is also revealing that the umbrella Indymedia site (like most of the member IMCs) has carefully preserved and archived the complete contents of the newswire back to 1999, as well as technical documents, email discussion lists, links to academic studies and news coverage of Indymedia in other outlets, and a host of other materials documenting the development of the network over time (an archival habit which has undoubtedly helped make it such an attractive case study for research). Chris Atton alludes to this static quality in his commentary on the predominance of "in-depth, discursive features and commentaries" over constantly refreshed "direct-action news" in Indymedia's 9/11 pages. "[T]he timeliness and dailiness we might expect from such contributions as part of an Internet media project is eroded the longer the pages remain static – the twenty-four-hour news cycle . . . is absent" (Atton, 2004, pp. 58–9).

To sum up, participatory journalism as a genre can be character-ized as fundamentally small scale and collaborative. Although it critiques and opposes the market-driven cynicism and detach-ment of the mainstream press, it has adapted the practices and values of professional journalism online as a method of trans-forming the content and production of the news, and to renew its role as a brake on government and corporate power.

In the next chapter, we move from the press and journalism as a watchdog of politics, to a genre with a direct involvement in politics and social movements – mediated mobilization.

CHAPTER 6

Getting People on the "Street"

Mediated Mobilization

A movement mobilizes because it has gathered the legacy and the resources of preexisting social structures and has reoriented them towards new goals of transformation.

(Melucci, 1996, p. 292)

[C]ommunication networks constitute, by and large, the public space in the network society. . . . Politics is media politics. . . . Therefore, the process of social change requires the reprogramming of the communication networks in terms of their cultural codes and in terms of the implicit social and political values and interests that they convey.

(Castells, 2009, p. 300)

In this chapter we turn to the way in which alternative political movements and activists use new media for mobilization – how technologies are reoriented toward transformational goals, as Alberto Melucci suggests, and indeed, as Manuel Castells argues, how networked technologies themselves are "reprogrammed" to become sites of action and change. What role do new media play in the conversion of people's shared ideas, identities, and interests into collective action that aims to change prevailing social, cultural, and political conditions? The fourth genre of alternative/activist new media, *mediated mobilization,* is concerned with the nature and distribution of power in communities and societies, and the promotion of radical and participatory democracy, where participatory democracy is defined as the widespread, direct involvement of citizens in both political processes and governance. Participatory democracy contrasts with the representative version, where politics and governance are delegated to appointed or elected proxies (see Lievrouw, 1994). Certainly, the genres discussed in the previous three chapters (related to popular culture, computing and information technologies, and journalism and the press) all take a critical view of different aspects of society and culture. By expressing an outsider or alternative perspective, they also aim to change public discourse and perceptions, and create the cultural and material conditions for what activists believe will be a better society. However, mediated mobilization goes a step further by using new media as the means to mobilize social movements – collective action in which people organize and work together as active participants in social change.

Of course, the use of electronic media in social and political movements is not new. Radio, motion pictures, and television helped promote and mobilize a "national unity culture" of consumption, popular entertainment, wartime solidarity, and economic production in the U.S. from the 1930s to the 1960s (Graham, 2000). The uses of print, radio, and motion pictures in mass political movements of both the right and left before World War II are well documented (Langman, 2005). Bruce Bimber (2003) shows the effects of different "information regimes" in U.S. political history, from the cultivation of party politics in the early nineteenth century, to the pluralism and rise of interest-group politics associated with industrialism and mass-produced print from the late nineteenth century through much of the twentieth, to the emergence of mass audiences and candidate-centered campaigning associated with broadcasting from the 1920s onward. As noted in Chapter 2, recent social movement theory and research has taken a distinctly communicative or "cultural" turn, focusing on the agency and action of movement participants, particularly how meaning is constructed and shared within movements and between movements and the larger society. Central problems include the symbolic and cultural representation of social movement issues, how issues and movements are framed discursively, and the "opportunity structures" for discourse and action repertoires afforded by media and information technologies (della Porta & Diani, 2006; Johnston & Noakes, 2005; Snow, 2004).

In terms of communication technologies and movements, mass media are well suited to the presentation of consistent, repetitive messages to large, heterogeneous audiences, shaping broad-based popular opinion, fostering mass consumption, and mobilizing mass political campaigns. In contemporary media culture, however, the "mass" view of society and media is being challenged by a more complex, dynamic view of society as made up of constantly reorganizing, interrelated networks of nodes, links, and flows (e.g., Castells, 1996). New media technologies help people seek, find, and assess information and each other. Mobilization and social movements today depend on people's abilities to cultivate relationships, seek and give advice, make recommendations, and amass and trade "reputation capital" and trust online (Madden et al., 2007; May, 2001; Shirky, 2008), as well as "get people on to the street" (Van Aelst & Walgrave, 2002, p. 480). Bimber (2003) argues that the contemporary, information-saturated social environment associated with ICTs and new media constitutes a "fourth information revolution" with important implications for politics.

In this chapter we begin with a review of the main points of social movement theories as outlined in Chapter 2, especially what these theories have to say about the process of mobilization. We also consider some recent research and debates regarding the rise of new, transnational social movements and radical politics facilitated by global digital networks. To illustrate mediated mobilization as a genre, a short sketch is presented that shows how the internet and related technologies have contributed to the growth of the worldwide anti-globalization, or *global justice*, movement since the late 1990s. The chapter concludes with a discussion of the key features that characterize the genre.

Social movements and mobilizing

We can recap points from the overview of theorizing about social movements in Chapter 2. *Collective behavior* theory frames movements as individual actors with the attitudes, emotions, and susceptibility to persuasion that individual people have. It focuses on the sudden, disruptive, and spontaneous quality of movements and the marginality or alienation of participants, or as sociologist Doug McAdam puts it, a "macro emphasis on social disorganization and [a] micro stress on isolation and marginality" (McAdam, 2003, p. 282). It is broadly based in "contagion" theories of communication and social influence, and tends to portray movements as essentially emotional or irrational outbreaks of group action.

Resource mobilization theory (RMT), in contrast, depicts movements as rational, collective efforts in which participants act deliberately and strategically to articulate grievances, identify and gather material and cultural resources, organize hierarchically, and employ tactics that will achieve their goals, usually through established institutional channels rather than by the disruption and overthrow of those channels. From this perspective, communication channels are seen as important resources for formulating and conveying movement aims, and cultivating support. RMT borrows some of its concepts from organizational theory, including issues of costs vs. benefits and incentives and disincentives for action.

By the 1960s and 1970s, RMT had become the predominant view among social movement theorists, particularly in the U.S. In response, *new social movement theory* was elaborated by European and American analysts who felt RMT could not adequately account for the new, identity-based movements that arose between the late 1960s and 1990s. New social movement theory emphasizes the sense of personal commitment, identity, and creativity among movement activists, who are more likely to be well-educated, white-collar professionals and creative "knowledge workers" than to be drawn from traditional industrial working classes or marginalized groups.

NSMs are notable for shifting away from centrally organized "causes," "campaigns," and particularistic "grievances," and toward more loosely organized affiliations and allegiances among participants based on their shared identities, values, and lifestyles. In NSMs activists tend to engage in "unconventional" or disruptive forms of action, and to disregard or even sabotage traditional institutional avenues for action and change. Activists in NSMs tend to live their lives in a way that reflects their political, social, and ethical values, and to engage in movement actions and commitments according to issues of the moment, framed within their larger concerns, shared values, and collective identities. Accordingly, communication in this strand of theory focuses on the expression of personal experience and identity, the creation and negotiation of images, the representations of causes and lifestyles, and so on.

Building on new social movement theory, recent theorizing about social movements has emphasized the mutability of movements, especially in the context of new media technologies. Theorists have focused on movements' heterogeneous, decentralized, or "swarming" network structures, the use of digital media technologies to create, sustain, and reorganize network ties among loosely affiliated alliances of movement participants, the norms and solidarities that unite movement participants and society at large, and the movements' fundamentally cultural and subjective qualities. This "culturalist" or framing approach, influenced by Erving Goffman's interactionist sociology, focuses specifically on repertoires of action, including communicative action, and discourse (Williams, 2004); indeed, it could be argued that contention over symbolic representations, frames, discourse, and the institutional and technological mediation of competing images and framing has become a principal mechanism of action in contemporary social movements. As Castells (2009) argues, power is now a matter of programming, reprogramming, and switching among socio-technical networks; and change arises from the contention among groups and interests engaged in that programming and reprogramming.

From whatever perspective, *mobilization* is a core concept across social movement theories. We can think of it as what makes a movement a movement, the process in which people convert their collective *concerns* into collective *action* to bring about change. "[I]n order to translate an identified interest into collective political action, individuals with similar interests must somehow find one another and discover that they share that common interest. They must further form, or reform, some kind of common will, organizational structure and identity" (Tambini, 1999, p. 317). Summarizing the classic discussion of mobilization by McAdam, McCarthy, and Zald (1988), Vince Carducci observes that in the process, "constituencies and capabilities are activated and associations created as mechanisms for taking action" (Carducci, 2006, p. 132). Moreover, through mobilization, movements acquire capabilities and resources they do not already possess:

> The current sociological terms for the process by which a social movement is created and begins to take action is "mobilization." . . . [it] is the process by which a social unit assumes, with relative rapidity, control of resources which it did not control before . . . the process by which a collective actor gathers and organizes its resources for the pursuit of a shared objective. . . . Mobilization is always a process of transfer of preexisting resource to the benefit of a new objective. (Melucci, 1996, pp. 289, 292)

Mobilization is arguably the most important, and the most problematic, aspect of social movement development. "The mobilization process, getting people on the street, has always been a difficult and unpredictable element in the movements' success" (Van Aelst & Walgrave, 2002, p. 480).

Unsurprisingly, different social movement theories tend to emphasize different mechanisms of mobilization. Collective behavior attributes mobilization to rapid social change that generates social disorganization and the breakdown of social order, which produces sudden, disruptive outbreaks of collective action. A classic example can be seen in the early days of the labor movement, which developed in response to rapid industrialization, urbanization, and the oppressive power of monopoly capitalism in the late nineteenth and early twentieth century.

As the name suggests, mobilization processes are the center-piece of resource mobilization theories, specifically the deliberate and strategic gathering, organization, and deployment of mate-rial and institutional resources in centrally organized campaigns that appeal to the overarching values and ideals of the larger soci-ety. Individual efforts and contributions tend to be downplayed in favor of "big picture" causes, values, institutional structures and forces. Here, classic cases would include the U.S. civil rights movement and the early feminist movement. These campaigns built strictly hierarchical organizational structures, led by rela-tively small numbers of charismatic leaders. These structures were used systematically to solicit movement participation (vol-unteers for marches, sit-ins, civil disobedience), financial and in-kind support for movement activities, media coverage, and so on. The leadership of both movements clearly and consist-ently articulated the movement's core values and aims, explicitly connected its values to those of the larger society, and pursued its aims through the dual channels of established institutions (legislatures and the courts) and innovative protest actions (e.g., non-violent civil disobedience).

In new social movements, mobilization is accomplished by cultivating collective identities, shared values, and a sense of belonging among people linked in diffuse, decentralized social and community networks. Activists generate and share sym-bolic representations of movement identities and values that challenge those of the larger culture. The subjective experiences of individual participants and their "microcontributions" are essential in the mobilization process (Garrett, 2006), especially to maintain the sense that movement participation is an ongoing commitment or lifestyle, thus creating a "permanent campaign" in which members participate or contribute on an as-needed basis, instead of being organized into disciplined, goal-directed drives. Examples of these types of movements include environ-mentalism, gay rights, and animal rights activism.

More recent theorizing has expanded on some of the main ideas of new social movement theory, particularly the connection between communication, ICTs, and mobilizing. Mobilization is seen as sporadic and emergent rather than sustained, more symbolic or narrative than material, as springing from norms, identities, and solidarities instead of specific grievances or movement organizations – and as tightly interwoven with the use of new media and information technologies.

Communication and mobilizing

Although the framing differs, communication and media/information technologies are implicated across all types of social movement theories. According to collective behavior approaches, media have the power to lead and shape public perceptions, opinions, and feelings. In resource mobilization theory, media and information technologies are resources to be employed and exploited like any others, whether to disseminate information among activists, frame issues, or inform and persuade key audiences. In new social movement theories, media and ICTs are the means for expressing and circulating activists' interests, values, and symbolic representations of issues and for shifting popular discourse and the perception of movement issues and even the staging ground for the movements themselves. In contemporary networked, transnational movements, "activists have used new digital technologies to coordinate actions, build networks, practice media activism, and *physically manifest their emerging political ideals*" (Juris, 2005, p. 192, emphasis added). That is, media and networked ICTs also enhance what social movement theorists call the *prefigurative* qualities of movements – they serve as sites where activists can model their values, ideals, and lifestyles, and live their personal and political commitments as an example for others to follow. In NSMs, media and information technologies not only provide channels for transmitting information, they actually constitute the real, practical field of action where movements themselves are created, contested, and played out.

This last point is particularly important because it marks a departure from the standard approach to communication in earlier social movement theory, where media and ICTs are viewed as tools to be used by movements – that is, they are secondary to movements' "real" work and goals of achieving social change. Social movement theories of all types tend to cast communication technologies as straightforward channels for transmitting information, reflecting a simple one-to-many, "mass media" or "broadcast" view of communication that is no longer current among most communication scholars (Carroll & Hackett, 2006; Downing, 2008; Poster, 1998; Tambini, 1999). In a discussion of NSM theories and development communication, for example, Robert Huesca points out that "new social movements literature proceeds with little, if any, sense of communication processes and often with naïve assumptions regarding the power of mass media" (Huesca, 2001, p. 416). The idea that the use of new media and information technologies might in fact *constitute* movements and action in themselves

> flies in the face of the conventional wisdom that the Internet and other digital media typically do little more than amplify or economize communication in political organizations. . . . The problem with these and dozens of other accounts of the Internet and politics is that they generally look at how established political institutions and organizations adapt the Internet to existing routines. (Bennett, 2003, p. 145)

Moreover, from the traditional point of view, mediated and interpersonal communication are fundamentally separate and different modes of communication, and the two serve different purposes in the mobilization process. At the "macro," or whole-society, level, media help movements "propagandize" and deliver their messages, while at the "micro," or local, relational, level, interpersonal communication helps to recruit participants and create loyalties that hold movements together. However, contemporary media scholars argue that in social movements today, as in society as a whole, the use of networked ICTs and new media crosses and integrates both levels. Indeed, the "mass" and "interpersonal" aspects of new media are seen as so interwoven as to be less and less useful as distinct categories of communicative action (a view reflected in the definition of new media in Chapter 1). From this perspective, engagement via new media is both symbolic *and* material. Communication, media, and ICTs not only express or represent movement messages, but in fact are how participants *make* and *enact* movements in a "politics of connections" (Carroll & Hackett, 2006, p. 93; see also Tambini, 1999). In his analysis of the movement against corporate globalization, Castells observes that "The *networking form* of the movement became the *networking norm* of the movement" (Castells, 2009, p. 340, emphasis in the original).

Keith Hampton (2003), for example, disagrees with researchers who separate the Internet 'from other ways people communicate'. His empirical work shows that large online networks of weak relational ties and the availability of interpersonal modes of online interaction, such as email, actually foster collective action. Bimber (2000) rejects the idea that there should be any distinction between traditional forms of civic engagement and those that employ new information technologies. Together with Andrew Flanagin and Cynthia Stohl (Flanagin, Stohl, & Bimber, 2006), he argues that all collective action (including social movements) is fundamentally communicative, and that movements occupy a "collective action space" defined by participants' *mode of interaction* (ranging from highly personal to highly impersonal) and their *mode of engagement* (ranging from flexibly networked and self-organizing, to strictly hierarchical and centrally controlled; the authors refer to these as "entrepreneurial" and "institutional," respectively). In collective action space, a variety of communicative strategies, relationships, and technological systems can be adapted according to the situation at hand.

The literatures on critical media studies, media activism, and political communication also suggest how important communication technologies are in social movements. Historically, researchers and activists in these fields have focused on the practices and products of major media, entertainment, and information industries (today's so-called *content industries*), especially popular media like television, cinema, and recorded music, and their role in democratic societies and politics. Recently, however, some of these scholars have shifted their focus to political and cultural activists' use of new media and ICTs to critique the mainstream, and, crucially, to produce and distribute content that reflects alternative, radical, or underrepresented viewpoints (e.g., McCaughey & Ayers, 2003; van de Donk et al., 2004). Scholars of media activism "distinguish between democratization *through* the media (the use of media, whether by governments or civil society actors, to promote democratic goals and processes elsewhere in society), and democratization *of* the media themselves" (Carroll & Hackett, 2006, p. 84, emphasis in the original; see also Bennett, 2003).

As we will see in the case study below, activist uses of new media and the internet have also been situated within the repertoire of "unconventional," non-state, "extra-parliamentary," or transnational protest actions and mobilization techniques associated with new social movements (Bennett, 2003; Coleman, 2005; Van Aelst & Walgrave, 2002). Some analysts suggest that because it combines mass media-style distribution of alternative or marginalized content with rich opportunities for social interaction, internet use fosters the formation and cultivation of counter-cultural or subcultural "spaces" where alternative views and identities can be worked out and shared (Kahn & Kellner, 2003, 2005). Others argue that the structure of new media networks fosters the mobilization of participants and movements across traditional spatial, political, ideological, and cultural boundaries and barriers (Bennett, 2003; Tambini, 1999). As pointed out in Chapter 3, media theorists and activists have argued that the use of new media supports the development of "autonomous" or "nomadic" communities and mobilization outside mainstream society, unique vantage points for political and cultural intervention in mainstream politics and culture

(Bey, 2003; Critical Art Ensemble, 1994). Other analysts have debated the potentials of the internet and related ICTs for creating "counter-publics" or extending new forms of the public sphere online (Cammaerts & van Audenhove, 2005; Dahlgren, 2005; Downey & Fenton, 2003; Langman, 2005; Poster, 1998).

Of course, not all observers are convinced that the use of ICTs, versus other types of media, makes a real difference with respect to political action or the distribution of power. Henry Jenkins and David Thorburn (2003) see such claims as thinly disguised technological determinism, or an extension of the "digital revolution" visions advanced by pundits and defenders of market capitalism. Frank Webster (2001) outlines the most significant changes in affluent societies in recent decades, ranging from the decreased role of working classes and traditional communities, growing globalization and declines in national sovereignty, and the pervasive presence of new technologies, especially media technologies. Yet he is skeptical, suggesting that observers today may be prone to presentism – the tendency to believe that one's own time is unusually significant and to overlook continuities with the past:

> . . . it is premature to announce the arrival of a new politics. To be sure there are interesting new expressions of politics in the current era. . . . Contemporary use of the Internet to mobilize protesters – as happened at Seattle, and later on at Washington, as well as, on a smaller scale, in London . . . is sociologically interesting . . . but evidence that [such phenomena] are indicative of profound transformations is rather slight. . . . while we can see innovation and imagination at work, the weight of established practices and political parties presses hard. (Webster, 2001, p. 10)

Similarly, Alan Scott and John Street (2000) maintain that the expressive, "unconventional" and carnivalesque quality of protest in contemporary social movements (both online and off) is nothing new, but can be traced to pre-Web forms of popular culture and analyzed from the perspective of resource mobilization theories.

In sum, we can say that communication and media technologies have always played an essential role in social movement mobilization. Indeed, social movements would scarcely be possible if participants could not interact, recognize, and articulate their shared values and goals, form and maintain relationships, share information and advice, represent issues and viewpoints, debate controversies, and express themselves and their interests, both in person and via media channels.

However, in the contemporary media context, we must reconsider some traditional binaries associated with movement mobilization and communication. The distinction between individual and collective action, or between global and local sites of action, for example, may become blurred when any movement participant has the ability to express ideas and shape broader movement aims in a discussion list, wiki, or Indymedia posting. The dividing line between the symbolic and material aspects of mobilization becomes less clear when digital technologies are both the means of expression and the expression itself, as in hacktivists' distributed denial-of-service (DDOS) actions against corporate or government websites. The conventional separation of interpersonal communication and mass media is unsustainable in interactions online that combine personal messaging, links to text documents and videos, ironic or critical mash-ups of mainstream media content, email, websites, blogs, and Twitter-style message sites with immediate global reach.

As Castells observes, for a social movement online, its "articulation over the Internet" becomes *"both its organizational form and its mode of action"* (Castells, 2009, p. 338, emphasis added). Contemporary movements manifest a "cultural logic of networking" or "network ideal" that is expressed in both the social/technical structures and the communicative actions among participants (Juris, 2005, p. 192). It is precisely this intersection and blending of message and channel, material and social, means and ends, offline and online, that is the distinctive characteristic of *mediated mobilization*.

Mobilization goes online: the global justice movement

Uses of the internet and related communication technologies in the anti-globalization, or *global justice*, movement have been so widely studied that the topic almost constitutes a subfield in its own right – what one reviewer has called the "post-Seattle literature" (Oleson, 2003, p. 229).[1] Some writers trace its origins to the Zapatista resistance in Chiapas, Mexico in the early 1990s, which publicized its grievances, aims, and activities on its own websites and used denial-of-service techniques to overload and disable opponents' sites. "By demonstrating the potential of Internet technologies, the Zapatistas arguably created a long-term shift in global social movement politics" (Chadwick, 2006, p. 127; see also Castells, 1997; Cleaver, 1998, 1994; Ford & Gil, 2001; Garrido & Halavais, 2003; Kahn & Kellner, 2004; Langman, 2005). For others, the critical starting point was the defeat of the Organization for Economic Cooperation and Development's draft Multilateral Agreement on Investment (MAI), which encountered worldwide opposition and outrage when it was leaked to activists and posted online in 1998: "[The MAI] was the first major inter-state economic negotiation where the media . . . the negotiators, the NGOs opposing the agreement and academics . . . all seem to agree that the Internet was a key tool, used effectively by opponents to prevent an agreement" (Smith & Smythe, 2001, p. 191; see also Bennett, 2003; Van Aelst & Walgrave, 2002).

However, the "Battle in Seattle" in 1999 – where the World Trade Organization (WTO) meeting was surrounded by tens of thousands of protesters who prevented delegates from attending, where anarchist protesters' clashes with police and attacks on property attracted worldwide media coverage, and where the first Independent Media Center was established and the Indymedia movement began – is most often credited with launching global justice as a *transnational* online movement (Juris, 2005, 2008; Kahn & Kellner, 2004, 2005; Keck & Sikkink, 1998). Among academics and activists alike, the 1999 WTO protest "has become recognized as a punctuating moment in the evolution of global activism" (Bennett, 2003, p. 144), "a major symbol of the anti-globalization struggle" (Van Aelst & Walgrave, 2002, p. 468).

By most accounts, activists' creative uses of internet and other digital communication technologies made Seattle a watershed moment. New media have played an indispensable role in the global justice movement by drawing together a wildly diverse range of groups and causes into a globally scattered, loosely articulated, self-organizing movement capable of responding to major multinational policy bodies and staging high-visibility events all over the globe. "[M]edia activism and digital network-ing more generally are among the most important features of contemporary anti-corporate globalization movements" (Juris, 2005, p. 191). "The global internet . . . is creating the base and the basis for an unparalleled worldwide anti-war/pro-peace and social justice movement during a time of terrorism, war, and intense political struggle" (Kahn & Kellner, 2004, p. 88). "These new kinds of Internet-based social movements, cyberactivism, are fundamentally new and require new kinds of theorization" (Langman, 2005, p. 44). New communication technologies have enabled what Lance Bennett calls a "new politics" that is fundamentally "different in its global scale, networked com-plexity, openness to diverse political identities, and capacity to sacrifice ideological integration for pragmatic political gain . . . impressive in its capacity to continuously refigure itself around shifting issues, protest events, and political adversaries" (Bennett, 2003, p. 143). Thus the global justice movement is not "anti-globalization" *per se* – in fact its own aims, scope, and actions are global: "[A]ctivist networks are engaging politically with non-state, transnational targets such as corporations and trade regimes, and . . . there is growing coordination of com-munication and action across international activist networks" (Bennett, 2003, p. 144; see also Juris, 2008; Langman, 2005). What activists object to is the neo-liberal, corporate, capitalist vision of globalization. Instead, they advance an alternative, socially centered vision ("global justice") that emphasizes social and political equity, fair trade, environmental responsibility, and direct participation of the poorest populations in global-scale economic decisions that affect them.

As detailed in Chapter 5, global justice activists in Seattle, in collaboration with programmers, technologists, and media producer/activists, created their own media production facilities and temporary technology labs. They provided on-the-ground coverage that provided a dramatically different perspective on the protest events from those in the mainstream press and broadcast media. The internet was used not only to distribute information, but also to recruit and instruct protest participants, to organize and publicize protest-related events, to feed Indymedia content to mainstream media, and to implement hacktivist actions against targeted organizations' websites.

Building on the success of the Seattle event, global justice activists went on to rally supporters and mobilize protests at virtually every major multilateral economic summit over the next decade (Castells, 2009). They also organized their own series of periodic "counter-summits," the annual World Social Forum (WSF) meetings (http://www.forumsocialmundial.org. br). These informal, festival-style events are designed as counterpoints to assemblies of the World Economic Forum. Some actions were more successful than others: for example, WSF gatherings grew from 50,000 participants in Porto Alegre, Brazil, in 2001, to 150,000 in 2005 (Castells, 2009; Langman, 2005). The Free Trade Agreement of the Americas (FTAA) summit in Miami, Florida, in November 2003 attracted thousands of protesters despite a massive show of force by local police. The 2003 WTO meeting in Cancún was disrupted and cancelled. Half a million people turned out for protests against the EU in Barcelona in March 2002 (Juris, 2005). On the other hand, actions against the IMF/World Bank meetings in Prague in October 2000, and against the FTAA in Québec City in 2001 drew many fewer participants and were marked by more violent encounters with police (Van Aelst & Walgrave, 2002).

Some critics are doubtful that movement communication and

mobilization online differ substantially in kind from the uses of media in traditional movements in the past (e.g., Wright, 2004). Any putative "internationalization" of movements online, they allege, benefits mainly activists in wealthy regions with good internet access (Tilly, 2004). Others note that even the most tech-savvy contemporary movements do not rely solely on the internet and new digital technologies, but use a mix of mass media and new media systems and techniques to communicate among their participants and with the wider public (Chadwick, 2006; Halleck, 2002; Kidd, 2003; Morris, 2004). As Bennett (2003) points out, and as noted in the discussion of Indymedia in the previous chapter, new media today often influence the coverage and agenda of mass media. Other observers claim that most movement groups, even those with network access and technological sophistication, tend to use them for routine communication functions and seldom take full advantage of the technology's capabilities and features (Stein, 2009).

However, the preponderance of research and scholarship on the global justice movement over the last decade suggests that activists' embrace of the internet and other digital technologies has expanded rapidly over the last decade, and has changed the nature of contemporary movements and activism in a way that is not fully accounted for by existing social movement theories. Several analysts, taking their cue from Castells's seminal work on identity, global networks, and new social movements (Castells, 1997), have asserted that new frameworks are needed for understanding large-scale, loosely organized, decentralized, transnational, intensively mediated movements like global justice. Lauren Langman, for example, calls these "Internetworked Social Movements" (ISMs) and contends that

> These new kinds of Internet-based social movements, cyber-activism, are fundamentally new and require new kinds of theorization. . . . the historically specific differences between ISMs and earlier movements have not yet been fully theorized within social movement theory, which has attempted to employ paradigms that emerged in earlier contexts. Nor has much

social theory, in general, addressed some of the more salient aspects of computer-mediated communication (CMC) and the kinds of electronically mediated connections, networks, communities, and identites that have emerged. The new realities of "network society" mandate rethinking social mobilization. (Langman, 2005, p. 44–5)

One of Manuel Castells's collaborators, Jeffrey Juris, has in fact proposed one such reframing of transnational activism, based on his experience as a global justice activist and anthropologist studying media activism in Europe and Latin America (Juris, 2005, 2008), that aligns with the idea noted in previous chapters, that new media are both "cultural material and material culture" (Boczkowski & Lievrouw, 2008). He argues that communication technologies are an integral feature of contemporary movements, inseparable from movement values, action, lifestyles, identities, and interests. Indeed it is only in the context of global information and communication networks that the alternative visions of society espoused by today's movement activists have been materially realized. "[T]he worldwide circulation of discourses, strategies, and tactics signals the emergence of a global web of alternative transnational counterpublics" (Juris, 2005, p. 196).

Juris (2008) argues that activists are not mere users of networked media and information technologies, but have actually absorbed the "cultural logic of networking" (p. 11) into all aspects of movement values and action, online and off. Open-source and peer-to-peer architectures, for example, are embodied in the very social organization and norms of new movements, as well as in the systems themselves. "[T]he network has also become a powerful cultural ideal, particularly among more radical activists, a guiding logic that provides a model of, and a model for, emerging forms of directly democratic politics" (p. 11). The "animating spirit behind this emerging political praxis," Juris says, is fundamentally "anarchist . . . libertarian" (p. 15). Expanding on Juris's main points, Castells describes movement uses of new technologies as "a *project of societal organization around networked self-management* . . . a new form of production and social organization based on the logic of open source . . . a postcapitalist order based on the principles of free software" (Castells, 2009, p. 343, emphasis in the original).

For example, an essential feature of contemporary transnational movements is the creation of technology centers or media labs, either as permanent organizations (e.g., Indymedia's Independent Media Centers) or as *ad hoc* bases during protests and other movement events. Such centers have become a routine feature of global justice protests and counter-summits like the World Social Forum meetings. Juris argues that these centers, which offer on-site technology facilities, network access, and support services, serve as laboratories for "experimenting" with alternative technologies and new, provisional forms of political and social organization, in line with the nomadic, autonomous, or rhizomatic social forms advocated by radical media activists and social theorists (Bey, 2003; Critical Art Ensemble, 1994; Deleuze & Guattari, 1987 [1980]). Tech centers allow activists to demonstrate and exemplify new, alternative, or "other" values and practices for the rest of society. Indeed, Alain Touraine's analysis of marginality and new social movements might apply just as well to movement tech centers: "a laboratory in which a new culture and a social counterproject are being elaborated" (Touraine, 1988 [1984], p. 106). Although they are used as much for play, socializing, and entertainment as they are for "serious" movement activities (Castells, 2009), they are as enmeshed in social movements today as they are in every other aspect of everyday life for the current generation of activists.

More broadly, the literature on the global justice activism suggests that networked communication technologies have served three main purposes in the movement to date. First, and most important, the internet has been an indispensable tool for coordination among diverse groups, especially in the process of organizing and staging live street protests, direct action, and "counter-summits" around the globe on a remarkably short turn-around cycle. (Table 6.1 shows a timeline of selected protest events since 1999 that have made substantial use of the internet and related technologies.)

Table 6.1. Timeline of global justice protest events and counter-summits with online/new media coordination, 1998–2009

Date		Protest venue/event	Counter-summits	Location(s)
1998		Organization for Economic Cooperation and Development (OECD) / Multilateral Agreement on Investment (MAI)*		[Posted online]
1999	June	Carnival Against Capitalism		Locations worldwide
	June	G8 Summit		Cologne (GER)
	Nov.–Dec.	World Trade Organization*		Seattle (USA)
2000	Jan.	World Economic Forum		Davos (SUI)
	Apr.	World Bank/International Monetary Fund		Washington, DC (USA)
	Sept.	World Economic Forum		Melbourne (AUSTRALIA)
	Sept.	World Bank/International Monetary Fund		Prague
	Nov.	G8 Summit		Montréal (CAN)
	Dec.	European Union Summit		Nice (FRA)
2001	Jan.		World Social Forum	Porto Alegre (BRA)
	Jan.	World Economic Forum		Davos (SUI)
	Apr.	Summit of the Americas (Free Trade Agreement of the Americas, FTAA)		Québec City (CAN)
	June	European Union Summit		Gothenburg (GER)
	June	World Bank		Barcelona (SPA)
	July	World Economic Forum		Salzburg (AUSTRIA)
	July	G8 Summit		Genoa (ITA)

Year	Month	Event	Social Forum	Location
2002	Jan.	World Economic Forum	World Social Forum	Porto Alegre (BRA)
				New York City (USA)
	Mar.	European Union Summit		Barcelona (SPA)
	June	World Bank Meeting		Oslo (NOR)
	June	G8 Summit		Calgary, Ottawa (CAN)
	July	No Border/Schengen Protest		Strasbourg (FRA)
	Sept.	G7		
		World Bank/Int'l Monetary Fund		Washington, DC (USA)
	Nov.		European Social Forum	Florence
2003	Jan.		World Social Forum	Porto Alegre (BRA)
	June	G8 Summit		Evian (FRA)
				Lausanne (SUI)
	June	European Union Summit		Thessalonika (GRE)
	Sept.	World Trade Organization 5th Ministerial Meeting		Cancún (MEX)
	Oct.	Regional World Economic Forum		Dublin (IRE)
	Nov.		European Social Forum	Paris (FRA)
	Nov.	Free Trade Agreement of the Americas		Miami (USA)
2004	Jan.		World Social Forum	Mumbai (IND)
	Apr.	European Economic Forum		Warsaw (POL)
	Oct.		European Social Forum	London (UK)
	Nov.	Asia-Pacific Economic Community		Santiago (CHILE)

Table 6.1. (continued)

Date	Protest venue/event	Counter-summits	Location(s)
2005	Jan.		World Social Forum	Porto Alegre (BRA)
	July.	G8 Summit		Gleneagles / Edinburgh (SCOT)
	Dec.	World Trade Organization 6th Ministerial Meeting		Hong Kong (PRC)
2006	Jan.		World Social Forum	Caracas (VEN), Bamako (MALI)
	Mar.		World Social Forum	Karachi (PAK)
	May		European Social Forum	Athens (GRE)
	Nov.	G20 Summit		Melbourne (AUSTRALIA)
2007	Jan.		World Social Forum	Nairobi (KEN)
	May	G8 Summit		Hamburg/Heiligendamm (GER)
	June	G8 Summit		Rostock (GER)
	Sept.	Asia-Pacific Economic Community		Australia
	Oct.	World Bank/International Monetary Fund		Washington, DC (USA)
2008	Jan.		World Social Forum	Locations worldwide
	Sept.		European Social Forum	Malmö (SWE)

2009	Jan.		World Social Forum	Belém (BRA)
	Mar.–Apr.	G20 Summit		London (UK)
	Apr.	World Bank/International Monetary Fund		Washington, DC (USA)
	July	G8 Summit		Rome (ITA)

*Although the global justice/anti-globalization movement was certainly active before 1998, the OECD/MAI protest and the WTO Seattle protest (shaded) are generally acknowledged as the first events to demonstrate broad-based, sophisticated, and effective use of the internet and related media for organizing protest actions, and provided the model for subsequent protest organizing.

Local organizers and their global colleagues tap into activist networks online to plan and debate future actions, recruit participants and volunteers, share organizational advice, solicit funds and other forms of support, and coordinate the myriad logistical aspects of bringing together tens of thousands of participants in one place and providing them with basic facilities, transportation, and technological support. Online, activists and organizers have overcome many of the physical barriers to communication that have hobbled movement organizing across national, cultural, and geographic boundaries in the past. Combined with the relative ease and cheapness of international air travel, online communication has certainly contributed to remarkably large protest turnouts in locations scattered from Porto Alegre to Montreal to Mumbai.

Obviously, not all activists can or do attend every event, and the "horizontal linkages" (Juris, 2005, 2008; see also Stein, 2009) across movement organizations, locations, and activists are often contingent and adaptable, made and broken as circumstances change. However, the ability of activists to employ communication technologies to mobilize people and events anywhere in the world on a more or less as-needed basis suggests that the movement operates as a "permanent campaign," as outlined in Chapter 2.

The second main use of the internet in the global justice movement has been as a platform to produce and distribute content. The Web is used to "advertise" movement activities, identities, concerns, and values to wider audiences, to provide counterpoints to opponents' views and mainstream press accounts, and to share information and build solidarity among allied activists and groups. This aspect of internet use is grounded in earlier forms of DIY media activism, media democracy, and tactical media, in which activists not only critique the mainstream, but also produce their own alternative content.

Here, the global IMC/Indymedia network has been perhaps the most effective channel for the production and distribution of movement-related content among activists and to the general public. The parallels with mass media are obvious: for example, Indymedia has deliberately organized itself along the lines of a traditional "newswire" or news service like the Associated Press or Reuters, with the difference that Indymedia is open to anyone who wants to contribute and engages in very little editorial "gate-keeping." But radical media online have also been subjected to increasing levels of legal harassment and outright censorship by authoritarian regimes as well as more "liberal" states (Juris, 2005; see also Chapter 5).

The third, least frequent, and least conventional, use of new media technologies among global justice activists has been for engaging in hacktivism, electronic civil disobedience (Wray, 1998), and similar interventions involving the technological infrastructure itself. These initiatives are not always techno-logically sophisticated. Tim Jordan and Paul Taylor (2004), for example, point out that global justice activists have preferred relatively low-tech techniques like distributed denial-of-service (DDOS) or "ping-storm" attacks over more efficient, centralized methods, in which (for example) a few programmers controlling automated programs and "botnets" can temporarily overwhelm target websites with millions of automatically generated page reload or information requests. Some activists consider "bad technology" like DDOS to be a more ethical form of electronic civil disobedience (ECD) because it is designed purposely to involve more people. It also requires individual protesters to make a deliberate choice whether to participate in a "blockade" action and thus open themselves to legal action (much as "live" protesters must decide whether to physically block a sidewalk or doorway to prevent summit delegates from entering a building, and face arrest and prosecution as a result).[2]

Obviously, of these three uses of the Internet, hacktivism and ECD carry the greatest degree of legal risk, especially as any entry into or manipulation of computer systems, even as innocu-ous pranks, has been criminalized and rigorously prosecuted in the post-9/11 climate. However, from the FloodNet actions of the Zapatista movement, meant to overload and disable hostile corporate and government websites, to DDOS actions against WTO websites during the Seattle protests and continuing "hacktivism" by activist programmers and technologists, such tactics have remained part of the direct action repertoire of the global justice movement.

Summary: mediated mobilization as a genre

Returning to the genre framework used throughout this book, it is clear that mediated mobilization is distinctive in terms of its scope, its position relative to society at large, and the agency/action of participants. With respect to scope, mediated mobilization is obviously collaborative. Indeed, from a certain perspective it can be seen as ultimately, and primarily, a process for promoting collaboration among like-minded people. Collaboration here takes a variety of forms, from interpersonal relationships and interaction, to the creation and sharing of ideas, opinions, and information via blogs, websites, wikis, email, and listservs, to participation in large-scale "live" protests, workshops, countersummits, and so on. Mobilization is not merely the collection and allocation of resources (people, time, funding, technology, space), it also creates a sense of belonging, solidarity, and collective identity among participants that is expressed through their collaborative activities.

In terms of the position of social movements relative to the larger society, mediated mobilization has also fostered movements that are distinctly heterotopic and subcultural. To a great extent social movements depend on activists' abilities to articulate and present their interests and concerns in contrast and opposition to the status quo, movements as insurgent forces existing "outside" the conventional institutions and practices of power, and as necessary and legitimate correctives and challenges to those institutions and practices. The subcultural qualities of the global justice movement, for example, are made explicit in the movement's opposition to the most powerful multinational economic institutions, to environmental and economic exploitation, and in its commitments to radical democracy, the interests of marginalized or oppressed communities, and so on. And, as many of the examples in this chapter have shown, and as several social movement theorists have argued, networked communication technologies have allowed movements to shift from relatively centralized, hierarchical organizational structures to highly decentralized, loosely affiliated contingent networks that link a wide variety of groups, actors, and interests without imposing a single dominant agenda or program of action. That is, movements have become increasingly heterotopic as they have adopted network "norms and forms" (Castells, 2009; Juris, 2008). "Precisely because they are multimodal, diversified, and pervasive, communication networks are able to include and enclose cultural diversity and a multiplicity of messages to a much greater extent than any other public space in history" (Castells, 2009, p. 300).

Finally, with respect to action and agency, mediated mobilization is fundamentally interventionist in purpose, practice, and ethos. At the broad, society-wide level, mediated mobilization helps movements intervene in the workings of social and political institutions, changing norms and values and reconfiguring the distribution of power and resources. At the middle-range level, mediated mobilization affects the organizing practices and structures of social movement organizations themselves. The use of networked ICTs has led activists to reject the traditional forms of movement organizations, including "vanguardism" and representative structures of movement participation, in favor of "messier," but more direct and participatory, forms of political organizing and action. Put differently, mediated mobilization has enabled a shift from an "intensive" form of movement organizing to a more "extensive" form. An important consequence of the "cultural logic of networking" has been a move toward increasingly flexible, adaptable, and "flat" social movement organizing. Such a form succeeds by assimilating the contributions of participants throughout every part of the network, not by the formulation of agendas and strategies by a centralized leadership structure that are subsequently passed down to the rank and file to be carried out. At the micro, interpersonal/individual level, the interventionist nature of mediated mobilization is most obvious in the "prophetic" or "prefigurative" activities of activists who put their values and commitments into practice in their everyday lives, as an example to others of how personal action can promote social and political change. Such modeling helps to cultivate collective identity within and across the different groups involved in the movement, creating a sensibility which feeds back upstream to movement organizing activities and the movement's broader social, cultural, and political aims.

The next chapter considers the final genre of alternative/activist new media. Like the other genres discussed so far, commons knowledge parallels and responds to a particular element within society and culture. As we have seen, culture jamming inverts the codes, content, and methods of popular culture to critique that culture. Alternative computing uses the techniques of system design and engineering as social and political critique, to intervene directly in the digital infrastructure and its institutional foundations. Participatory journalism adopts the ethics and practices of journalism and the press as a commentary on and corrective to the failures of the news industry and to provide new arenas for news, opinion, and analysis that are neglected or marginalized by the mainstream. In mediated mobilization, political and cultural activists employ the internet and digital media to overcome the informational, geographic, and cultural limitations of conventional social movement organizing. They create new networked movements that are more flexible, inclusive, loosely articulated, and extensive than traditional movements – and possibly more effective forms of resistance to global-scale economic and social power and forces for social change. In commons knowledge, the scope widens even further, to the very forms of organized knowledge itself – how it is generated, organized, and evaluated, who decides what is worth knowing, and why.

CHAPTER 7

Challenging the Experts

Commons Knowledge

Wikipedia is just an incredible thing. It's fact-encirclingly huge, and it's idiosyncratic, careful, messy, funny, shocking, and full of simmering controversies – and it's free, and it's fast. . . . It's like some vast aerial city with people walking briskly to and fro on catwalks, carrying picnic baskets full of nutritious snacks.

(Baker, 2008, p. 6)

Somebody who reads Wikipedia is "rather in the position of a visitor to a public restroom," says Mr. [Robert] McHenry, Britannica's former editor. "It may be obviously dirty, so that he knows to exercise great care, or it may seem fairly clean, so that he may be lulled into a false sense of security. What he certainly does not know is who has used the facilities before him."

(*Economist*, 2006a, p. 15)

When asked what the "2.0" of "Web 2.0" means, most Internet users will point to so-called *social media* – social network sites like Facebook and MySpace, the "microblogging" site Twitter, tagging and bookmarking sites such as Digg.com or del.icio. us, Q&A sites like Answerbag and Answers.com, or the spectacularly successful collaborative encyclopedia, Wikipedia. More literary users, such as the author Nicholson Baker and Robert McHenry of the *Encyclopedia Britannica*, both of whom are quoted above, tend to invoke vivid metaphors to describe – and excoriate – their experiences.

Whereas Web 1.0, *circa* the 1990s, opened up an imponderably large universe of documents and information on demand,[1] the twenty-first-century Web 2.0 links this power of global information search and retrieval with the personal involvement, interaction, and collaborative creativity of people linked to one another in complex, far-flung social and technological networks. The internet has grown beyond its initial mode as a vast library and document repository into something more like a cultural festival in which anyone can perform, contribute, comment, and debate – "one lovely big amusement park," to use Geert Lovink's phrase (1997, p. 59). Compared with Web 1.0, Web 2.0 is fundamentally *social*.

This broad expansion of the character of online communication and information, from the documentary to the interactive, from the storehouse to the festival, is the pivotal development underlying the fifth genre of alternative and activist new media. Just as the genres discussed in preceding chapters reflect and respond to other aspects of society and culture – journalism and the press, technological systems and infrastructure, popular culture, political and social movements – what I am calling *commons knowledge* provides an alternative and complement to the expert-driven, disciplinary, institutionalized, and authoritative process of knowledge creation, distribution, and gatekeeping that has evolved in modern societies. At its best, commons knowledge revives the sort of dedicated amateur scholarship associated with the natural philosophers, the *philosophes*, and the birth of early modern science and letters. At its worst, it generates an appalling morass of misinformation, rumor, incivility, libel, partisan rants, uninformed "opinion," and unverifiable claims. Either way, what is important about commons knowledge projects is that they have opened new arenas for collaborative knowledge production that increasingly rival the traditions, conventions, and privileges of expert authorities and institutionalized knowledge itself.

At first glance, commons knowledge may not appear as overtly "alternative" or "activist" as the other genres discussed so far. Wikipedia hardly seems as radical a project as electronic civil disobedience, an Indymedia blog, or mobilizing a G8 protest via Twitter. However, in Chapter 1 alternative and activist new media were defined as those that "employ or modify the communication artifacts, practices, and social arrangements of new information and communication technologies to challenge or alter dominant, expected, or accepted ways of doing society, culture, and politics." In this chapter I hope to show that commons knowledge fits this definition. As alternatives to the very institutional and disciplinary bases of knowledge "authorities," open-source collaborations like Wikipedia and folksonomic projects like del.icio.us and Digg.com may in fact constitute significant challenges to the assumptions and privileges of professional expertise and established, institutionalized power. A growing literature on commons-based knowledge production suggests that, contrary to critics' objections, the scope and quality of these online projects are comparable to those of many traditional authoritative resources in print and other formats, which may help explain their dramatic growth and acceptance as generally reliable, useful information sources.

In the rest of this chapter, I survey some key studies and what they suggest about the development of commons knowledge online, including its strengths and weaknesses. I propose several broad characteristics that distinguish commons knowledge from more conventional, institutionally sanctioned forms of knowledge production, and thus qualify projects like Wikipedia or folksonomies as genuinely alternative and activist. I provide a short case study of Wikipedia as today's paradigmatic example of commons-based knowledge production, including research findings about its collaboration process, growth patterns, quality assurance practices, and stance relative to more traditional, authoritative information sources. I close, as with the preceding chapters, with a brief summary of the features of commons knowledge as a genre of alternative and activist new media.

From collaboration to crowdsourcing

Collaboration is not uniquely human, but it could certainly be considered a defining feature of human action and culture. Virtually every aspect of human affairs, from architecture to zoology, is collaborative to some extent; it would be difficult to imagine the workplace, education and scholarship, entertainment, agriculture, politics, commerce, family life, or most any other arena of society in which people do not act together to achieve some purpose or outcome. So it is hardly surprising that people would carry this "real life" preference for doing things together into the online setting, or that people would devise tools and techniques for collaborating at a distance, from telephone calls and messenger services to wikis, teleconferences, and other forms of what has come to be called *computer-supported cooperative work*, or CSCW.[2]

However, beginning in the 1990s, the highly flexible networks of links among people, systems, places, and information resources afforded by the internet opened new possibilities for collaboration, especially for projects with specific goals that could benefit from many small contributions of hundreds or even thousands of participants. This style of online collaboration is often traced to "distributed" software development projects, in which numerous, geographically dispersed contributors share their efforts and mutually fill in, edit, or amend each other's work, more or less continuously.

The software engineer and open-source pioneer Eric Raymond famously likens this mode of software development to a "bazaar" in which innumerable interactions among diverse buyers, sellers, and browsers maximize opportunities for finding new and interesting ideas and for identifying and correcting or eliminating bad ones. He contrasts this model with the more traditional "cathedral" approach, in which a hierarchy of craftspeople is assembled and centrally directed toward the completion of a single, complex, pre-defined goal. Each style has its place, but the bazaar model, he argues, is far better suited to mobilizing creativity on a massive scale, to find solutions to intricate, interlinked problems, or to identify and correct errors in large, complex projects. To use Raymond's memorable phrase (mixed metaphors notwithstanding), "with enough eyeballs, all bugs are shallow" (Raymond, 2001, p. 30). This approach was a defining feature of early free software and open-source software projects, such as the GNU operating system created by Richard Stallman and his colleagues, and, later, the Linux operating system and its many spin-offs, versions, and "builds" (which today run the majority of servers and routers that comprise the internet).[3]

By the late 1990s the remarkable success of these projects, especially their capacity for rapid, community-driven self-correction and "repair" as well as extraordinary innovativeness at low cost, had become widely admired alternatives to "closed," strictly proprietary software development as practiced by industry giants like Microsoft and IBM (Kelty, 2008). Advocates also emphasized the ethics of free software and open-source projects. In contrast to centrally organized and directed project management, proponents consider free software and open-source projects to be more meritocratic and egalitarian. The contributions and shared "authorship" of all participants are recognized (rather than crediting only project leaders, lone inventors, or subsuming myriad contributions under a single corporate label). This generates "reputation economies" that can provide powerful motivations for innovation and excellence among collaborators, as is common among hobbyists, amateur enthusiasts, club members, and so on (Ciffolilli, 2003). Such projects also sustain a longer tradition of sharing software as a public good within a community of peers (Stallman, 2002).

To date, open-source collaborative models have been most closely associated with computing and software development (although their foundations clearly lie in the peer review practices of academic scholarship and science). However, a similar logic has been applied in other areas and to other types of complex projects with "commons" or "public goods" qualities and large numbers of potential participants, using the internet as a shared platform for "mass collaboration" (Fallis, 2009).[4] The open-source approach has been applied across a range of fields, from pharmaceuticals, to musical composition and creative writing, to open-source journalism (see Chapter 5). Among open-source advocates, conventional copyright is rejected in favor of alternative approaches to intellectual property like "copy-left" (based on Stallman's original GNU Public License) and

Creative Commons licenses. Under these terms, copyrights are still claimed, but holders agree to make their works available free for others to use in the creation of new works, so long as the copyright holder is properly acknowledged and the original itself is not appropriated *in toto* (examples of Creative Commons licenses are available at http://www.creativecommons.org).

In recent years, a number of observers have picked up on the open-source idea and the virtues of commons-based, collective, and open-source models of production and society versus privatization. Scholarly and popular authors alike have extolled the power of "crowdsourcing" (Howe, 2008), "the wisdom of crowds" (Surowiecki, 2004), and "collective intelligence" (Lévy, 1999) in everything from marketing to politics to scientific discovery. The statistical patterns and economic forces underlying mass-scale collective action have been characterized in terms of "commons-based peer production" (Benkler, 2007), the "tipping point" (Gladwell, 2000), or "long tail" distributions (Anderson, 2008), in which the cumulation of small events can generate sudden, massive changes or unexpected systemic consequences, and even "Wikinomics" (Tapscott & Williams, 2008).

Some writers argue that the benefits of commons-based models of collaboration extend far beyond the rigorous egalitarianism of free and open-source software. Collective knowledge production, they say, has the potential to enhance the autonomy and liberty of individuals, and to strengthen deliberative and participatory democratic practices against the prerogatives of technocratic elites and the growing dominance of experts in every corner of social life (Benkler, 2007; Surowiecki, 2004).

Not all observers are so positive, however. Critics see three main problems with collective or commons-based peer production. The first is that such projects are exploitative because they depend on volunteer contributions and the "free labor" of participants (DeLong, 2003). Thus collective projects create alienation, extract "surplus value" from the labor of legions of creative workers, and enrich investors, much as factory work does in the context of industrial capitalism (Terranova, 2009 [2000]). In a critique of what they call the "creative industries," Lovink and Rossiter point out,

> The peer-to-peer formats of production are fantastic, for sure. But there is no redistribution of absent revenues to creative producers. This contradiction inside digital capitalism is only further accelerating and takes us in to [sic] unknown territories. There will be no Hegelian synthesis in which the aspiring billions make money through "friends." . . . You go and perform your concerts, you install a company's IT requirements, you design viral memes, you wait on a restaurant table. There is a logic of equivalence at work here, but it's not going to make you rich fast. If anything, it's going to rapidly sap any creative juices out of you. (Lovink & Rossiter, 2007a, p. 11)

A second objection to collective knowledge production comes from critics who disagree that the accumulation of contributions by lay enthusiasts and "amateurs" can or should be compared to the benefits of expertise and technocratic elites, or that peer production is necessarily democratic by definition (Keen, 2007). These critics contend that claims for the power of online peer production are based on a relativist view of knowledge that is vacuous and even morally hazardous, if anyone's views on a topic can be considered as valid as anyone else's. Moreover, the deluge of fragmented ideas, opinions, issues, and events produced by anyone and everyone online – in the form of memes, streams, buzz, mobs, or "viral culture" – prevents sustained attention and a reasoned, coherent understanding of the world (Wasik, 2009). As former Silicon Valley entrepreneur Andrew Keen observes, "This undermining of truth is threatening the quality of civil public discourse, encouraging plagiarism and intellectual property theft, and stifling creativity. . . . Instead of more community, knowledge, or culture, all that Web 2.0 really delivers is more dubious content from anonymous sources, hijacking our time and playing to our gullibility" (Keen, 2007, p. 17).

A third criticism is that collective knowledge production processes in themselves are no guarantee of quality, and that advocates tend to overstate the effectiveness of open-source or peer production as self-regulating or "self-healing" processes (Duguid, 2006). Robert McHenry, the former editor-in-chief of the *Encyclopedia Britannica* who compares Wikipedia to a public toilet in the quote that opens this chapter, also refers to it as a "faith-based encyclopedia" (McHenry, 2004) that embodies "the moist and modish notion of community and some vague notions about information wanting to be free" (*Economist*, 2006a, pp. 14–15).

Paul Duguid (2006) is deeply skeptical about two presumed "laws of quality" associated with peer production, arguing that they are more articles of faith than rigorously tested principles. The first is Eric Raymond's maxim, quoted earlier, that "given enough eyeballs, all bugs are shallow." Raymond credits Linus Torvalds, the originator of Linux, with the original idea, thus Duguid calls it "Linus's Law." Unlike peer-produced content such as that compiled in Wikipedia or indexed at Digg.com, Duguid says, open-source software is developed by competent experts who are literally peers scrutinizing their colleagues' work. Ultimately, software "solutions must compile and run . . . [but] What might it mean to "compile" a Project Gutenberg submission? How might a Wikipedia entry be said to run? Or to crash? . . . Software projects do not generally let anyone contribute code at random" (Duguid, 2006).

Second, Duguid charges that a kind of implicit, and unexamined, Darwinism underlies claims that good work will naturally rise to the top and drive out the bad in collaborative, peer-produced projects, if the number of collaborators is large enough. Calling this belief "Graham's Law" after a remark by programmer Paul Graham in an essay on open-source (Graham, 2005), Duguid (2006) charges that "Graham's implication that continuous tinkering only makes things better is highly suspect. It is hard to see why entropy would be indefinitely suspended by peer production."

Anthropologist Chris Kelty (2008) takes a more nuanced view, acknowledging that the approach and logic of free and open-source software can be seen everywhere in contemporary society, including

> Connexions and Creative Commons, open access, Open Source
> synthetic biology, free culture, access to knowledge (a2k),
> open cola, open movies, science commons, open business,
> Open Source yoga, Open Source democracy, open educational
> resources, the One Laptop Per Child project, to say nothing of
> the proliferation of wiki-everything or the "peer production" of
> scientific data or consumer services. (Kelty, 2008, p. 302)

Kelty sees these developments as part of a larger cultural landscape in which society's attitudes and relationships to knowledge
and power are undergoing a major reorientation. Nonetheless,
he cautions that, given the complexity of coding, and that the
affinity among programmers is based on ethical commitments
and beliefs about technology that are specific to the culture of
computing, the correspondence between open-source software
development and other types of projects may only go so far.
Indeed, to strict adherents of the free and open-source software
philosophy and "movement," many of the most widely hailed
peer-produced projects hardly count as "free" or "open-source" at
all: although participants may contribute and change the content
of the system, they are not permitted to modify or intervene in
the fundamental design of the system itself. Or, as media critic
Geert Lovink notes,

> Over the last few years, the creative struggles of the multitudes
> have produced outputs on many different layers: the dialectics
> of open sources, open borders, and open knowledge. Yet the
> deep penetration of the concepts of openness and freedom into
> the principle of struggle is by no means a quick compromise to
> the cynical and greedy neoliberal class. (Lovink, 2008, p. 193)

Commons knowledge vs. institutionalized knowledge

Before turning to the case of Wikipedia, we can summarize a few
main characteristics that distinguish commons knowledge from
more traditional, institutionally sanctioned forms of knowledge
production and circulation – characteristics that qualify commons

knowledge as "alternative" and "activist." The point here is not to argue that commons knowledge projects are necessarily superior or that they supersede traditional approaches to knowledge creation and gatekeeping. Indeed, authoritative knowledge institutions, professions, and informal commons-based knowledge production are increasingly articulated and overlapping, as universities, libraries, academic disciplines, scholarly societies, cultural institutions, and government agencies link to online resources or create commons-based, peer-produced projects of their own (Borgman, 2007). Examples include the Public Library of Science (PLoS; see http://www.plos.org) or Cornell University's ArXiv project (http://www.arxiv.org), which provides open, public access to "e-print" (online pre-print) research articles in physics, mathematics, non-linear science, computer science, quantitative biology, and statistics. Rather, the characteristics outlined here help demonstrate how commons knowledge has become a prominent feature of the contemporary landscape of social media and Web 2.0, and an increasingly credible rival and complement to more authoritative, institutional forms of knowledge.

The Alexandrian ideal

The first defining characteristic of commons knowledge projects is what might be called their "Alexandrian" ambitions. The term derives from the Library of Alexandria, Egypt, founded around 300 BCE, which was the largest collection of Greek writings then existing, and reputed to contain all the recorded knowledge of the ancient world. Its collection was gradually decimated between the first century BCE and the seventh century CE (MacLeod, 2004). In the modern era, scholars, librarians, and archivists have pursued the ideal of restoring the Alexandria library in modern form, principally by building up comprehensive collections, such as those held in national libraries (e.g., France's Bibliothèque Nationale or the Library of Congress in the U.S.) or other major cultural institutions (e.g., the New York Public Library or the Bodleian Library at Oxford University), but also by establishing standardized metadata and methods of "universal" document classification that allowed collections to be organized and shared among cooperative networks of organizations. The United Nations Educational, Scientific, and Cultural Organization (UNESCO) and a number of other international cultural organizations have also joined forces to support a New Library of Alexandria, or Bibliotheca Alexandrina, in Egypt, which combines both physical and digital library collections, a cultural center, and a planetarium, among other facilities (see http://www.bibalex.gov.eg/).

By the early twentieth century, in the wake of the horrors of World War I, prominent intellectuals and visionaries like H.G. Wells and Paul Otlet insisted that understanding among nations, world peace, and the prevention of another catastrophic war would only be realized by collecting and organizing "all the knowledge in the world" into a single collective repository of world culture open to all (Rayward, 2003, 2008; Wells, 1938; Wright, 2008). Together with colleagues, Otlet, one of the founders of the documentation movement in Europe, actually created a purpose-built repository for a vast collection of documents in Brussels called the Mundaneum (Rayward, 1999, 2003, 2008; Wright, 2008). The collection was organized according to a unique scheme called the Universal Decimal Classification (UDC), which became the basis of classification systems that are still in use today. Although projects like the Mundaneum did not endure for long after World War II, the philosophy behind it and Wells's "World Brain" helped inspire the establishment of non-governmental forums for international deliberation and mediation, such as the League of Nations and later the United Nations (Rayward, 1999, 2003, 2008).

Crucially, this twentieth-century incarnation of the Alexandrian ideal was later reinvented by Vannevar Bush, an engineer and administrator at the Massachusetts Institute of Technology who became the Director of the U.S. Office of Scientific Research and Development (OSRD) during World War II. His experiences convinced him that scientific and social progress was being held back by poor access to recorded knowledge and pressures toward increasing specialization that prevented collaboration across disciplines.

> There is a growing mountain of research. But there is increased evidence that we are being bogged down today as specialization extends. The investigator is staggered by the findings and conclusions of thousands of other workers – conclusions which he cannot find time to grasp, much less to remember, as they appear. Yet specialization becomes increasingly necessary for progress, and the effort to bridge between disciplines is correspondingly superficial. . . . The summation of human experience is being expanded at a prodigious rate, and the means we use for threading through the consequent maze to the momentarily important item is the same as was used in the days of square-rigged ships . . . . (Bush, 1945, pp. 101–2)

In his seminal essay in *The Atlantic* in 1945, entitled "As We May Think," Bush outlined his proposal for a device called memex. Based on computing, photocell, microfilm, and telephone technologies, memex would allow users to search for, retrieve, view, and annotate any document from vast networked collections on a screen mounted into an ordinary desktop. Today, the ideas that Bush proposed in his essay are often credited as the prototypes of hypertext, search engines, even the World Wide Web itself. But for the present discussion, the key point is that Bush, like Wells, Otlet, and others before him, recognized the potential power of linking diverse collections of information into extensive, comprehensive networks. His vision was a direct influence on generations of librarians and information scientists who sought to make collections of information more complete, more relevant, and more accessible for anyone, anywhere, at any time, using ICTs.

It is no surprise, then, that the Alexandrian ideal has carried over into the online context, as libraries have made not only their catalogs but also whole collections available via the internet. *Digital library* projects have been underway since the earliest days of networked computing, but they have proliferated since the introduction of browsers and the Web in the early 1990s (Borgman, 2007). Indeed, a major digital library hosted at the University of California, Santa Barbara, which provides scientific and teaching materials for the study of geography, is called the Alexandria Digital Library (Goodchild, 2004; see also http://alexandria.ucsb.edu), and a new, digital Bibliotheca Alexandrina has been established in Egypt, as noted above. In their popular book *Wikinomics*, Don Tapscott and Anthony Williams (2008) argue that digital librarians, the institutions collaborating in the Google Books project, and other "new Alexandrians" (p. 151) are at the forefront of moves toward a new era of collaborative science and scholarship.

Although the Alexandrian idea of comprehensiveness and quality originated with "bricks and mortar" libraries, it has developed in some different directions online.[5] Where physical, institutional libraries must establish formal resource-sharing agreements with other institutions (typically in the form of union lists, such as today's WorldCat, or interlibrary loan relationships), and then physically retrieve and ship materials from one location to another, much the same service can be accomplished online through a system of hyperlinks and downloads. As a result, from the user's point of view, access to particular works seems less and less tied to particular institutions or locations.

The Web also encourages a sense that the total capture and collection of all information and cultural materials online is both possible and desirable – in some ways it has helped make the Alexandrian ideal part of popular culture. This idea is certainly implicit in many of the most ambitious digital library projects online, including the Internet Archive (http://www.archive.org), Google Books and Google Scholar, and of course commons knowledge projects like Wikipedia. The idea is somewhat naïve – as noted previously, only a fraction of all the world's information is already or likely ever to be posted online. However, in comparison with printed publications and other physical materials, the relative ease of locating and retrieving documents online encourages information seekers to narrow their searches to whatever is available via the Web, to forget or neglect other sources, and ultimately to assume that if something is not available online, it must not exist.

Thus, the Alexandrian ideal has its critics. Jean-Noël Jeanneney (2007) points out that the lopsided dominance of English over other languages in publishing is becoming more, not less, pronounced online, and such cultural inequities are being exacerbated and reinforced by projects like Google Books. In fact, Google Books has become the prime target for growing ranks of critics, despite its claims that the project will provide access to vast collections of out-of-print and scarce materials that publishers no longer distribute. Librarians, for example, worry that although the intent behind the project may be benign and egalitarian, ultimately Google or any other single entity with the power to collect and monopolize the bulk of the world's recorded knowledge also has the power to choose who has access and to charge exorbitant rates for the privilege (Darnton, 2009; Pasquale, 2007). Many publishers and booksellers (including major rivals and incumbents like Amazon.com) are wary of Google's enormous reach and Google Books's potential to erode their markets (Helft, 2010).

Folksonomic organization of information
In his classic book *The Order of Things*, Michel Foucault recounts a fable in a story by the writer Jorge Luis Borges:

> Borges . . . quotes "a certain Chinese encyclopedia" in which it is written that "animals are divided into: (a) belonging to the Emperor, (b) embalmed, (c) tame, (d) sucking pigs, (e) sirens, (f) fabulous, (g) stray dogs, (h) included in the present classification, (i) frenzied, (j) innumerable, (k) drawn with a very fine camelhair brush, (l) et cetera, (m) having just broken the water pitcher, (n) that from a long way off look like flies." (Foucault, 2002 [1966], p. xvi)

To some observers, the second distinctive aspect of commons knowledge may seem to have more in common with Borges's Chinese encyclopedia than with more familiar and authoritative systems of organizing information. Social media and commons knowledge sites often use "folksonomies" to order, sort, and organize information, and to establish relationships among information resources (Marlow et al., 2006). The word is a play on "taxonomy," a formal classification system that fits objects into specific categories or *taxa*. The categories are designed to be accurate and standardized representations of reality, and category labels are established by experts using specialized terminology ("controlled vocabularies") and thesauri of descriptive keywords. The classifier's job is to assign items to these expert-defined categories using the proper descriptors – a system called *metadata*. Common examples of traditional classification systems using standardized vocabularies and metadata include the Dewey Decimal Classification and the Library of Congress Subject Headings, which are used to organize the collections of most public and academic libraries in the U.S. (see Figures 7.1 and 7.2).

Folksonomies, on the other hand, are more local, informal, practical, and even playful "open organization" systems of classification, created by ordinary users of information (Hammond et al., 2005; Shirky, 2005). Instead of authoritative, stable categories and terminology, the user of a document or other piece of information creates a link to the resource (a "bookmark") and then assigns his or her own categories, labels, or terminology (called "tags") to indicate to others what the linked resource is, or is about: tags are essentially shorthand signifiers that recommend and point others to the resource. The tagger can revise or delete tags as needed, and can link the item to others that seem most relevant to him or her – which also helps tell others what the tagged material is about. Although people certainly use bookmarks and tags to organize resources for their own use, tags are also intended to communicate the user's understanding of the materials to others – thus making tags fundamentally communicative and social, and a distinguishing feature of Web 2.0.

When these informal tags and links are aggregated on an internet-wide scale (as in del.icio.us or Digg.com, for example),

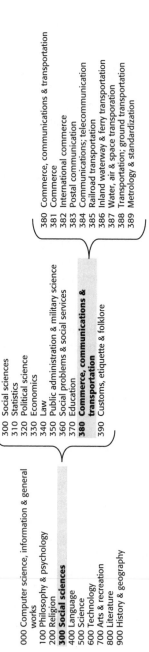

000 Computer science, information & general works
100 Philosophy & psychology
200 Religion
300 Social sciences
400 Language
500 Science
600 Technology
700 Arts & recreation
800 Literature
900 History & geography

300 Social sciences
310 Statistics
320 Political science
330 Economics
340 Law
350 Public administration & military science
360 Social problems & social services
370 Education
380 Commerce, communications & transportation
390 Customs, etiquette & folklore

380 Commerce, communications & transportation
381 Commerce
382 International commerce
383 Postal communication
384 Communications; telecommunication
385 Railroad transportation
386 Inland waterway & ferry transportation
387 Water, air & space transportation
388 Transportation; ground transportation
389 Metrology & standardization

Source: Copyright 2020 OCLC Computer Library Center, Inc., 6565 Kilgour Place, Dublin, Ohio 43017-3395, USA.

Figure 7.1. Selected classifications from the Dewey Decimal Classification, Edition 22 (2003)

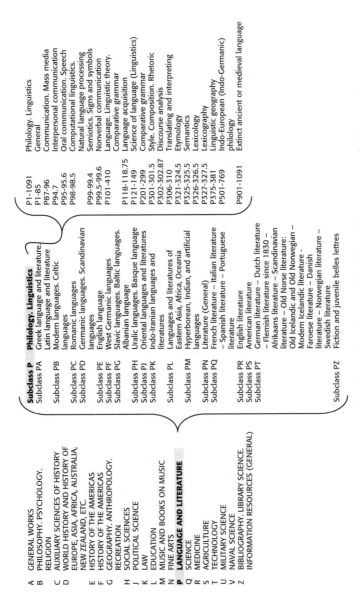

Figure 7.2. Library of Congress Subject Headings classification for Class P (Language and Literature)

A	GENERAL WORKS
B	PHILOSOPHY. PSYCHOLOGY. RELIGION
C	AUXILIARY SCIENCES OF HISTORY
D	WORLD HISTORY AND HISTORY OF EUROPE, ASIA, AFRICA, AUSTRALIA, NEW ZEALAND, ETC.
E	HISTORY OF THE AMERICAS
F	HISTORY OF THE AMERICAS
G	GEOGRAPHY. ANTHROPOLOGY. RECREATION
H	SOCIAL SCIENCES
J	POLITICAL SCIENCE
K	LAW
L	EDUCATION
M	MUSIC AND BOOKS ON MUSIC
N	FINE ARTS
P	**LANGUAGE AND LITERATURE**
Q	SCIENCE
R	MEDICINE
S	AGRICULTURE
T	TECHNOLOGY
U	MILITARY SCIENCE
V	NAVAL SCIENCE
Z	BIBLIOGRAPHY. LIBRARY SCIENCE. INFORMATION RESOURCES (GENERAL)

Subclass P

Subclass PA	Greek language and literature. Latin language and literature
Subclass PB	Modern languages. Celtic languages
Subclass PC	Romanic languages
Subclass PD	Germanic languages. Scandinavian languages
Subclass PE	English language
Subclass PF	West Germanic languages
Subclass PG	Slavic languages. Baltic languages. Albanian language
Subclass PH	Uralic languages. Basque language
Subclass PJ	Oriental languages and literatures
Subclass PK	Indo-Iranian languages and literatures
Subclass PL	Languages and literatures of Eastern Asia, Africa, Oceania
Subclass PM	Hyperborean, Indian, and artificial languages
Subclass PN	Literature (General)
Subclass PQ	French literature – Italian literature – Spanish literature – Portuguese literature
Subclass PR	English literature
Subclass PS	American literature
Subclass PT	German literature – Dutch literature – Flemish literature since 1830 – Afrikaans literature – Scandinavian literature – Old Norse literature: Old Icelandic and Old Norwegian – Modern Icelandic literature - Faroese literature – Danish literature – Norwegian literature – Swedish literature
Subclass PZ	Fiction and juvenile belles lettres

Philology. Linguistics

P1-1091	Philology. Linguistics
P1-85	General
P87-96	Communication. Mass media
P94.7	Interpersonal communication
P95-95.6	Oral communication. Speech
P98-98.5	Computational linguistics.
P99-99.4	Natural language processing
P99.5-99.6	Semiotics. Signs and symbols
P101-410	Nonverbal communication Language. Linguistic theory. Comparative grammar
P118-118.75	Language acquisition
P121-149	Science of language (Linguistics)
P201-299	Comparative grammar
P301-301.5	Style. Composition. Rhetoric
P302-302.87	Discourse analysis
P306-310	Translating and interpreting
P321-324.5	Etymology
P325-325.5	Semantics
P326-326.5	Lexicology
P327-327.5	Lexicography
P375-381	Linguistic geography
P501-769	Indo-European (Indo-Germanic) philology
P901-1091	Extinct ancient or medieval language

they form broader folksonomies, generated bottom-up by creators and users, which can have very different categories and terminology than top-down, standardized classification systems. Where traditional classification systems tend to be organized into hierarchical, nested lists of institutionally approved terms, folksonomic and tagging systems are better represented by the "tag clouds" that have become a familiar feature of social networks and other social media websites (see Figure 7.3). Indeed, the emergence of major folksonomic systems has only been possible in the context of the massive, global-scale generation and circulation of information and documents made possible by the World Wide Web.

The introduction of user tagging is often traced to early browsers like Mosaic, which allowed users to record and share bookmarks (Hammond et al., 2005). The bookmarking website del.icio.us, launched in 2003, was the first large-scale forum for sharing bookmarks and tags. Since then, similar systems that allow users to point to or annotate content for other users have become routine parts of many Web 2.0 sites, including Flickr, Facebook, YouTube, Technorati, Twitter, and so on. On sites like Wikipedia, interlinking and tagging essentially serve the same purpose as an index in a traditional print encyclopedia. A survey conducted in late 2006 by the Pew Internet and American Life Project found that nearly a third of all American internet users had already used tagging and bookmarking online (Rainie, 2007).

Tagging and folksonomies have provoked a lively debate among information scientists and librarians, who see the trade-offs between the personalization, adaptability, and creativity of folksonomic classification and the powerful search and retrieval capabilities of systems based on controlled vocabularies and systematic thesauri (Taylor & Joudrey, 2008). Google, for example, has been held up as the prime example of a "natural language" search tool (that is, it allows users to search using whatever terms seem most appropriate or meaningful to them). It nonetheless has enormous power to retrieve highly relevant links as

Figure 7.3: Tag cloud visualization of word frequency in a single document.

Source: Many Eyes visualization project, *Tag Cloud Guide*, IBM Almaden Labs. http://manyeyes.alphaworks.ibm.com/manyeyes/page/Tag_Cloud.html.

a result of its proprietary Page Rank algorithm, which accumulates and analyzes the results of millions of searches over time to refine the results returned in subsequent searches. However, a natural-language search engine like Google is considered an unsuitable tool for highly technical, targeted, or specialized types of searches, where better results can be achieved by using search terms that are specific to the discipline or field in question. In these cases folksonomic tagging can be idiosyncratic, unreliable, and ultimately too dependent on the variable perceptions of individual users to generate dependable and consistent search results over the long term and across social and cultural contexts.

On the other hand, a strength of folksonomies and natural-language search systems is that they allow users to frame questions and seek information on their own terms, in ways that are most meaningful and useful to them individually, and that may be more faithful to knowledge "in the world" than to elite or culturally biased classification systems (Olson, 2002; Shirky, 2005). As the Google experience shows, the accumulation of natural-language searches can provide a powerful representation of how information is understood and used collectively in society, and a representation that is dynamic and changes as social and cultural perceptions change. Few people are likely to be willing or able to consult complex technical thesauri of terms for every casual Web browsing session, especially as information becomes more idiosyncratic and diverse. Furthermore, bottom-up tagging schemes can have the serendipitous consequence of revealing unanticipated and fruitful connections among ideas and resources that might otherwise be obscured by authoritative, hierarchical systems (Weinberger, 2008).

Folksonomic classification may seem ironic or counterintuitive in one respect: although tagging, linking, bookmarking, and so on, have been practical only in the comprehensive, "Alexandrian" context of the browser-driven World Wide Web, to date no overarching, single, authoritative system has emerged for classifying and organizing the vast range of information resources and materials available online. There is no ultimate, privileged, or stable viewpoint from which the order of all available information might be determined or imposed – a situation that contrasts dramatically with the visions of information organization pioneers like Otlet, Wells, and Bush, and even of the original Alexandrians themselves. Hope Olson, a historian and philosopher of information classification, has observed that traditional classificationists, such as Melvil Dewey and Charles Cutter, saw strict hierarchy as a way of "organizing the mob of information into an orderly army using the tool of logic" (Olson, 2004, p. 604). Online, however, the organization of information is always radically incomplete, fragmented, and in flux. From the perspective of established disciplines, expert knowledge, and the cultural institutions that support them, this is a crucial weakness of Web-based information. From the perspective of people engaged in their everyday interests and pursuits, however, the ability to rearrange and reassemble the categories of knowledge opens all kinds of possibilities for creativity, cultural openness, and change.

Distrust of knowledge authorities
When the Alexandrian scope and ambitions of commons knowledge projects are combined with the idiosyncratic, folksonomic sensibility that drives the tagging and organization of so much information, one result is the third characteristic of commons knowledge: participants in projects like Wikipedia, Digg.com, open-source software development, and so on, tend to take a broadly anti-authoritarian perspective. To some extent, this anti-authoritarian streak has its origins in the countercultural mistrust of knowledge authorities already seen in hacker culture and alternative computing, where expertise is based on "no other criteria than technical virtuosity and accomplishment (by hacking alone and not 'bogus' criteria such as degrees, age, race, or position)" (Nissenbaum, 2004, p. 197).

However, critics of peer production allege that participants in commons knowledge projects are outright dismissive of or openly hostile to academic, scientific, or other institutionally or professionally sanctioned claims of knowledge authority.

> It has been suggested that Wikipedia exhibits *anti-intellectualism* and actively deters people with expertise from contributing. . . . experts rarely receive any deference from other contributors . . . [and] have to fight it out just like anyone else to get their views to stick in the encyclopedia. [Thus they are] unwilling to put in the effort to create content that might simply be removed by an unqualified individual with an axe to grind. (Fallis, 2008, p. 1665, emphasis in the original)

Some argue that the anti-authoritarian attitude is a serious shortcoming of commons knowledge projects: ". . . Wikipedia's inclination toward ordinary users may keep experts at bay, though these are the exact individuals they need" (Duguid, 2006). In a recent article published in an academic philosophy journal, Wikipedia founder Larry Sanger acknowledges that "Wikipedia has challenged traditional notions about the roles of experts in the Internet Age" and that "egalitarian online communities might challenge the occupational roles or the epistemic leadership roles of experts."[6] Nonetheless, he concludes that "There is little support for the notion that the distinctive occupations that require expertise are being undermined. It is also implausible that Wikipedia and its like might take over the epistemic leadership roles of experts." Wikipedia articles, Sanger says, "are edited by knowledgeable people to whom deference is paid, although voluntarily" (Sanger, 2009, p. 52).

In a discussion of how peer production works, and echoing themes from analyses of hacker culture, Tapscott and Williams (2008) focus on the self-selection and volunteerism of participants, contending that what participants oppose is not expertise *per se* but claims of privilege or priority based solely on professional qualifications or institutional affiliation: "Expertise is by no means shunned on Wikipedia, but 'credentialism' is clearly discouraged. A Ph.D. in astrophysics may just as well find him- or herself arguing over the nature of the universe with an eager high school student (or worse, an astrologer) as with a peer with equivalent training" (Tapscott & Williams, 2008, p. 74). As the philosopher and information scientist Don Fallis points out, amateurism is not equivalent to lack of knowledge: ". . . people who voluntarily choose to write on a particular topic are likely to have at least some degree of reliability on that topic. Indeed, there are many amateur ornithologists, amateur astronomers, and so on who do not have academic credentials but who have quite a bit of expertise" (Fallis, 2008, p. 1670).

Clay Shirky, a technology pundit and Associate Teacher in the Interactive Telecommunications program at New York University, argues that the unprecedented availability of new online tools for expression and group action has generated a new era of what he calls "mass amateurism" with important consequences for professional privilege and knowledge gatekeeping. He recounts his own early experience in a small, start-up web design firm when AT&T became one of their first clients. Shirky and his colleagues used a programming language called Perl, one of whose main strengths was almost immediate, informal, volunteer technical support from the community of other Perl users. The engineers from AT&T, on the other hand, insisted that the project use an "industrial-strength," proprietary programming language developed by AT&T, C++.

> We explained that there was a discussion group for Perl programmers, called comp.lang.perl.misc, where the Perl community hung out, asking and answering questions. Commercial support was often slow, we pointed out, while there were people on the Perl discussion group all day and night answering questions. We explained that when newcomers had been around long enough to know what they were doing, they in turn started to answer questions, so although the system wasn't commercial, it was self-sustaining. The AT&T guys didn't believe us. We even showed them how it worked; we thought up a reasonably hard question and posted it. . . . Someone answered it before the meeting with AT&T was over. But not even that could convince them. They didn't care if it worked in fact, because they were already sure it wouldn't work in theory. (Shirky, 2008, pp. 256–7)

Mass amateurism, Shirky believes, has helped reverse the traditional relationship between "filtering" (editing and agenda-setting) and publishing. When anyone can be a publisher, publishing comes first, with review and revision later. Mass amateurism has made the roles of participants in commons knowledge projects more flexible and elided clear distinctions between readers, writers, and editors, and between experts and amateurs. As we saw in the earlier chapter on the changing nature of journalism and the role of journalists, the emerging role of amateurs also poses a fundamental threat to the worldview and prerogatives of some media professions, which continue to see their practices as indispensable even as the conditions that created them change: "In any profession, particularly one that has existed long enough that no one can remember a time when it didn't exist, members have a tendency to equate provisional solutions to particular problems with deep truths about the world" (Shirky, 2008, p. 59).

The distrust of authority in commons knowledge projects extends beyond credentialed experts to other forms of knowledge authority and gatekeeping, such as organizational owners and managers. Wikipedians' objections to founder Larry Sanger's early insistence on reserving the right to delete anything in Wikipedia became a factor in his resignation from the project (Shirky, 2008). In 2007 users of the social networking site Digg. com staged a massive protest against the site's suppression of postings by participants that included the decryption key for copying HD-DVDs.[7] Digg's management had removed all materials referring to the code in response to legal threats from an HD-DVD industry group and its own lawyers' advice. However, the storm of criticism from Digg's core users, alleging that Digg had betrayed its own community-driven values, created such negative publicity that Digg founder Kevin Rose publicly acceded to the community's demands. He acknowledged that "after seeing hundreds of stories and reading thousands of comments, you've made it clear. You'd rather see Digg go down fighting than bow down to a bigger company. We hear you, and effective immediately we won't delete stories or comments containing the code and will deal with whatever the consequences might be" (http://en.wikipedia.org/wiki/Digg).

Wikipedia as commons knowledge

As noted at the start of this chapter, perhaps no commons knowledge project has provoked as much interest, participation, or sharp debate as Wikipedia. Since its launch in early 2001, numerous profiles and histories of Wikipedia have been published in both the academic and popular press, and scores of scientific studies have examined its growth, dynamics, and usage. Broadly speaking, the most intensive scrutiny has centered on two main issues: Wikipedia's breathtaking growth and popularity as a basic reference for a remarkably wide sweep of topics in numerous languages; and persistent worries about its quality – its credibility, accuracy, validity, and even (among philosophers) its epistemic value.

Both concerns grow out of what one of its founders, Larry Sanger, calls Wikipedia's intrinsic "paradox" (Sanger, 2009, p. 52): that a reasonably reliable, comprehensive information resource can be created and sustained through a collaborative process among thousands of amateur enthusiasts and contributors, with relatively little reliance on (or deference paid to) professional subject-matter experts. The questions of what constitutes legitimate knowledge, and who decides, lie at the heart of continuing debates about Wikipedia. Ultimately the challenge to expert-driven, institutionally sanctioned, centralized knowledge production represented by Wikipedia may make it and other commons knowledge projects some of the most potentially revolutionary or disruptive expressions of alternative/activist new media.

Indeed, many analyses of Wikipedia's operations, policies, and methods begin with some variation on a theme of incredulity that such a project can even exist, never mind flourish, in the first place. "Paradoxically, this seemingly chaotic process has created a highly regarded reference on the Internet" (Lih, 2004, p. 1). "I'm sure I wasn't the only person who decided, on first hearing how it worked, that it would never be worth much. I was wrong" (Dalby, 2007, p. 3). "[Wikipedia is] a source of wonder: its essential idea – that a useful encyclopedia can be created by allowing *anyone* to create and edit articles – seems absurd" (Priedhorsky et al., 2007, p. 259, emphasis in the original). "To many, [Wikipedia's] approach – so vulnerable to mistakes, ignorance and malice – seems a flatly ridiculous way of producing a serious reference tool. The mystery of Wikipedia is that despite the obvious potential drawbacks of its openness, it has enjoyed significant success" (Viégas, Wattenberg & Dave, 2004, p. 575).

The story of Wikipedia's evolution has been retold many times (e.g., Rosenzweig, 2006; Schiff, 2006), not least on Wikipedia itself (http://en.wikipedia.org/wiki/History_of_Wikipedia). However, a few main historical points help to illustrate how its seemingly counterintuitive, collaborative model of knowledge production reflects the three characteristics of commons knowledge – the Alexandrian ideal, folksonomic knowledge generation and organization, and a tendency toward a distrust of knowledge authorities, or at least their presumed privileges.

Wikipedia's Alexandrian ambitions

Wikipedia went "live" in early 2001 as a strategy to increase the volume of contributions to an expert-driven, strictly peer-reviewed project, Nupedia, which had encountered difficulty recruiting contributors and generating a critical mass of content. Jimmy Wales, whose company Bomis originated the Nupedia project, hired a doctoral candidate in philosophy, Larry Sanger, to manage and oversee Nupedia. According to Wikipedia's history page, Sanger came up with the idea of using a wiki-based system to boost Nupedia's growth in a dinner conversation with wiki developer Ben Kovitz. Some of Nupedia's editors were skeptical, but Wales embraced the idea and set up the initial wiki in January 2001. Today both Sanger and Wales are acknowledged as originating the wiki-based encyclopedia idea and credited as co-founders of Wikipedia.

Volunteer contributions to Wikipedia began to accumulate almost immediately, particularly after approving notices in Slashdot, Kuro5hin, and mainstream media like *The New York Times* appeared in its first year. In the early stages, articles were often assembled from original contributor text and passages from older, authoritative sources in the public domain, such as the 1911 edition of the *Encyclopedia Britannica*, among other classic reference works. Today, Wikipedia articles are written and edited entirely by contributors, but "The fragments from original [reference] sources persist like those stony bits of classical buildings incorporated in a medieval wall" (Baker, 2008, p. 8).

The accumulation of articles in the English-language Wikipedia accelerated dramatically from the start; as one writer observed, "Very swiftly, Wikipedia became the tail that swallowed the dog (Nupedia)" (Rosenzweig, 2006, p. 121). It took one month for English Wikipedia to compile its first 1,000 articles, and five years to accumulate 1 million articles (in comparison, Nupedia generated only twelve articles in its first, pre-Wikipedia year). Between the beginning of 2006 and the end of 2009 that number more than tripled. As of this writing (mid-2010) the number of articles stands at over 3,200,000, which constitutes only about 20 percent of the total of over 15 million Wikipedia articles in over 270 languages (daily updates are available at http://en.wikipedia.org/wiki/Wikipedia:About).[8]

Anyone may contribute to Wikipedia; indeed its huge contributor base has been one of its most powerful features. Currently, Wikipedia has approximately 12.4 million registered contributors, although an unknown number of contributors are not formally registered. However, some Wikipedians are far more active participants than others. Soon after the project began, a relatively small core of very active contributor-editors took the lead in creating and refining Wikipedia content, and this pattern of participation (an example of a highly skewed, "long tail" distribution common across many types of social activities, whether on- or offline) has persisted over time. Of the 12.4 million contributors currently registered, about 300,000 contribute or edit once a month, and roughly 50,000 make five or more edits per month. Just 5,000 contributors, or about four-tenths of one percent of all registered Wikipedians, make 100 or more edits per month (see http://en.wikipedia.org/wiki/Wikipedia:Editor_statistics#Demographics). Nonetheless, the total population of contributors has risen as steeply as the number of articles over time. If a relative handful of Wikipedians are responsible for most editorial traffic on the site, it is also true that an ever wider and more diverse variety of people have joined the effort and have vastly enlarged the scope and range of topics and interests included in the project.

As these figures suggest, from its inception Wikipedia's ambitions have been unabashedly Alexandrian. Some scholars (and Wikipedia's own history page) have situated the project within the larger chronicle of attempts to collect, classify, and make accessible all of the world's knowledge, and cite the library of Alexandria, Otlet's Mundaneum, Wells's World Brain, and Bush's memex, among other influences (e.g., Rosenzweig, 2006). Stacy Schiff (2006) argues that Wikipedia can be seen as the latest manifestation of an "encyclopedist impulse" that dates at least to the eighteenth century. The Wikimedia Foundation's global-scale vision is also evident in its support for developing and supporting versions in any language with an interested community of contributors to support it, and Wikipedia's increasing internationalization over time. Jimmy Wales has said that his goal is to "distribute a free encyclopedia to every single person on the planet in their own language" (quoted in Schiff, 2006, p. 38).

Folksonomy and Wikipedia
Despite Wikipedia's rapid success, differences between the two founders quickly emerged about the best ways to generate not just *more* content, but *better* content, and how to discourage malicious, incorrect, frivolous, or self-serving contributions and editorial changes. Wales favored a hands-off, folksonomic

approach, leaving the community as free as possible to self-regulate, to contribute, edit, and create links among whatever material they chose, and to identify and amend errors through a consensus process with a minimum of top-down policy decrees and intervention. Sanger – the former doctoral student in philosophy – was more concerned about accuracy and the potential for spreading mis- or disinformation. He advocated "gentle" but decisive gatekeeping with more editorial authority for the most active Wikipedians and clear policy guidelines. Sanger himself introduced the first guideline in 2001, which (perhaps ironically in retrospect) was "ignore all rules"; it was quickly followed by other "non-negotiable" core principles that still shape Wikipedia contributions today, including the Neutral Point of View (NPOV) principle and the expectation that content should be verifiable and derived from reliable sources. Over time the major elements of Wikipedia editorial policy and philosophy have been codified into "Five Pillars" (see http://en.wikipedia.org/wiki/Wikipedia:Five_pillars).

When Bomis's revenues declined with the dot.com bust in 2002, Sanger left the organization and Wikipedia. After his departure he founded Citizendium, a new effort to build an authoritative, peer-reviewed, wiki-based encyclopedia. He has also become an increasingly vocal critic of Wikipedia's knowledge-production model and the value of the content itself (Sanger, 2009; Schiff, 2006).

But even after Sanger's departure, the folksonomic versus authority-control positions hardened into a heated rivalry between two camps of Wikipedians. One group, calling themselves *inclusionists*, adopted a liberally hands-off line. Editorial policy, they said, should restrict content as little as possible, uphold community values of openness and participation, and include whatever contributors wished to add, no matter how minor or eclectic the topic. Their opposition, the *deletionists*, held that vigilant editorial intervention by the most knowledgeable or experienced Wikipedians was necessary to prune unserious, unimportant, false, fraudulent, or "nonnotable" contributions, reduce vandalism, and improve and maintain the quality of content overall. By 2007 their differences had flared into waves of argument and content purges, prompting author and inclusionist Wikipedian Nicholson Baker to complain that "a lot of good work – verifiable, informative, brain-leapingly strange – is being cast out of this paperless, infinitely expandable accordion folder by people who have a narrow, almost grade-schoolish notion of what sort of curiosity an on-line encyclopedia will be able to satisfy in the years to come" (Baker, 2008, p. 10). Despite his support for editorial gatekeeping, Larry Sanger (2009) continues to insist that he is a solid inclusionist. Despite his faith in the self-correcting power of open participation, Jimmy Wales eventually endorsed the creation of authoritative editorial committees and administrators, and has personally taken on new oversight powers as a sort of "editor of last resort" for particularly controversial or difficult cases (Cohen, 2009).

As Wikipedia has become an ever more important first-line resource, its overseers have tried to walk a narrow path between the sometimes shambolic energy, creativity, and participatory mission of the original project and the adoption of formal policies and rule structures that enhance its authoritativeness and trustworthiness, but move Wikipedia away from its original vision. Inclusionist Wikipedians insist that the community's values, intensely participatory culture, and consensus-based shared governance processes take care of most content quality problems. Yet a variety of more formal safeguards have been instituted over time, including automated content-checking programs, prohibitions against editing one's own biographical page, increased review steps for all biographies of living persons, limits on page creation and deletion privileges, and other formal editorial guidelines and rules (Cohen, 2009). The rules have often been instituted in response to episodes of abuse involving vandalism, libelous material, alleged copyright infringement, or contributors misrepresenting their credentials or expertise. Nonetheless, Nicholson Baker laments the recent proliferation of "rules and policy banners at every turn – there are strongly urged warnings and required tasks and normal procedures and notability guidelines and complex criteria for various decisions – a symptom of something called *instruction creep*: defined in Wikipedia as something that happens 'when instructions increase in number and size over time until they are unmanageable'" (Baker, 2008, p. 10, emphasis in the original).

Wikipedia and knowledge authorities

At the same time, Wikipedia's reputation for providing generally reliable (if rudimentary, incomplete, or under-digested) information has grown, even among dubious university instructors, legal authorities, and mainstream media and news organizations. A key turning point for Wikipedia's reputation came in 2005, when the journal *Nature* asked expert reviewers to compare pairs of science articles on the same topics from Wikipedia and the *Encyclopaedia Britannica*, without revealing which article in the pair came from which source. Fifty article pairs were originally selected for the study, of which forty-two usable evaluations were returned. The reviewers reported more minor errors of fact, omissions, or misleading statements in Wikipedia than *Britannica* (162 versus 123, respectively, or an average of about 3.9 errors per article in Wikipedia versus 2.9 errors in *Britannica* articles). They also found that Wikipedia articles were often not as well written or organized as their *Britannica* counterparts. However, both sources had an equally low number of "serious errors" across all articles reviewed – just four each for Wikipedia and *Britannica* (Giles, 2005). Critics cited problems with the research design, and *Britannica*'s representatives rejected outright any suggestion that the two sources were in any way comparable as reference tools. But proponents argued that Wikipedia's potential for quick amendment and correction would eventually bring it up to *Britannica* standards.

Wikipedians' preoccupation with minutiae and statistics, and with providing exhaustive, up-to-the-minute records of Wikipedia editing histories for analysis by anyone who downloads the data, has sparked something of a gold rush of Wikipedia research, with investigators bent on solving the mystery of how trustworthy information can be generated by legions of mostly anonymous, non-expert amateurs. Empirical studies have shown, for example, that Wikipedia articles are perceived as more credible by reviewers who are expert in those topics than by non-expert reviewers (Chesney, 2006). Some have found that articles that persist the longest tend to be written by a small fraction of very active Wikipedia contributors, and that the domination of this fraction is increasing (Priedhorsky et al., 2007). Others argue that although historically, a minority of "elite" Wikipedians have generated most of its content, the workload has shifted recently to include many more average participants (Almeida, Mozafari & Cho, 2007; Kittur et al., 2007). Correlations have been established between the average article's quality and the number of edits it undergoes (Wilkinson & Huberman, 2008). Other researchers caution that adding editors to an article only increases article quality if the editors coordinate their work in appropriate ways, and that inappropriate types of coordination can harm article quality (Kittur & Kraut, 2008).

With respect to vandalism, several studies have demonstrated that erroneous information deliberately inserted into Wikipedia articles is rapidly repaired. In 2004 a team of researchers from IBM and the MIT Media Lab developed a graphic tool for visualizing "revert wars" (intensive series of content additions and removals by partisan editors). Their data showed that half of "mass deletes" of Wikipedia pages (malicious deletion of 90 percent or more of a page's content) were repaired in under three minutes, and half of malicious edits involving the insertion of obscenities were repaired in less than two minutes (Viégas, Wattenberg & Dave, 2004). A 2007 study at the University of Minnesota found that the probability of a typical article being damaged, though increasing, is small. The authors also found that 42 percent of damage incidents across all Wikipedia page views were "repaired essentially immediately" (Priedhorsky et al., 2007, p. 265). In another, more anecdotal case, 36 percent of false statements inserted into biographical articles about philosophers were corrected within forty-eight hours (Magnus, 2009). The relative immediacy of repairs in Wikipedia contrasts dramatically with the glacial pace of similar corrections in traditional academic peer review and publishing.

On the whole, and with some important exceptions, this literature suggests that Wikipedia's success is due largely to its sheer size and what might be called (*pace* Paul Duguid's [2006] critique of the implicit Darwinism espoused by open-source proponents) the diverse and intensely competitive "speciation" within its knowledge "ecology," in contrast to the reliance on centralized disciplinary authority and elite expertise that define traditional scholarship and knowledge institutions. "[T]here is much theoretical and empirical evidence that large collaborative projects, such as *Wikipedia*, can actually be fairly reliable. . . . When groups are sufficiently large and diverse, they can often come up with better information than experts on a topic" (Fallis, 2009, p. 2). Wikipedia is expansive and unfinished by design, and makes no pretense of being a fixed, definitive, or universal catalog of all knowledge (Mattus, 2009). As such it is used differently than conventional encyclopedias (Magnus, 2009). For better or worse, the knowledge of Wikipedia is the knowledge of amateurs, "lovers" of a topic in the etymological sense, of passionate hobbyists and fan culture, of dedicated volunteers and people with a lot of time on their hands (Baker, 2008).

Summary: commons knowledge as a genre

As with the other genres presented thus far, we close this chapter with a brief review of the genre characteristics that distinguish commons knowledge. Regarding their scope, commons knowledge projects are clearly collaborative – indeed, on a scale that dwarfs the levels of participation seen in other types of alternative and activist new media discussed in previous chapters. In this respect commons knowledge differs from quintessentially small-scale genres like culture jamming and alternative computing. Examples such as Wikipedia, and to a lesser extent tagging sites like Digg.com, may even be classic examples of systems with network effects or network externalities, where the resource becomes vastly more valuable to users the larger and more comprehensive it becomes. In commons knowledge projects the effect works on two levels: the number of participants involved and the size of the resource produced. The two are co-determining, because the quality of the resource and its capacity for correction and self-repair becomes greater as the number of participants grows, and more participants are drawn to use, and especially to contribute to, the resource as it becomes more comprehensive and diversified. Of course, the "downside" of network effects is the risk of lock-in, where systems can become so large and entrenched that the economic and social costs of building or switching to an alternative become prohibitive and thus discourage innovation. There are already signs that Wikipedia's sheer mass and reach are both accelerating its adoption among new users, and discouraging potential rivals.

The position or stance of commons knowledge projects relative to mainstream society and institutions seems to be in transition. Wikipedia, for example, began life with a distinctly subcultural sensibility. It attracted a dedicated corps of adept insiders who took a skeptical view of authority and professional expertise. They created a heterotopic community of Wikipedians that defied the conventions of authoritative scholarship, with a staunchly communitarian ethos, a predilection for wide-open debates over the smallest points of fact or interpretation, and an adherence to consensus-driven editorial decision-making. Although Wikipedia articles themselves are written and delivered in an almost comically deadpan prose style (perhaps a consequence of the increasing reliance on style and content rules), the "backstage" interactions among page editors – which anyone can view using a page's "talk" option – often take a humorous or ironic view of the content and sources they deal with. A small confraternity of Wikipedians continues to play the central role in guiding the site's activities, mission, and decision-making. However, as the ranks of contributors swell and become more diverse, and as casual contributors devote more time and effort to the project (even if not as much as the handful of top-ranked Wikipedians), we might anticipate corresponding shifts in governance and deliberation processes to reflect a more broad-based community with a wider range of viewpoints and values.

Commons knowledge projects are also notable for their forms of action and agency. Often, projects like Digg.com, del.icio.us and Wikipedia are not expressly interventionist at the outset – certainly not in the same way as most of the other genres. They are not necessarily designed to interfere with or intrude upon other sites and resources; indeed, they often begin as "complementary" to other forms of expression (e.g., bookmarking websites for easy retrieval later; tagging links to web-based content on a personal social network page or blog; see also Hammond et al., 2005). Wikipedia itself was established as a sideline to drive content to another, more conventional reference resource. In these cases commons knowledge projects are set up to act essentially as metadata – that is, to frame, label, recommend, or direct users to other sources of information. Tags, bookmarks, and links (like their library catalog counterparts, subject headings and keywords) are markers of similarity and difference, and thus suggest that the information categorized under certain labels also has a given order or meaning.

However, as in the case of Wikipedia, linking, labeling, and directing often lead to the generation of more elaborate systems of purpose-built material that is organized according to the project's own native classification scheme or ontology, which may bear little resemblance to a hierarchical taxonomy. (One writer has compared the difference between formal taxonomies and folksonomies to the difference between "trees and piles of leaves"; Weinberger, 2006.) In any given Wikipedia article, readers are presented with links to a myriad of other links within Wikipedia, as well as to a wide range of other resources and materials outside Wikipedia. Indeed, views of early versions of Wikipedia articles, available through the Internet Archive's

Wayback Machine, reveal that many early pages relied far more on links to other sites and sources than to original text (see http://www.archive.org). These links not only provide the reader with additional depth and context on the topic, but also help to validate and corroborate the information in the text of the Wikipedia article itself.

Moreover, as pointed out by librarians and information scientists specializing in metadata and classification, metadata schemes and ontologies do not simply mirror some larger, objective reality; in a very material sense, they are cultural statements about the world and what is known (and not known) about it. Ontologies are created by particular people in particular social contexts who make certain assumptions about the nature of the world and society. Metadata systems are thoroughly socialized and constructed, and this is as true for the tag clouds on Facebook as it is for Otlet's Universal Decimal Classification system or the Library of Congress Subject Headings (Andersen & Skouvig, 2006; Olson, 2002; for a general introduction to information organization, see Taylor & Joudrey, 2008, as well as the Wikipedia page on Library Classification, http://en.wikipedia.org/wiki/Library_classification).

The difference between commons knowledge and more formal ontologies and classification tools, however, is its perishability. The technological platforms that make Wikipedia and other collaborative, peer-produced resources possible also make them highly changeable and unstable. In contrast, authority-controlled systems like those used by the Library of Congress, the Computing Classification System of the Association for Computing Machinery, or the National Library of Medicine's Medical Subject Headings (MeSH), for example, are so stable and authoritative that they can be difficult to update, even when new terms or classifications are needed. For the proponents of commons knowledge projects, their fluidity and flexibility are a defining strength. For detractors, they are a serious problem that opens resources to unauthorized interference and thus makes them fundamentally unreliable.

In the final chapter, we summarize the overall framework and types of projects presented so far. But we also move to a more general discussion of the implications of alternative and activist new media for understanding communication and engagement with media. As I hope to show, reception and consumption – the paradigmatic forms of engagement with mass media systems and content – are giving way to more complex repertoires of engagement based on the reconfiguration of media technologies and remediation of content and interpersonal communication. Collective "audiences" still exist, of course, but they are increasingly fragmented and complemented by new practices of individual "users" and small, self-selecting, interpersonal groups. In the next chapter we consider alternative and activist new media as the leading indicator of a shift in perspective in communication study, from mass media to mediation.

CHAPTER 8

New Media, Mediation

Alternative, activist, oppositional, and radical media were once "fringe" by definition. The few activists with access to print shops, broadcast studios, and airwaves, monopolized telecommunications systems, or closely held academic mainframes could hardly pose much of a threat to entrenched media industries and institutions, and their legal and political allies. Certainly, powerful interests still set much of the communications agenda today, and they protect their privileges jealously. But they must do so in a cultural and media environment where anyone with a mobile telephone or tablet computer and an internet connection has the same potential to reach listeners, viewers, and readers as a major television network or political party. Media culture in the digital age has become more personal, skeptical, ironic, perishable, idiosyncratic, collaborative, and almost inconceivably diversified, even as established industries and institutions seek to maintain their grip on stable messages and audiences and to extend their business models online.

In the preceding chapters, a range of alternative and activist new media genres and projects have been presented to illustrate how political and cultural activists, artists, journalists, engineers, librarians and archivists, subcultures and fans, hobbyists – essentially anyone passionate enough to express and organize themselves in ways that challenge, modify, or work around mainstream "ways of doing culture" – have become central players in the contemporary digital culture landscape. By combining an aesthetic sensibility of *dérive*, collage, and disjuncture drawn from Dada and Situationism, the anti-authoritarian and identity-driven values of contemporary social movements, and the hit-and-run tactics of radical and underground media, new media activists have found the open technological platforms of networked computing and telecommunications to be fruitful arenas for action and expression. They have created innovative modes of social and cultural engagement that question, parody, and debate the assumptions and prerogatives of mainstream institutions and power. In the process, they may be redefining what counts as "mainstream" in a post-mass media age.

The principal aim of this book has been to assess the scope and scale of this changing environment by surveying the opportunities for oppositional and alternative viewpoints and agendas afforded by new media and information technologies. Projects have been loosely organized into five main genres, each of which corresponds to a particular aspect of society or cultural practice. *Culture jamming* uses the images, ideas, and discourse of popular culture and commerce to critique and subvert that culture. *Alternative computing* projects design, adapt, hack, and rebuild the material infrastructure of computing, media, and information technology. *Participatory journalism* adopts the values and practices of mainstream news production and public opinion to cover issues, concerns, perspectives, and communities that are ordinarily sidelined by the mainstream press. *Mediated mobilization* merges online and "live" social network relations to organize and represent new social and political movements on a global scale. *Commons knowledge* projects employ folksonomic, bottom-up methods of collaboration and peer production to collect, organize, classify, and evaluate information in systems that challenge or serve as counterpoints to institutionally sanctioned, expert consensus and knowledge.

Genres (and thus projects) vary along three main "dimensions" of characteristics or features. The small-scale, collaborative character of alternative and activist projects indicates their *scope*. The *stance* of different genres relative to mainstream society and culture is indicated by their ironic, subcultural, and heterotopic qualities. A genre's or project's potential for *action* or *agency* is suggested by the degree to which it is interventionist or perishable. Comparing the genres along these axes, some are clearly more persistent or longer-lived than others. Some tend to separate themselves or create more autonomous spaces for action apart from mainstream society, while others seek to integrate themselves into everyday work life, learning, politics, and play. Some encourage direct social/cultural/technological participation or intervention, or constitute such intervention themselves. Some genres and projects are massively collaborative, enlisting thousands or even millions of participants; others may reflect the efforts of small collectives or just a handful of dedicated insiders. Some genres and projects take themselves quite seriously, but many are wickedly funny, using humor and irony to persuade and recruit supporters and participants.

Technology and action: reconfiguration and remediation

In addition to this general framework for characterizing alternative and activist new media projects, I have suggested that projects and genres are the product of an ongoing, complementary, and mutually determining relationship between the *reconfiguration* of communication technologies and the *remediation* of communicative action – expression, interaction, social relations, and meaning.

Reconfiguration is the ongoing process by which people adapt, reinvent, reorganize, or rebuild media technologies as needed to suit their various purposes or interests. As they innovate, users combine new and old techniques, or adapt combinations of familiar technologies in new ways; indeed, this feature distinguishes new media from traditional mass media systems.[1] New media technologies are *recombinant*, the product of the hybridization of existing technologies and innovative techniques, and they are continuously renewed in the process (Lievrouw & Livingstone, 2006). This quality allows us to keep thinking of new media as "new." Nor is reconfiguration inherently teleological. Although their creators may have some immediate purpose or use in mind, reconfigured technologies are often perceived, adopted, and appropriated by others in unanticipated ways – reinvented, sabotaged, adapted, hacked, ignored.

Alternative computing, for example, virtually defines reconfiguration in its interventionist, libertarian stance toward technological systems and its commitment to creating and defending open systems and information resources. Chris Kelty (2008) observes that "geeks" (computing professionals and amateur experts) do not just argue *about* technology, they argue "with and through it," using software and hardware design *as* persuasion and rhetoric – as when a designer builds a prototype system and calls it a "proof of concept," for example. In mediated mobilization and contemporary social movements, communication technologies are not merely the means for representing and conveying a political agenda. They are themselves arenas and spaces of relationships and action, and tools for intervention (e.g., denial-of-service attacks), which are continuously reorganized and reconfigured as movement priorities change. As Manuel Castells puts it, for today's global justice movement the internet and related technologies are "both its organizational form and its mode of action" (Castells, 2009, p. 338).

Remediation is the process by which people construct new meanings and expressions out of existing and novel forms of interaction, social and institutional relationships, and cultural works. Jay Bolter and Richard Grusin's concept of remediation is a point of departure here: taking their cue from Marshall McLuhan's famous axiom about old media becoming the content of the new, they define remediation as "the representation of one medium in another" (Bolter & Grusin, 1999, p. 45). In their scheme, remediation includes straightforward repackaging (e.g., transferring still photographs or sound recordings on audiotape to CD), augmentation or enhancement (e.g., online newspapers or encyclopedias that combine hyperlinked audio and motion images with conventional text), refashioning (e.g., "tiled" windows on a computer desktop or television screen, perceived by the viewer as a composite whole), and absorption (e.g., online games that employ the cinematic character and plot devices of feature films).

Clearly, media technology figures prominently in Bolter and Grusin's theory, although in a somewhat "dematerialized" way. Their main focus is actually the mutability and intertextuality of content; media are framed more as broad cultural formations that generate various types of content than as specific configurations of technological devices, practices, and organizing that exist in particular times and places with certain material affordances and features. As used by Bolter and Grusin, remediation incorporates channel and content together, although the symbolic or representational aspect of remediation takes precedence over its material nature as something that people *do*. Thus I suggest a greater emphasis on remediation as a material practice and form of social and cultural engagement, including individual expression, interaction, and social relations as well as the generation, circulation, and use of content.

The examples in the preceding chapters suggest that remediation extends well beyond the representation of one medium in another to a variety of other forms. For example, commons-based peer production, as in open-source software development and collaborative projects like Wikipedia, is notable for the *mobilization* of collective creativity and knowledge, and the *integration* of "microcontributions" by legions of loosely affiliated collaborators into coherent, emergent bodies of work, governed by public debate among the collaborators themselves. Time can also play a role in remediation. We might recall that a defining strategy of new social movements, which has been particularly effective in the online context, is *prophecy*, in which activists act out the future changes and values they desire in their present lives on- and offline, to convey "the message that the possible is already real" (Melucci, 1994, p. 125).[2] And in the alternative/ activist new media context, perhaps the classic form of remediation is the *hack*, in McKenzie Wark's memorable sense of creating "the possibility of new things entering the world. Not always great things, or even good things, but new things. . . . in any production of knowledge where data can be gathered, where information can be extracted from it, and where in that information new possibilities for the world produced, there are *hackers hacking the new out of the old"* (Wark, 2004, §004, emphasis added).

From repackaging, to prophecy, to the hack, remediation borrows, modifies, samples, and remixes existing content, forms, and expressions to create new works, relationships, interactions, and meanings. It could be argued that remediation lies at the heart of any type of creativity. However (and again in line with Bolter and Grusin), I have argued that digital media technologies have fostered remediation on an unprecedented scale, making it a hallmark of contemporary creative work and media culture.

Culture jamming provides some of the most dramatic and entertaining examples of remediation. Whether in the form of surveillance camera dramatics, ®™ark's underwriting of the spoof websites and WTO-crashing antics of the Yes Men, the deadpan clip-art cartoons of Get Your War On, or Jonah Peretti's meme-driven "Nike Media Adventure," culture jamming projects depend on the pastiche and subversion of common cultural images and ideas. Participatory journalism and Indymedia projects take a less humorous line, but also select and recombine mainstream news and commentary with intensely local (and partisan) reporting and opinion on issues and stories that are ordinarily ignored by major media outlets. (Ironically, and recalling the cycle of cross-appropriation between subcultures and mainstream society discussed in Chapter 3, Indymedia sites themselves are increasingly monitored by mainstream news organizations for leads and story ideas.) Commons knowledge projects also exemplify remediation processes. Their flexible, volunteer networks of participants help create, collect, critique, evaluate, amend, and reorganize diverse materials into useful and fairly trustworthy information resources. They demonstrate that remediation depends on the vital interplay between sociality and knowledge, and a view of knowledge that is not merely the accumulation of abstract facts or discoveries, but a constantly changing understanding that is expressed, documented, circulated, validated, revised, and even forgotten or lost, collectively.

As discussed to this point, reconfiguration and remediation relate to technology and action, respectively. However, they do not exist independently, but mutually implicate and reconstitute each other in a larger, dialectical process of *mediation*. Mediation as a theoretical approach in communication research and scholarship is discussed at more length below, but with respect to alternative and activist new media projects, the cases presented in the preceding chapters demonstrate how reconfiguration and remediation shape one another. For example, in the effort to "remediate" and intervene in the uniformly negative mainstream news coverage of protests by global justice movement activists at the 1999 World Trade Organization meeting in Seattle, techs sympathetic to the movement adapted and reconfigured donated, off-the-shelf hardware and open-source software to create a new web-based publishing platform (and thus the first Independent Media Center) (Juris, 2008). The platform allowed journalists and movement activists alike to create and post content continuously as events in the street unfolded. Their live, alternative coverage often contradicted mainstream accounts and effectively challenged the twenty-four-hour news cycle of the corporate broadcast and print media. In turn, the new platform itself, and the "Indymedia news model" it fostered (Platon & Deuze, 2003), were rapidly adopted by other nascent IMCs around the world, becoming the foundation of a global network of alternative, open-source, participatory news outlets.

The *Hacker Quarterly*/DeCSS case provides another example of the interrelationship between reconfiguration and remediation. By reporting the Decrypt Content Scrambling System (DeCSS) technique, invented by a Norwegian teenager to reconfigure media products (DVDs) so that they could be run on computers with open-source operating systems (i.e., by disabling their digital rights management restrictions), Eric Corley and the *Hacker Quarterly* attracted the legal sanctions of movie studios intent on preventing the dissemination of knowledge about anti-DRM methods. The subsequent court-ordered restraints on Corley's press and speech rights prompted worldwide outrage within the technology community, who responded with a campaign of republishing and remediating the code as visual art, performance, poetry, t-shirts, as well as software, long after DeCSS itself – although still illegal –had become obsolete.

Mediation: beyond activism

The interplay of reconfiguration and remediation, then, is evident across the different genres of alternative and activist new media. However, in the remainder of this chapter I would like to go one step further and suggest that mediation, comprising reconfiguration and remediation as mutually determining processes, can be a useful analytic framework for studying the relationship between communication and society and cultural/social change, beyond the specific context and concerns of political and cultural activism. As we will see, the concept of mediation has been elaborated and debated for decades within the communication field, though for much of that time it has remained at the periphery of theorizing and research. However, in recent years it has attracted increased interest among scholars seeking an approach for understanding communication and social change that is more relevant than the linear, production–consumption and sender–receiver models of media influence that have prevailed in the discipline to date.

Historically, communication research and scholarship, based in theories of industrial production and consumption, mass society, and mass persuasion, have focused on what "the media" – as technologies and as institutions – *produce* and what those products do *to* the people, societies, and cultures that *consume* them. However, as new media technologies, practices, and social arrangements become ever more entwined, and especially as complex, constantly reorganizing, networked forms of social and technological organization absorb and recombine with familiar hierarchical structures in many social settings (as forcefully argued by Yochai Benkler [2007], among others), the linear notions of media influence and effects that have dominated communication study since the early twentieth century are losing their explanatory power. Rather than thinking of communication as something "the media" do, it may be more useful to frame the relationship between communication and society in terms of mediation, keeping in mind the dual senses of the term: technological channels and social/interpersonal involvement and intercession. In place of (or perhaps in addition to) linear message transmission and channel effects, we should consider the reconfiguration of technological systems and the remediation of expression, interaction, social relations and structures, and content as two emergent, reflexive, recombinant, and interdependent processes.

The next section presents a brief account of how the concept of mediation has evolved in communication research and scholarship, especially in response to the development of networked telecommunications and computing technologies and the growing use of computers as media since the 1970s. (The discussion is a summary of the main points in earlier work; see Lievrouw, 2009.) This overview is followed by a discussion of mediation as a theoretical framework; and the chapter concludes with some observations about the implications of the mediation perspective for the study of communication and media in society.

From the mass to mediation: three "moments" in communication study

Since the 1970s, the rise of new media technologies, and the innovative modes of communication associated with them, have contributed to two shifts within the communication discipline. First, they have helped broker something of a *rapprochement* between mass media and interpersonal communication research, since new media support both content production/ reception and interpersonal "computer-mediated communication" (CMC). Second, within the critical media studies tradition, new technologies and modes of communication have opened new opportunities for studying the intersections between human behavior and action, and institutional forms and forces. Early modes of CMC, including teleconferencing, computer bulletin boards, videotext and email, and even more traditional forms like the humble telephone call, did not fit easily into the discipline's traditional subfields, and raised new questions about the theoretical and empirical distinctions between content and form, message and medium, and process and effects. Where mass media researchers tended to see technology instrumentally, as the insertion of systems into the human interaction process, and channels as variables in their own right, a small but growing cadre of new media scholars rejected channel-centric frameworks and developed new theoretical approaches, or adapted concepts from other fields, in their analyses of what Gary Gumpert (1988) called the "media nexus" – the intersection between communication technologies and interpersonal interaction.

Moves toward reconceptualizing the relationship between technology and communication correspond to three broad "moments" in the field. The first began with Elihu Katz and Paul Lazarsfeld's (2006 [1955]) formulation of the "two-step flow" theory of mass media effects, which, contrary to theories of strong, direct media effects, hypothesized an indirect "media to conversation to opinion" persuasion process (Katz, 2006 [1955], p. xxiii). This line of theory and research also contrasted with "scientific," linear models of communication influenced by information theory and telecommunications, particularly the work of telecommunications engineers Claude Shannon and Warren Weaver (1963 [1949]). David Berlo and others adapted information theory into the famous "sender–message–channel–receiver," or SMCR, model (Berlo, 1960); soon SMCR and similar transmission-type models became a staple of introductory communication texts. But they also encountered a rising tide of criticism from scholars who charged that although such models nominally described the one-way, few-to-many distribution patterns of mass media, they bore little resemblance to human communication and the experience of interaction and shared understanding (Golding & Murdock, 1978; Peters, 1986; Reardon & Rogers, 1988).

Two-step flow was the progenitor of two streams of theory that departed from linear models of communication and influence (Katz, 2006 [1955]). *Decision* studies focused on the persuasion process, on "active audiences," their selective reception and interpretation of media messages, and how audiences construct and share meaning about media and everyday life. "Uses and gratifications" theory, one of the most influential frameworks in this stream between the 1960s and 1980s, assumed that audience members are active and engaged, bring their own purposes and meanings to media content, and make rational choices among media and messages according to their particular needs and interests.

Diffusion studies, on the other hand, focused on the spread of new ideas and interpersonal influence within social networks: how people share information, seek and give advice, form affiliations and loyalties, build communities, and so on. Diffusion research also framed communication in terms of imitation and "contagion" processes of influence, rather than focusing on persuasion *per se*. Though they differed in emphasis, both streams emphasized the interrelationship of interpersonal interaction and media messages in the communication process, and rejected simple linear notions of message transmission and "powerful media" wielding unopposed power over pliant, passive audiences.

The second moment was a "crisis" in mass media studies generated by the dramatic growth of networked media, telecommunications, information retrieval, and computing systems in the 1970s and 1980s. At first, media researchers paid little attention to the new technologies, since they did not fit conceptual distinctions between mass media and interpersonal/small group communication, or notions of powerful media technologies and institutions exerting generalized social effects. For example, voice telephone conversations are typically dyadic, simultaneous interactions; however, because they lack many qualities of face-to-face contact, until the 1970s most interpersonal researchers considered them poor substitutes for "real" interaction. Similarly, in the early 1980s, teletext and videotex systems like BBC's Ceefax or Canada's Telidon delivered content to subscribers on demand; video teleconferences connected meeting participants in multiple locations via live audio and video links. But these systems had little relation to traditional analyses of broadcasting based on mass audiences and widespread, predictable changes in attitudes and behavior.

Nonetheless, communication researchers – particularly those in organizational communication, communication policy studies, and social-psychological studies of interaction and small group process – soon began to shift their focus toward the convergence of older mass media systems with newer digital technologies, and to emerging modes of CMC such as email and computer conferencing. Some argued that traditional media theories and methods could be adapted to the study of new media. Others looked outside the communication discipline (e.g., to organization studies or science and technology studies) for different concepts and approaches that seemed suited to emergent and continuously reorganizing technical and social networks. The move within the communication discipline in the 1980s from large-scale surveys and experimentation toward more reflexive, subjective, and qualitative methods also played an important role in generating new approaches to the study of networked communication technologies.

The third moment arrived in the early 1990s, when American universities and government agencies handed over the non-profit, research- and education-driven internet to private-sector firms. The introduction of browsers, search engines, server–client architectures, and the protocols of the World Wide Web made the internet easily accessible in most homes and workplaces for the first time, and attracted the interest of communication scholars with more critical and cultural interests, including those from the media studies tradition.[3] Like the organizational researchers and social psychologists before them, initially critical and cultural scholars applied familiar concepts and theories to the analysis of online and mobile communication. In particular, they invoked a "cultural transmission" view of media, including new media, as powerful influences in the reproduction and reinforcement of dominant cultural ideologies, political power structures, and economic interests. The internet, like the mass media systems that preceded it, was seen mainly as a channel for distributing cultural products or texts to be deciphered, critiqued, and resisted. Online representations of gender, sexuality, ethnicity, and class, and their influence on people's senses of self or identity, were intensely debated.

Over the last decade, a new generation of new media researchers has helped drive a more culturally oriented shift in theorizing and empirical research about new media. These younger scholars, who have grown up with online interaction and culture, have tended to emphasize the intensely personal, participatory, playful, and performative quality of newer "social media." For them, new media and mediation have become domesticated (Silverstone, 1999, 2005, 2006), almost banal (Lievrouw, 2004). An increasingly seamless and always-on, always-there web of interaction, expression, relationships, social organizing, and creative culture is part of everyday life, on- and offline. Rather than framing the internet as some sort of separate "cyberworld" that shadows or reflects "real" life, contemporary scholars of digital culture recognize that society and technology are mutually determining and even dialectic. In this context, mediation has emerged as a central concept in theorizing about new media.

For example, Johan Fornäs suggests that mediation should be a foundational concept in new media studies: ". . . our communication society is based on mediations between texts and people, in that people pass and meet each other through texts, just as texts pass and encounter each other through people" (Fornäs, 2002, p. 104). Stefaan Verhulst (2007) argues for a "new mediation ecology" for communication and media policy. Participants in two panels at the International Communication Association

(ICA) conference in 2007 debated a cluster of related concepts, including mediatization, transmediation, medium theory, media logics, remediation, and the "mediatic turn"; the respondent Nick Couldry (2008) called these "new terms to understand the intensification of media influence in social life." In her 2008 Presidential Address to the ICA entitled "On the Mediation of Everything," my colleague Sonia Livingstone recounted the growing "mediation" literature, assessed the political and cultural implications of differing etymological variations on mediation, and concluded that there is indeed a conceptual shift underway in new media studies that may facilitate the exploration of "the possible and actual mediation of everything" (Livingstone, 2009, p. 13).

Two influential media theorists, Roger Silverstone and Jesús Martín-Barbero, have helped to establish the concept of mediation as central to new media scholarship. Silverstone, for example, critiques the traditional, modernist view that media technologies, and thus mediation itself, distort or corrupt an otherwise ideal, symmetrical experience of interpersonal interaction. The study of communication must encompass both communication technology and communicative action in the continuous and dialectical "circulation of meaning, which is mediation" (Silverstone, 1999, p. 13). Silverstone (2005) suggests that mediation, as the defining condition of contemporary experience, is "a fundamentally dialectical notion which requires us to address the processes of communication as both institutionally and technologically driven and embedded" (p. 189), and requires that media scholars "return to the issue of interpersonal communication" (p. 190). Moreover, analysts cannot "simply presume linearity in media effects or media influence. Mediation is not all one way . . . ownership does not determine content; content does not determine reception" (p. 191). Ultimately, mediation "is both literal and metaphorical" (p. 203).

Similarly, Martín-Barbero criticizes both the instrumentality of North American communication research and the critique of cultural imperialism embodied in dependency theory, which has been a core framework in Latin American communication research (Martín-Barbero, 2004, 2006). Both, he says, reduce communication and the role of media to "mere ideological reproduction" (Martín-Barbero, 2006, p. 281). Based on his analyses of the role of media in Latin American social and political movements, he argues that people are capable of acting and engaging with media on their own terms, and that culture is not simply imposed by elites through media channels. Culture (i.e., the practices of people in everyday life) and media are mutually determining, and multiple cultural representations are negotiated and put into circulation in global markets through the process of mediation (Martín-Barbero, 1993). He opposes Frankfurt School-style dualisms of high and low culture and of the material and symbolic in media. Instead he shows how the everyday and local become part of an ongoing process of cultural change, where meaning is established and modified in a "complex fabric of mediations that articulates the relations between communication, culture and politics" (Martín-Barbero, 1993, p. 281). For Martín-Barbero, "*mediation* is the social and cultural process that functions between various levels in the field of communication. . . . hegemony and counter-hegemony . . . overlap through a process of cultural circulation: there [is] a constant interaction and borrowing of styles, recycled, then *mediated* as a reflection of the original style" (Berry & Theobald, 2006, pp. 198–9, emphasis in the original).

In a recent article Martín-Barbero (2006) sketches out four types of mediations. The categories are part of a much more complex theoretical framework, but at the risk of oversimplification, they can be summarized as follows. *Institutionality* mediates between production processes and cultural "matrices," i.e., practices and conventions, to produce social structures. *Technicity* mediates between production and industrial "formats," generating new techniques and methods. *Rituality* mediates between industrial formats and people's reception/consumption "competences," resulting in regular patterns of action over time. *Sociality* mediates between people's competences and their cultural practices, creating social relationships and affinities. Although a detailed analysis and comparison is outside the scope of this chapter, it would be a useful exercise to map Martín-Barbero's scheme of mediations onto the three-part definition of new media infrastructure proposed in Chapter 1 (comprising technological artifacts, social and cultural practices, and institutional arrangements and organizing), or to compare his mediations to the dialectic relation between reconfiguration and remediation proposed here, to explore how the different approaches might be applied in further empirical work.

Mediation and themes in communication study

As a concept in communication study, mediation has evolved in parallel with certain themes or trends in the field, particularly as networked computing and telecommunications have overtaken print on paper, cinema, and broadcasting as the primary platforms for communication technology. (Indeed, to a great extent these trends have created the need for new analytical frameworks.) First, analysts have tended to move away from accounts of "powerful" or dominant media and their subsequent effects or impacts, and toward resituating interpersonal interaction as an indispensable and definitive part of media engagement and use. Put differently, this can be seen as a move from a theoretical and empirical focus on *channels* as independent factors or variables in the communication process, and toward more emphasis on people's communicative *action*.

Second, across the various subfields of communication research and scholarship, there has been a gradual rejection of a purely *transmission* or conduit view of communication – that is, models that depict the process as the movement or transfer of message/content "objects" from senders to receivers and back (although traces of this view can still be detected in discussions that cast internet users as "both" producers and consumers, or, less elegantly, "prosumers"). In contrast to this view, there has been growing interest in *meaning-based* definitions of communication influenced by theories of interactionism, intersubjectivity, and relational models of social action.[4] Everett Rogers and Larry Kincaid, for example, define communication as "a process in which the participants create and share information with one another in order to reach a mutual understanding" (Rogers & Kincaid, 1981, p. 63). Elsewhere I have defined it as "coordinated action that achieves understanding or shares meaning" (Lievrouw, 2001, p. 13). This increased focus on contexts and meanings may also represent the "interiorization" of concepts of communication, in both the spatial and subjective senses – communication as an essentially domestic, personal, or local phenomenon, and as the highly personal, shared, and context-dependent experiences of the people involved (Lievrouw, 2004).

A third theme in communication study that has fostered the mediation view is the growing acknowledgement of communication as action that responds to and is situated within complex fields of relations, systems, and roles, rather than as isolated episodes of expression/production or reception/consumption. That is, the *network* metaphor has become a governing framework for understanding communication as a socially constitutive process as well as individual or group action. This aspect is reflected in communication scholars' continuing search for theories that bridge mass and interpersonal processes, as suggested in the discussion above and in Chapter 1 (Lievrouw, 2009). The broader turn in social theory in the 1970s and 1980s toward approaches that united social structure and action as inseparable, mutually constitutive phenomena[5] also encouraged the development of theoretical frameworks which posit the dialectical co-production and complex articulation of public and private contexts, of material conditions and symbolic expressions, and of technologies and practice. In these accounts, media are not merely technical or institutional systems that intervene in or "contain" an otherwise unmediated process of human expression and interaction.[6] Communication technologies, interpersonal relationships, institutional and organizational structures, and individual action all comprise complex socio-technical networks that are both *resources* for, and themselves *manifestations* of, communication and culture.

Thus, the definition of mediation has shifted over the course of three "moments" in communication study and in relation to larger concerns and themes in the field. Once understood as a technological intervention between parties in an interaction, or between personal experience and a larger reality, today mediation can be defined as the continuous and mutual reshaping of communicative action and communication technology that actually *constitutes* experience (Boczkowski & Lievrouw, 2008; see also Jouet, 1994). It entails both technological tools and interpersonal and social intervention, negotiation, and organizing. Mediation is thus reconceptualized as a field of articulations and co-productions between public and private, world and home, structure and action, material and symbolic, technology and experience.

Mediation as a theoretical framework

To summarize, mediation comprises an ongoing, mutually shaping relationship between people's uses of communication technology (reconfiguration) and their communicative action (remediation) that produces social and technological change. In contrast to traditional conceptions of "the media" that emphasize the influence of powerful technologies and institutions on individuals and society, mediation actually constitutes social relationships and experience. Through reconfiguration and remediation, media artifacts, practices, and arrangements become both the means and the ends of communication, "cultural material and material culture" (Boczkowski & Lievrouw, 2007, p. 955).

Figure 8.1 illustrates the principal elements of the mediation framework proposed here and suggests some dynamics of the process. The central part of the figure indicates the continuous, mutually constitutive interrelationship between reconfiguration

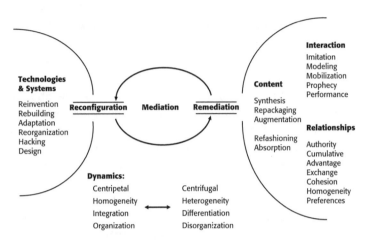

Figure 8.1. New media and mediation.

and remediation. The reconfiguration of technologies and systems, shown at the left, can take a number of forms, such as reinvention, rebuilding, adaptation, reorganization, hacking, design, and so on. At the right, remediation processes are organized into three groups: the remediation of *content*, of *interaction*, and of *relationships*. Content remediation includes processes similar to the types proposed by Bolter and Grusin, such as synthesis, repackaging, augmentation, refashioning, and absorption. Remediation of interaction includes imitation or modeling processes and performance; other examples more specific to activism have been introduced in previous chapters, including mobilization and prophecy. The remediation of relationships is exemplified by processes like social cohesion or exchange, the negotiation of authority, or the cumulative advantage or "long-tail" processes that characterize social networks, where some actors may attract more relationships or enhanced reputations than others.

Mediation is also subject to dynamics that can "push" cultural change in different directions. For example, Henry Jenkins (2006) has suggested that media "convergence" can result in either centripetal (centralizing) or centrifugal (dispersing) types of change. Mediation might also encourage cultural homogeneity, on one hand, or more heterogeneity, on the other: for example, mass media are often regarded as culturally homogenizing while newer ICTs and particularly Web 2.0 have been seen as more socially and culturally heterogeneous and heterotopic (Lievrouw, 1998). Mediation may generate greater social integration in one setting or greater differentiation in another (Lievrouw, 2001). At the broadest level, mediation might also be seen in successive waves of social, cultural, or technological organization versus disorganization, or emergence, as suggested by self-organizing systems theory (Monge & Contractor, 2003).

These dynamics indicate that the relationship between reconfiguration and remediation is not always symmetrical or predictable. The two processes can certainly confirm, reinforce, or create new alignments between technology structures/systems and communicative content or action. However, because they intervene in usual or accepted practices, they can also disrupt existing or entrenched alignments. For example, Nupedia's adoption of innovative wiki software in 2001 failed as a tactic for generating expert contributions to an online reference work. However, almost by accident, it also created a shared space in which a vast, global community of amateur (and mostly uncredited) contributors could assemble and quarrel over bits of sometimes authoritative, often idiosyncratic, and wildly miscellaneous information. The result – Wikipedia – has become one of the most widely used online resources over the last decade. Nonetheless, it remains controversial among institutional authorities and critics who worry that it undermines expertise and legitimate knowledge, and that it is too easily manipulated or sabotaged to be considered a definitive, reliable information source.

A fuller theoretical elaboration of mediation is outside the scope of a single short chapter, but as a final point we can say that mediation is not unique to new media and ICTs. Obviously, technologies (semaphore, printing, Twitter) and action (speech, fashion, political campaigning, making art) are always implicated in communication across social and cultural contexts, times and places. However, different modes or patterns of mediation may emerge under different conditions. By focusing on mediation, rather than "the media" themselves, we may open the way for a new phase of critical and empirical inquiry in the study of communication.

In this book, the mediation approach has been used to help theorize alternative and activist new media projects. I have also suggested that it provides a new and potentially powerful way to think about the interdependence and mutual shaping of communicative action and communication technology in society more generally. The key point is that people's expressions and interactions are inseparable from the devices and methods they use to create, sustain, or change them. This relationship is a moving target, or perhaps more accurately a moving window, for viewing communication as the fundamental mechanism of social change. Although various modes of communication, institutional structures, or technological systems may appear to remain stable over time, in fact mediation is a continuous process of countless small adaptations – interrelated reconfigurations and remediations that gradually produce new practices, artifacts, and social arrangements, and thus whole infrastructures, like the changes that occur when small parts of a building or machine are replaced over time. The structure or device is never destroyed or discarded *in toto*, but at some point the piecemeal replacements create a new object. Whether this process occurs rapidly or slowly depends on the extent to which people find different ways to reconfigure technological artifacts and/or remediate their communicative expressions, interactions, and relationships over time.

The last word might go to Jay Bolter and Richard Grusin, whose ideas have enriched and illuminated the present discussion. They argue that it is not possible to separate mediation and reality, or to separate some kinds of mediations from others: "The events of our mediated culture are constituted by combinations of subject, media, and objects, which do not exist in their segregated forms. *Thus, there is nothing prior to or outside the act of mediation*" (Bolter & Grusin, 1999, p. 58, emphasis added). From a vantage point at the edges or "frontiers" of culture, alternative and activist new media projects may be models for this new understanding of mediation, communication, and social change at the center.

Notes

1 I use the term "ecology" in the etymological sense noted by the *Oxford English Dictionary*, i.e., the discipline or "order of the house," in contrast to the common biological usage denoting the interrelationship of plants and animals with their natural surroundings. The latter sense underlies much of the influential work in media ecology studies, but my purpose here is more limited and I want to distinguish the present discussion from the larger theoretical contributions and frameworks of media ecology, and its connections with Toronto School-type medium theory.

2 My emphasis on reconfiguration and remediation in the new media context is similar to Christopher Kelty's argument that designers and expert users of the internet and related technologies constitute a *recursive public* that not only engages in discourse *about* technology but also *with* and *through* it (see Chapter 4; Kelty, 2008). I would argue that this concept applies not just to expert technologists, but also to many "ordinary" users of media and information technologies, if in a more limited or less sophisticated way.

3 For example, Zittrain (2008) warns that the recent proliferation of more purpose-built digital devices such as internet-enabled mobile phones or "readers" like Amazon's Kindle or Apple's iPad is a deliberate strategy that allows manufacturers to restrict users' abilities to adapt devices to new uses or applications.

4 The ubiquity of new media also gives them the quality of being "always already," an idea related to Heidegger's concept of *Dasein* or being-in-the-world, and his analysis of technology as being ready-to-hand or taken for granted until it breaks down and thus becomes "visible" to the user. The idea was later elaborated by Jacques Derrida (*toujours déjà*) as a quality of experience that makes it difficult to imagine that the world was ever different in a time prior to the present – a common sensibility among younger new media

users, who may have no recollection of a time before web browsers or pushbutton telephones, for example, or in the celebratory pages of industry publications like *Wired*. The sociologist Leigh Star, together with her colleagues, has also adapted many of Heidegger's ideas about technology in her theoretical discussions of technology *infrastructure* (Star & Bowker, 2006; Star & Ruhleder, 1996). The definition of new media advanced here builds on a number of key ideas from Star's work.

5 Indeed, national rates of "broadband" connectivity (i.e., high-speed internet access via coaxial cable, satellite, or digital subscriber line [DSL] connection) have recently been added to the list of national or economic development indicators used by international agencies like UNESCO and the Organization for Economic Cooperation and Development (see *Economist*, 2008b; OECD, 2008; and the OECD Broadband Portal, http://www.oecd.org/sti/ict/broadband).

6 The present discussion provides only a general sketch of the much larger field of genre studies and analysis in communication and other disciplines. More detailed overviews can be found in Bazerman (1988, 1995), Chandler (2000), Freedman & Medway (1994), McQuail (2005), Miller (1984), and Yates & Orlikowski (1992). For discussions of genres in the context of the World Wide Web, see Agre (1998), Crowston & Williams (2000), Dillon & Gushrowski (2000), Miller & Shepherd (2004), and Yates, Orlikowski & Okamura (1999). The points in this section are drawn mainly from these sources.

CHAPTER 2 THE ROOTS OF ALTERNATIVE AND ACTIVIST NEW MEDIA

1 For a more comprehensive overview of the art and history of Dadaism, including an excellent collection of images, see the website for the 2006 exhibit on Dada organized by the National Gallery of Art in Washington, D.C. and the Centre Pompidou in Paris (http://www.nga.gov/exhibitions/2006/dada/cities/index.shtm).

2 In the 1970s and early 1980s, well before the internet existed as a popular medium, *détournement* was revived and reappropriated as a key element of punk style, especially in the UK. For more detail about the influence of Debord's ideas and Situationism in punk and other youth subcultures, see Chollet (2004), Ford (2005), Hebdige (1979), and Marcus (1989, 2002).

3 As late as 1990, in a comprehensive overview of social theory, the prominent American sociologist James Coleman still saw emotion and indoctrination as key factors in collective action, in which he included "such phenomena as mob behavior, systems of trust, public opinion, social movements, emergent charismatic authority, audience behavior, fads, and fashion" (Coleman, 1990, p. 43).

4 In some ways, the affiliation between project activists and the communities they interact with resembles the concept of *parasocial interaction*, which has been used by mass media scholars since the 1950s to describe audience members' emotional involvement with or attachment to particular media personalities or characters (for a further discussion, see McQuail, 2005). However, the sense of community online differs in some respects, notably that in online communities there is much more opportunity for "meeting" and interacting with others than in traditional media contexts. Online projects are often deliberately designed "social spaces" that also permit community members to post, rate, recommend, or "tag" informational resources, give and seek advice, adopt pseudonyms and avatars, and much more (a particularly good overview of the notion of online community is found in Jones, 1998). With traditional media programs, in contrast, "involvement" of the audience is ordinarily restricted to the psychology of reception and some occasional interaction among audience members, rather than with program producers or personalities. Indeed, the efforts of particularly keen or persistent fans to follow, contact, or interact with popular media personalities are often seen as pathological, and are outlawed in most U.S. jurisdictions, notably California and New York.

5 In previous work (Lievrouw, 1998, 2001), I have suggested that heterotopic spaces, such as online sites and projects, are thus sites for *heterotopic communication*, a distinctive style of communicative action that facilitates the communication of difference. Heterotopic communication employs simulation and spectacle as sources of information; exhibitionism/voyeurism as communicative styles, linked to an awareness of surveillance; the competitive use of knowledge as a commodity, based on widespread horizontal and vertical information inequities; the presentation of a global or universal "face" on what are essentially parochial interests; and the strategic use of public and private domains as frames for engagement.

6 Some critics have argued that the term "digital archive" should be

considered an oxymoron because it yokes together two concepts with diametrically opposed definitions of reality: the virtual immateriality of digital information and the tangible substance of the physical archive (Laermans & Gielen, 2007).

CHAPTER 3 MONKEYWRENCHING THE MEDIA
MACHINE: CULTURE JAMMING

1 Wikipedia's assessment of the essay is supported in part by Dery's own contributions to the entry's "talk page" discussion (see http://en.wikipedia.org/wiki/Talk:Culture_jamming).
2 Dawkins was apparently unaware of the extensive literature that already existed in economics, sociology, and communications on the *diffusion of innovations*, which accounts for the ways that new ideas and practices diffuse among acquaintances in a social system over time (Rogers, 2003), preferring instead to portray the process as essentially adaptive and deterministic, using a biological metaphor.
3 In a scathing parody that echoes the tactics of ®™ark, Frank and Mulcahey (2000) offer a corporate prospectus for a "lifestyle and deviance merchant," Consolidated Deviance, Inc.: ". . . the nation's leader . . . in the fabrication, consultancy, licensing, and merchandising of deviant subcultural practice." Consolidated Deviance's main products are SubCults™, including Grunge™, Poststructuralism™, and PostRock™. (In fact, Frank and his colleagues helped reveal a list of "grunge speak" terms, such as "lamestain" and "harsh realm," published in the *New York Times* in 1997, as a hoax; see the *Grunge speak* entry in Wikipedia, http://en.wikipedia.org/wiki/Grunge_speak.) The ConDev prospectus claims that

> the company's greatest asset is a highly educated and highly motivated work force. The vogue of cultural studies has dovetailed nicely with the conglomeration of the Culture industry and the worldwide assault on the wage, giving rise to a glut of savvy and underemployed pop culture pundits. This work force, though almost exclusively privileged, highly educated and acutely leveraged, is generally willing to work for low wages and few benefits. It is also indifferent, even hostile, to labor organization efforts. And unlike entry-level workers in most industries, the company's fresh post-college recruits are valued for their youth, inexperience and bad attitudes. (pp. 73, 77)

This humorous treatment prefigures later, more somber, analyses of the "free labor" involved in creating and maintaining websites and online content, including blogs, social networks, multiuser games, wikis, and so on (Castronova, 2003; Lovink & Rossiter, 2007b; Terranova, 2009 [2000]).

4 The term "skunkworks" originated with a renowned R&D installation established by the Lockheed Martin Corporation to develop new military aircraft during World War II, and which continues to design advanced aircraft systems today (Bennis & Biederman, 1997; see also http://www.lockheedmartin.com/ aeronautics/skunkworks/index.html).

5 The Thing still serves arts organizations in New York City, but NTT/Verio's tactic of cutting off internet access for organizations it deems undesirable continues. In 2007, Verio terminated access to cryptome.org, "a website concerned with encryption, privacy, and government secrecy" that specializes in posting documents that governments consider sensitive or incriminating (Slashdot, 2007; see also Cryptome's response at http://cryptome.org/cryptome-shut. htm).

CHAPTER 4 "HACKING THE NEW OUT OF THE OLD": ALTERNATIVE COMPUTING

1 I am indebted to David Hakken, who introduced me to the phrase "alternative computing" at the 2004 meeting of the Society for Social Studies of Science meeting in Paris, during a panel discussion of free/libre/open-source software (FLOSS) projects in developing regions of the world. In the early 1990s Hakken traced the roots of an "alternative" approach to computing practice to both the utopian view of computer technology widespread in popular culture, and a more pragmatic perspective on software development and implementation in the workplace, *participatory design* (PD). PD originated in the Nordic countries in the 1970s and 1980s and involved both management and workers in the process of designing industrial automation systems (see Hakken, 1993; Hakken & Andrews, 1993). Since 1992, PD techniques and projects have been the central focus of the Participatory Design Conferences, co-sponsored by Computer Professionals for Social Responsibility and the Association for Computing Machinery.

2 For a fuller discussion of the focus on progressive/left projects versus conservative/right projects in the study of alternative media,

see Atton (2004), Bailey, Cammaerts & Carpentier (2008), and Downing et al. (2001).

3 The background of Easter eggs and their history is available at http://www.mackido.com/EasterEggs/HistoryOfEggs.html. An archive of Easter egg "finds" in software, games, DVDs, and other media, and directions for launching them, is available at the Easter Egg Archive, http://www.eeggs.com. (For example, an otherwise hidden flight simulator game can be launched within recent versions of Google Earth with the keystroke combination Ctrl+Alt+A in Windows operating systems or Command+Option+A in Mac OS X.) The Easter eggs entry in Wikipedia (en.wikipedia.org/wiki/Easter_egg_(media)) contains a short history of some early Easter eggs in computer software and hardware, including those built into versions of Unix, the TOPS-10 operating system for Digital Equipment Corporation's PDP-10 mainframe computer, all Microsoft operating systems prior to XP, and even the Hewlett-Packard Scanjet 5P printer. In recent years the entertainment industry has appropriated the "Easter egg" idea and now movie studios, television networks, and recorded music companies routinely build hidden features into their products as a marketing tactic.

4 Some writers trace the origins to MIT in the 1960s, where the term "hack" referred to any kind of spectacular campus prank, especially involving the school's iconic architecture (see Peterson, 2003; Thomas, 2002).

5 The 2600/DeCSS case is explored at greater length by, *inter alia*, Eschenfelder & Desai (2004), Lessig (2001), and Litman (2001). The present discussion is based on these sources, as well as details of the case provided in legal documents, the archives of 2600, the Electronic Frontier Foundation, among others.

6 For nearly three decades, this "outsider" aspect of computer culture, and the implications of computer-mediated communication for identity, have been incisively documented and analyzed by the psychologist Sherry Turkle. In a seminal essay entitled "Computer as Rorschach" (Turkle, 1980), she argues that computers, as communication media, are "projective devices" that allow socially awkward individuals, like some of the engineering and computer science graduate students she studied at MIT, to express and present themselves more confidently than in face-to-face situations (see also Turkle, 1984, 1995). In fact, the "identity play" afforded by the use of pseudonyms, avatars, and alternate identities and characters became a common feature of computer-mediated communication, even among novice internet users, by the early 1990s and a popular focus

of study among academics and social commentators. Although the phenomenon was probably never as prevalent as the cultural studies literature seemed to suggest, it certainly persists today in popular forms like multiplayer role-playing games and virtual worlds like Second Life, for example.

CHAPTER 5 "BREAKING THROUGH THE
INFORMATION BLOCKADE": PARTICIPATORY
JOURNALISM AND INDYMEDIA

1 In the present discussion I use the term "readers" broadly, to denote people who select and follow the news across any media platform – text, still and moving images, and sound – and who may also contribute to or comment on news coverage, as well as "consume" it. I prefer this term because it suggests active engagement with the news, in contrast to other concepts like "audience" (which emphasizes reception, especially in the mass-media sense) or "user" (which carries a more technology-driven, computer-centric, or instrumental connotation). For a further discussion of the difficulties involved in characterizing people's engagement with new media, see the introduction to the second edition of the *Handbook of New Media* (Lievrouw & Livingstone, 2006).

2 Strictly speaking, the term "Indymedia," capitalized, applies only to news and opinion sites affiliated with Independent Media Centers. Recently, however, the word "indymedia," lower-case, has been applied to a variety of web-based alternative, radical, or critical news sites employing the practices or philosophies of public, civic, citizen, participatory, or open-source journalism. Because the present chapter uses the original IMC-based movement as its principal example, the word is capitalized in this discussion.

3 A complete bibliography is beyond the scope of this chapter. However, the summary and case study here are drawn from Indymedia documents archived at http://docs.indymedia.org, as well as numerous academic studies and commentaries (see, e.g., Atton, 2002, 2003, 2004; Bailey, Cammaerts & Carpentier, 2008; Beckerman, 2003; Bennett, 2003; Deuze, 2003; Downing, 2003, 2008; Downing et al., 2001; Halleck, 2002, 2003; Hyde, 2002; Jankowski & Jansen, 2003; Kidd, 2003; Morris, 2004; Pavis, 2002; Pickard, 2006a, 2006b, 2008; Platon & Deuze, 2003; Tarleton, 2000).

4 A general description of Indymedia open-publishing policy is

available at https://docs.indymedia.org/Global/FrequentlyAskedQ
uestionEn#newswire; a more detailed editorial policy is posted on
the Indymedia UK site, http://www.indymedia.org.uk/en/static/
editorial.html.

5 See the posting by Chucko on the Indymedia imc-process
   listserv, http://archives.lists.indymedia.org/imc-process/2000-
   December/000261.html.

6 The case is discussed in detail, with supporting documentation,
   on the EFF website (http://www.eff.org/cases/indymedia-server-
   takedown) and on the Indymedia documents archive (https://docs.
   indymedia.org/Global/AhimsaAnalyticReflection).

7 For a concise overview of the cold war origins of the cultural
   imperialism critique, see Sturken & Cartwright (2009, pp. 397–9).
   The debate between the market-driven "free flow" perspective and
   the opposing "new world information order" (NWIO) view espoused
   by developing and non-aligned nations, which champions the right
   to communicate as a fundamental human right, was captured in
   a report prepared for UNESCO in 1980 by a special commission
   chaired by Sean MacBride (MacBride Commission, 2004 [1980]).
   More recently, some critics on the left have acknowledged that, in
   practice, NWIO has been used by authoritarian governments as a
   justification for propagandizing their own populations or blocking
   access to news or information from outside sources (Teer-Tomaselli,
   2007).

CHAPTER 6 GETTING PEOPLE ON THE "STREET":
MEDIATED MOBILIZATION

1 The case study presented here is drawn from a number of selected
   sources, including Almeida & Lichbach (2003); Bennett (2003);
   Castells (2009); Juris (2005, 2008); Kahn & Kellner (2004, 2005);
   Langman (2005); and Van Aelst & Walgrave, (2002), among other
   works.

2 Andrew Calabrese (2004) describes the characteristics of non-
   violent civil disobedience (CD), which has an established history
   as a form of political communication and protected speech in
   U.S. legal tradition. He argues that much of what has been called
   "electronic civil disobedience" does not qualify as such because it
   does not meet two core requirements. First, the person undertaking
   CD must be identifiable and publicly accountable for his or her
   actions (thus open to the risk of prosecution and being a victim of

the very injustice in question). Second, legitimate civil disobedience may be disruptive, but cannot be violent, deliberately intended to injure persons or destroy property; otherwise it forfeits its moral authority as protest. ECD actions are frequently anonymous, with little risk of consequence for individual activists, and some actions are deliberately destructive, not just disruptive. However, Calabrese says, to the extent that electronic civil disobedience meets these two tests, it should be considered legitimate political speech and must be protected in any democratic political system.

CHAPTER 7 CHALLENGING THE EXPERTS: COMMONS KNOWLEDGE

1 Despite popular complaints that the internet has created an information "flood" or "overload," librarians and information scientists report that the amount of information available online is just a small fraction of all the information held in the world's libraries and archives, much less that held in other organizations and collections. As noted in Chapter 2, the "deep," "dark," or "invisible" Web includes broken or inaccessible websites. It also encompasses information resources such as statistical databases, scientific data, multimedia files, content derived from forms, or content locked behind commercial and security firewalls (see Sherman & Price, 2001; Wikipedia entry, "Deep Web," http://en.wikipedia.org/wiki/deep_web).

2 The study of CSCW is an academic specialization in its own right that developed in the 1980s and 1990s among scholars in a variety of fields, including organization studies and management, organizational communication, human factors engineering and human–computer interaction, and anthropology, among other fields. An overview of CSCW developments can be found in the proceedings of the annual conferences on Computer Supported Cooperative Work sponsored by the Association for Computing Machinery (archive available through the ACM portal, http://portal.acm.org), and the annual European Computer Supported Cooperative Work conference (ECSCW; see http://www.ecscw.org/). The Wikipedia entry for "Computer Supported Cooperative Work" also provides a good general introduction to the field's main ideas and history (http://en.wikipedia.org/wiki/Computer_supported_cooperative_work).

3 Interviews with Raymond, Richard Stallman, Linus Torvalds,

and other leaders of the free software and open-source software movements are included in the documentary *Revolution OS* by filmmaker J.T.S. Moore (2003).

4 In contrast to privately owned property, *public goods* are resources held in common by members of a community for their collective benefit because they are both *non-excludable* (i.e., impractical or impossible to withhold from any member) and *non-rival* in consumption (i.e., use by one or all members does not "use up" the resource or keep others from using it). Classic examples of public goods are public highways, traffic signs or signals, air, or – prior to the cable television era – broadcast radio and television signals. Goods with only one of these characteristics, but which are essential for members' or the community's well-being, are often regarded as public goods in practice: examples include water, sewage, and electrical systems, which are limited in supply, but are necessary for members' survival and ethically cannot be withheld. Since the 1990s some have argued that the internet, online services like Google, and indeed collected knowledge itself have both characteristics and should be considered public goods in a global-scale commons (see, e.g., Spar, 1999; Stiglitz, 1999).

5 As electronic resource sharing has grown, the legal situation for libraries and other collections has become more complicated and restrictive. New legal barriers to cross-institutional sharing have been erected, mainly in the form of contracts with publishers and other vendors that override libraries' traditional first sale and fair use rights (Farb, 2006). These elements of traditional copyright law have ensured that libraries and other institutions can loan materials and allow patrons limited copying privileges for personal and educational use. However, these provisions are increasingly sidelined as copyright holders have attempted to exercise even greater control over, and thus revenue generation from, digital publications than they had from books, journals, films, audio recordings, and other physical formats, by requiring users to agree to restrictive contractual licensing agreements.

6 *Epistemology* is the branch of philosophy that deals with how knowledge is created and acquired. The *epistemic value* of an information source – that is, whether it should be considered a "true" or reliable source of knowledge, and not misleading or erroneous – depends on a variety of factors, including the evidence supporting it (its *justification*), its accuracy or verifiability, and agreement among experts about its value. Other epistemic values include the *power* of an information source (i.e., how much

knowledge it provides), its *speed* (how fast it provides knowledge), and its *fecundity* (how many people can acquire knowledge from it; Goldman, 1999). Don Fallis (2008) argues that Wikipedia, Digg. com, and other collaboratively generated information resources should be judged not solely on their absolute reliability, but on the basis of a variety of epistemic values.

7 Parallels with the earlier Decrypt CSS dispute (see Chapter 4) led blogger Chris Shiflett to describe the Digg HD-DVD controversy as 'DeCSS 2.0' (see http://shiflett.org/blog/2007/may/learning-from-Digg-decss-2.0).

8 Wikipedia's commitment to making all information about its operations public, and Wikipedians' own fascination with facts and figures, can be seen in the numerous Wikipedia pages devoted to its vital statistics. See, e.g., http://en.wikipedia.org/wiki/Wikipedia:Statistics; and http://en.wikipedia.org/wiki/Wikipedia:Modelling_Wikipedia%27s_growth.

CHAPTER 8 NEW MEDIA, MEDIATION

1 It remains to be seen whether mass media systems facing serious market challenges, such as print or broadcasting, will be willing or able to adapt their relatively stable technical/institutional architectures and "learn the trick" of technological reconfiguration and hybridization as a way to survive in the contemporary media landscape. This seems to be the hope underlying the recent introduction of new devices and platforms like Apple's iPad, Amazon's Kindle book reader, and online television distribution schemes like Hulu, for example, although these systems are designed to be difficult to reconfigure and retain "pay wall"-type revenue models carried over from publishing and pay television.

2 Prophecy also characterizes simulations, virtualization, and other visualization techniques that have been applied so effectively in new media. Whether in scientific studies of climate change, high-energy physics, or proteomics, or in more entertaining forms like multiplayer online games or computer-generated effects in motion pictures, the creation of new "worlds" as ideal models or alternatives to existing, "real world" conditions has become a staple of online culture and research, one in which the general public as well as elite scientists and special effects designers can participate.

3 In a 1999 interview with the Communication Initiative Network, Colombian communication researcher Jesús Martín-Barbero

observed that the "expansion and inter-penetration of cultural studies and communication" and a general shift toward cultural analysis was the most important intellectual development in the communication discipline of the time (see http://www.comminit.com/en/node/149538). Martín-Barbero is also a leading theorist of mediation whose work is discussed at more length later in this section.

4 To some extent this development may signal a revival of interest in Chicago School interactionism, which was a major influence on the communication discipline from the outset (see Rogers, 1994).

5 In social theory, perhaps the paradigmatic example is Anthony Giddens's theory of structuration (Giddens, 1979, 1984).

6 Actor-network theory, which attributes agency to both people and technological systems enmeshed in complex networks of relations, is another important example of this type of theory (see Latour, 2005; Law & Hassard, 1999). A basic introduction is available on Wikipedia (http://en.wikipedia.org/wiki/Actor_network_theory).

References

Abbate, J. (1999). *Inventing the Internet*. Cambridge, MA: MIT Press.

ADILKNO (Foundation for the Advancement of Illegal Knowledge) (1994). *Cracking the movement: Squatting beyond the media* (trans. L. Martz). New York: Autonomedia. (Originally published as *Bewegingsleer: Kraken aan gene zijde van de media*. Amsterdam: Uitgeverij Ravijn, 1990.)

Agre, P.E. (1998). "Designing genres for new media: Social, economic, and political contexts." In S.G. Jones (ed.), *Cybersociety 2.0: Revisiting computer-mediated communication and community*, pp. 69–99. Thousand Oaks, CA: Sage.

Alexander, J.C. (1996). "Collective action, culture and civil society: Secularizing, updating, inverting, revising and displacing the classical model of social movements." In J. Clark and M. Diani (eds.), *Alain Touraine*, pp. 205–234. London and Washington, DC: Falmer Press. (Originally published by Routledge, transferred to digital printing 2006.)

Alexander, J.C. (2006). *The civil sphere*. New York and Oxford: Oxford University Press.

Allen, D.W. (2003). "Rtmark: Viral activism and the meaning of 'post-identity.'" *Journal of the Midwest Modern Language Association*, 36(1), 6–24.

Almeida, P.D. and Lichbach, M.I. (2003). "To the Internet, from the Internet: Comparative media coverage of transnational protests." *Mobilization: An International Journal*, 8(3), 249–72.

Almeida, R.B., Mozafari, B., and Cho, J. (2007). *On the evolution of Wikipedia*. Presented at the first International Conference on Weblogs and Social Media, ICWSM 2007, Boulder, CO, March 26–8. Association for the Advancement of Artificial Intelligence.

Altheide, D.L. and Snow, R.P. (1988). "Toward a theory of mediation." In J.A. Anderson (ed.), *Communication Yearbook 11*, pp. 194–223. Newbury Park, CA: Sage.

Anarchy and the AoC (1993). *Declaration of digital independence*. Retrieved May 11, 2010: http://en.thehackademy.net/madchat/esprit/tetes/fuck/fuck0314.txt.

Andersen, J. and Skouvig, L. (2006). "Knowledge organization: A socio-historical analysis and critique." *Library Quarterly*, 76(3), 300–22.

Anderson, C. (2006). *"Actually existing" citizen journalism projects and typologies: Part 1. Blog post, Unpacking My Library*, July 31. Retrieved May 5, 2010: http://indypendent.typepad.com/academese/2006/07/index.html.

Anderson, C. (2008). *The long tail: Why the future of business is selling less of more* (1st paperback edn). New York: Hyperion.

Anderson, J.A. and Meyer, T. P. (1988) *Mediated communication: A social action perspective*. Newbury Park, CA: Sage.

Asen, R. (2000). "Seeking the 'counter' in counterpublics." *Communication Theory*, 10(4), 424–46.

Atton, C. (2002). *Alternative media*. London: Sage.

Atton, C. (2003). "Reshaping social movement media for a new millennium." *Social Movement Studies*, 2(1), 3–15.

Atton, C. (2004). *An alternative Internet*. New York: Columbia University Press.

Bailey, O., Cammaerts, B., and Carpentier, N. (2008). *Understanding alternative media*. London: Open University Press.

Baker, N. (2008). "The charms of Wikipedia." *New York Review of Books*, March 20, 6–10.

Barbrook, R. (2001). "HyperMedia freedom." In P. Ludlow (ed.), *Crypto anarchy, cyberstates, and pirate utopias*, pp. 47–58. Cambridge, MA: MIT Press.

Bazerman, C. (1988). *Shaping written knowledge: The genre and activity of the experimental article in science*. Madison: University of Wisconsin Press.

Bazerman, C. (1995). "Systems of genres and the enactment of social intentions." In A. Freedman and P. Medway (eds.), *Genre and the new rhetoric*, pp. 79–88. London: Taylor & Francis.

Beckerman, G. (2003). "Edging away from anarchy: Inside the Indymedia collective, passion vs. pragmatism." *Columbia Journalism Review*, September/October, 27–30.

Benjamin, W. (1968). "On some motifs in Baudelaire." In *Illuminations* (trans. H. Zohn; ed. and with an introduction by H. Arendt), pp. 155–94. New York: Schocken Books. (Originally published as *Illuminationen*. Frankfurt am Main: Suhrkamp Verlag, 1955.)

Benkler, Y. (2007). *The wealth of networks: How social production transforms markets and freedom*. New Haven, CT and London: Yale University Press.

Bennett, W.L. (2003). "Communicating global activism: Strengths and vulnerabilities of networked politics." *Information, Communication & Society*, 6(2), 143–68.

Bergman, M.K. (2001). "The deep web: Surfacing hidden value." *Journal of Electronic Publishing*, 7(1). Online journal DOI, retrieved May 5, 2010: http://dx.doi.org/10.3998/3336451.0007.104.

Berlo, D.K. (1960). *The process of communication: An introduction to theory and practice*. New York: Holt.

Berry, D. and Theobald, J. (2006). *Radical mass media criticism: A cultural genealogy*. New York: Black Rose Books.

Beschastnikh, I., Kriplean, T., and McDonald, D.W. (2008) *Wikipedian self-governance in action: Motivating the policy lens*. ICWSM 2008: Proceedings of the Second International Conference on Weblogs and Social Media. Seattle, WA, March 30–April 2, pp. 27–35. Association for the Advancement of Artificial Intelligence.

Best, S. and Kellner, D. (1999). "Debord, cybersituations, and the interactive spectacle." *SubStance*, 28(3), Issue 90, 129–56.

Bey, H. (2003). *The Temporary Autonomous Zone, ontological anarchy, poetic terrorism* (2nd edn with new preface). Brooklyn, NY: Autonomedia. Retrieved May 5, 2010: http://www.hermetic.com/bey/taz_cont.html.

Bimber, B. (2000). "The study of information technology and civic engagement." *Political Communication*, 17, 329–33.

Bimber, B. (2003). *Information and American democracy: Technology in the evolution of political power*. Cambridge and New York: Cambridge University Press.

Boczkowski, P.J. (2004). *Digitizing the news: Innovation in online newspapers*. Cambridge, MA: MIT Press.

Boczkowski, P.J. and Lievrouw, L.A. (2008). "Bridging STS and communication studies: Scholarship on media and information technologies." In E. Hackett, O. Amsterdamska, M. Lynch, and J. Wajcman (eds.), *New handbook of science, technology and society*, pp. 951–77. Cambridge, MA: MIT Press (published in cooperation with the Society for Social Studies of Science).

Bolter, J.D. and Grusin, R. (1999). *Remediation: Understanding new media*. Cambridge, MA: MIT Press.

Borgman, C.L. (2007). *Scholarship in the digital age: Information, infrastructure, and the Internet*. Cambridge, MA: MIT Press.

Bourges, H. (ed.) (1968). *The French student revolt: The leaders speak*. New York: Hill and Wang.

Bowman, S. and Willis, C. (2003). *WeMedia: How audiences are shaping the future of news and information*. Reston, VA: The Media Center at the American Press Institute. Retrieved May 5, 2010: http://www.hypergene.net/wemedia/.

Boyd, A. (2003). "The web rewires the movement." *The Nation*, July 17. Retrieved May 5, 2010: http://www.thenation.com/issue/august-4-2003

Braman, S. (2002). *Defining tactical media: An historical overview*. New

York: Virtual Casebook Project, New York University. Retrieved May 5, 2010: http://www.nyu.edu/fas/projects/vcb/case_911/reverberations/braman2.html.

Brock, G. (2008). "Pencilled out." *Times Literary Supplement*, November 28, 23.

Broder, A., Kumar, R., Maghoul, F., Raghavan, P., Rajagopalan, S., Stata, R., Tomkins, A., and Wiener, J. (2000). *Graph structure in the Web*. IBM Almaden Research Center. Retrieved May 5, 2010 from the Internet Archive: http://web.archive.org/web/20000815202357/www.almaden.ibm.com/cs/k53/www9.final.

Bush, V. (1945). "As we may think." *The Atlantic*, July, 101–8. Retrieved May 5, 2010: http://www.theatlantic.com/doc/194507/bush.

Calabrese, A. (2004). "Virtual nonviolence? Civil disobedience and political violence in the information age." *Info: The Journal of Policy, Regulation and Strategy for Telecommunications*, 6(5), 326–38.

Caldwell, R. (2003). "The guru of conscientious consumption." *Toronto Globe & Mail*, January 18, R11.

Cammaerts, B. and van Audenhove, L. (2005). "Online political debate, unbounded citizenship, and the problematic nature of a transnational public sphere." *Political Communication*, 22(2), 179–96.

Carducci, V. (2006). "Culture jamming: A sociological perspective." *Journal of Consumer Culture*, 6(1), 116–38.

Carr, C. (2003). "Dow v. Thing: A free-speech infringement that's worse than censorship." *Village Voice*, January 17. Retrieved May 5, 2010: http://www.villagevoice.com/2003-01-21/news/dow-v-thing/1.

Carr, D. (2008). "Mourning old media's decline." *New York Times*, October 29, B1.

Carroll, W.K. and Hackett, R.A. (2006). "Democratic media activism through the lens of social movement theory." *Media, Culture & Society*, 28(1), 83–104.

Castells, M. (1996). *The rise of the network society. The information age: Economy, society and culture, vol. 1*. Oxford: Blackwell.

Castells, M. (1997). *The power of identity. The information age: Economy, society and culture, vol. 2*. Oxford: Blackwell.

Castells, M. (2009). *Communication power*. Oxford and New York: Oxford University Press.

Castronova, E. (2003). "On virtual economies." *Game Studies*, 3(2). Retrieved May 5, 2010: http://www.gamestudies.org/0302/castronova/.

Chadwick, A. (2006). *Internet politics: States, citizens, and new communication technologies*. New York and Oxford: Oxford University Press.

Chandler, D. (2000). *An introduction to genre theory*. Retrieved May 5, 2010: http://www.aber.ac.uk/media/Documents/intgenre/intgenre1.html.

Chavoya, C.O. (2004). "The Surveillance Camera Players." In N. Thompson and G. Sholette (eds.), *The interventionists: Users' manual for the creative disruption of everyday life*, pp. 83–6. North Adams, MA: MASS MoCA Publications, distributed by MIT Press.

Chesney, T. (2006). "An empirical examination of Wikipedia's credibility." *First Monday*, *11*(11), November 6. Retrieved October 17, 2009: http://firstmonday.org/issues/issue11_11/chesney/index.html.

Chollet, L. (2004). *Les situationnistes: L'utopie incarnée*. Paris: Gallimard.

Ciffolilli, A. (2003). "Phantom authority, self-selective recruitment and retention of members in virtual communities: the case of Wikipedia." *First Monday*, 8(12). Retrieved May 5, 2010: http://firstmonday.org/htbin/cgiwrap/bin/ojs/index.php/fm/issue/view/165.

Cleaver, H. (1994). "The Chiapas uprising." *Studies in Political Economy*, *44*, 141–57.

Cleaver, H. (1998). *The Zapatistas and the international circulation of struggle: Lessons suggested and problems raised*. Paper presented at the INET98 Conference, Geneva, Switzerland, July. Retrieved August 8, 2010: http://www.eco.utexas.edu/faculty/Cleaver/lessons.html.

Cohen, J.E. (2003). "DRM and privacy." *Berkeley Technology Law Journal*, 18, 575–617.

Cohen, J.E. (2006). "Pervasively distributed copyright enforcement." *Georgetown Law Journal*, 95(1), 1–48.

Cohen, N. (2009). "Slowing down wiki writers." *New York Times*, August 25, B1, B5.

Coleman, J.S. (1990). *Foundations of social theory*. Cambridge, MA: The Belknap Press of Harvard University Press.

Coleman, S. (2005). "The lonely citizen: Indirect representation in the age of networks." *Political Communication*, 22(2), 197–214.

Collins, J. (1995). *Architectures of excess: Cultural life in the information age*. London: Routledge.

Couldry, N. (2008). "Mediatization or mediation? Alternative understandings of the emergent space of digital storytelling." *New Media & Society*, 10(3), 373–91.

Cramer, F. (2009). "Ubermorgen.com's hyperactive melancholy." In A. Ludovico (ed.), *Ubermorgen.com: Media hacking vs. conceptual art/Hans Bernhard and LIZVLX*, pp. 186–7. Basel: Christoph Merian Verlag.

Critical Art Ensemble (1994). "Nomadic power and cultural resistance." In *The electronic disturbance*, pp. 11–30. New York: Autonomedia. Retrieved May 5, 2010: http://www.critical-art.net/books/ted/.

Crowston, K. and Williams, M. (2000). "Reproduced and emergent genres of communication on the World Wide Web." *The Information Society*, 16, 201–15.

Crozier, M. (1996). "Alain Touraine: A pioneer in the new French sociology." In J. Clark and M. Diani (eds.), *Alain Touraine*, pp. 9–16. London and Washington, DC: Falmer Press. (Originally published by Routledge, transferred to digital printing 2006).

Cubitt, S. (2006). "Tactical media." In K. Sarikakis and D.K. Thussu (eds.), *Ideologies of the Internet*, pp. 35–46. Cresskill, NJ: Hampton Press.

Cudmore, J. (2009). *Who's behind the hoax?* CBC News, December 14. Retrieved May 5, 2010: http://www.cbc.ca/politics/insidepolitics/2009/12/whos-behind-the-hoax.html.

Dachy, M. (2006). *Dada: The revolt of art* (trans. L. Nash). New York: Abrams. (Originally published as *Dada, la révolte de l'art*. Paris: Gallimard, 2005.)

Dahlgren, P. (2005). "The Internet, public spheres, and political communication: Dispersion and deliberation." *Political Communication*, 22(2), 147–62.

Dalby, A. (2007). "Wikipedia(s) on the language map of the world." *English Today* 90, 23(2), 3–8.

Darnton, R. (2009). *The case for books: Past, present and future.* New York: PublicAffairs.

Dawkins, R. (1976). *The selfish gene.* Oxford: Oxford University Press.

Debord, G. (1981a). "Theory of the dérive." In K. Knabb (ed. and trans.), *Situationist International anthology*, pp. 50–4. Berkeley, CA: Bureau of Public Secrets. (Originally published in *Internationale Situationniste*, 2, 1958.)

Debord, G. (1981b). "Detournement as negation and prelude." In K. Knabb (ed. and trans.), *Situationist International anthology*, pp. 55–6. Berkeley, CA: Bureau of Public Secrets. (Originally published in *Internationale Situationniste*, 3, 1959.)

Debord, G. (1981c). "Instructions for taking up arms." In K. Knabb (ed. and trans.), *Situationist International anthology*, pp. 63–4. Berkeley, CA: Bureau of Public Secrets. (Originally published in *Internationale Situationniste*, 6, 1961.)

Debord, G. (1994). *The society of the spectacle* (trans. D. Nicholson-Smith). New York: Zone Books. (Originally published as *La société du spectacle*. Paris: Buchet-Chastel, 1967.)

Debord, G. (2003). *In girum imus nocte et consumimur igni* (film soundtrack). Trans. K. Knabb (from the original film, released 1978). Retrieved May 5, 2010: http://www.bopsecrets.org/SI/debord.films/ingirum.htm.

Debord, G. and Wolman, G.J. (1981). "Methods of detournement." In K. Knabb (ed. and trans.), *Situationist International anthology*, pp. 8–14. Berkeley, CA: Bureau of Public Secrets. (Originally published in *Les Lèvres Nues*, 8, May 1956.)

Deleuze, G. and Guattari, F. (1987). *A thousand plateaus: Capitalism and schizophrenia* (trans. B. Massumi). Minneapolis: University of Minnesota Press. (Originally published as *Mille plateaux*, Vol. 2 of *Capitalisme et schizophrénie*. Paris: Les Éditions de Minuit, 1980.)

Delio, M. (2002). "DMCA: Dow what it wants to do." *Wired*, December 31. Retrieved August 1, 2010: http://www.wired.com/politics/law/news/2002/12/57011.

della Porta, D. and Diani, M. (2006). *Social movements: An introduction* (2nd edn). Malden, MA and Oxford: Blackwell.

DeLong, J.B. (2003). "Any text. Anytime. Anywhere. (Any volunteers?) The mechanics of a universal library are simple. The tricky part: Harnessing the free labor." *Wired* 11.2. Retrieved January 14, 2010: http://www.wired.com/wired/archive/11.02/view.html?pg=5.

Dery, M. (1990). "The Merry Pranksters and the art of the hoax." *New York Times*, December 23. Retrieved August 16, 2010: http://www.nytimes.com/1990/12/23/arts/the-merry-pranksters-and-the-art-of-the-hoax.html.

Dery, M. (1993). "Culture jamming: Hacking, slashing and sniping in the empire of signs." Westfield, NJ: *Open Magazine Pamphlet Series*. Retrieved May 5, 2010: http://www.markdery.com/archives/books/culture_jamming/#000005#more.

Deuze, M. (2001). "Online journalism: Modelling the first generation of news media on the World Wide Web." *First Monday*, 6(10). Retrieved September 15, 2009: http://firstmonday.org/issues/issue6_10/deuze/index.html

Deuze, M. (2003). "The web and its journalisms: Considering the consequences of different types of newsmedia online." *New Media & Society*, 5(2), 203–30.

Deuze, M. (2006). "Participation, remediation, bricolage: Considering principal components of a digital culture." *The Information Society*, 22(2), 63–76.

Diani, M. (2003). "Networks and social movements: A research programme." In M. Diani and D. McAdam (eds.), *Social movements and networks: Relational approaches to collective action*, pp. 299–319. Oxford and New York: Oxford University Press.

Diani, M. and Eyerman, R. (1992). "The study of collective action: Introductory remarks." In M. Diani and R. Eyerman (eds.), *Studying collective action*, pp. 1–21. London and Newbury Park, CA: Sage.

Dickerman, L. (2005). "Introduction." In *Dada: Zurich, Berlin, Hannover, Cologne, New York, Paris* (with essays by B. Doherty, D. Dietrich, S.T. Kriebel, M.R. Taylor, J. Mileaf, and M.S. Witkovsky), pp. 1–15. (Catalogue of an exhibition held at the Centre Pompidou, Paris, October 5, 2005–January 9, 2006; the National Gallery of Art, Washington, February

19–May 14, 2006; and the Museum of Modern Art, New York, June 18–September 11, 2006.) Washington, DC: National Gallery of Art.

Dillon, A. and Gushrowski, B.A. (2000). "Genres and the Web: Is the personal home page the first uniquely digital genre?" *Journal of the American Society for Information Science*, 51(2), 202–5.

Downey, J. and Fenton, N. (2003). "New media, counter publicity and the public sphere." *New Media & Society*, 5(2), 185–202.

Downing, J. (2003). "The independent media center movement and the anarchist socialist tradition." In N. Couldry and J. Curran (eds.), *Contesting media power: Alternative media in a networked world*, pp. 243–57. Lanham, MD: Rowman & Littlefield.

Downing, J. (2008). "Social movement theories and alternative media: An evaluation and critique." *Communication, Culture & Critique*, 1(1), 40–50.

Downing, J., with Ford, T.V., Gil, G., and Stein, L. (2001). *Radical media: Rebellious communication and social movements*. London: Sage.

Duguid, P. (2006). "Limits of self-organization: Peer production and 'laws of quality.'" *First Monday*, 11(10). Retrieved May 5, 2010: http://first-monday.org/htbin/cgiwrap/bin/ojs/index.php/fm/issue/view/204.

Durlak, J.T. (1987). "A typology for interactive media." In M.L. McLaughlin (ed.), *Communication Yearbook 10*, pp. 743–56. Newbury Park, CA: Sage.

Dutton, W.H. (2009). "The fifth estate emerging through the network of networks." *Prometheus*, 27(1), 1–15.

Eco, U. (1986). "Towards a semiological guerrilla warfare." In *Travels in hyperreality* (trans. W. Weaver), pp. 135–50. New York: Harcourt Brace Jovanovich.

Economist (2006a). "The wiki principle (in: Among the audience: A survey of new media)." April 22, 14–15.

Economist (2006b). "Who killed the newspaper?" August 26, 9–10.

Economist (2006c). "More media, less news." August 26, 52–4.

Economist (2008a). "Nomads at last: A special report on mobile telecoms." April 12, Technology Quarterly section, 3–5.

Economist (2008b). "The broadband myth." May 23.

Egbert, D.D. (1970). *Social radicalism and the arts: Western Europe*. New York: Alfred A. Knopf (a Borzoi Book).

Eschenfelder, K.R. (2005). "Chasing down the social meaning of DeCSS: Investigating the Internet posting of DVD circumvention software." *Bulletin of the American Society for Information Science & Technology*, 31(5), 21–4.

Eschenfelder, K.R. and Desai, A.C. (2004). "Software as protest: The unexpected resiliency of U.S.-based DeCSS posting and linking." *The Information Society*, 20(2), 101–16.

Eyerman, R. (1992). "Modernity and social movements." In H. Haferkamp and N.J. Smelser (eds.), *Social change and modernity*, pp. 37–54. Berkeley, Los Angeles, and Oxford: University of California Press.

Fallis, D. (2008). "Toward an epistemology of Wikipedia." *Journal of the American Society for Information Science and Technology*, 59(10), 1662–74.

Fallis, D. (2009). "Introduction: The epistemology of mass collaboration." *Episteme*, 6(1), 1–7.

Farb, S.E. (2006). *Negotiating use, persistence and archiving: A study of academic library and publisher perspectives on licensing digital resources.* Unpublished Ph.D. dissertation. Los Angeles, CA: University of California, Los Angeles, Department of Information Studies.

Flanagin, A.J., Stohl, C., and Bimber, B. (2006). "Modeling the structure of collective action." *Communication Monographs*, 73(1), 29–54.

Ford, S. (2005). *The Situationist International: A user's guide.* London: Black Dog Publishing.

Ford, T.V. and Gil, G. (2001). "Radical internet use." In J. Downing, with T.V. Ford, G. Gil, and L. Stein, *Radical media: Rebellious communication and social movements*, pp. 201–34. Thousand Oaks, CA and London: Sage.

Fornäs, J. (2002). "Passages across thresholds: Into the borderlands of mediation." *Convergence*, 8(4), 89–106.

Foucault, M. (1986). "Of other spaces." *Diacritics*, 16(1), 22–7.

Foucault, M. (2002). *The order of things: An archaeology of the human sciences.* Oxford and New York: Routledge Classics. (Originally published as *Les mots et les choses*. Paris: Éditions Gallimard, 1966.)

Frank, T. (1997). "Why Johnny can't dissent." In T. Frank and M. Weiland (eds.), *Commodify your dissent: The business of culture in the new Gilded Age*, pp. 31–45. New York: W.W. Norton.

Frank, T. (2000). "New consensus for old: Cultural studies from left to right." In *One market under God: Extreme capitalism, market populism, and the end of economic democracy*, pp. 276–306. New York: Doubleday.

Frank, T. and Mulcahey, D. (1997). "Consolidated Deviance, Inc." In T. Frank and M. Weiland (eds.), *Commodify your dissent: The business of culture in the new Gilded Age*, pp. 72–8. New York: W.W. Norton.

Freedman, A., and Medway, P. (eds.) (1994). *Genre and the new rhetoric.* London: Taylor & Francis.

Gamson, J. (2003). "Gay Media, Inc.: Media structures, the new gay conglomerates, and collective sexual identities." In M. McCaughey and M.D. Ayers (eds.), *Cyberactivism: Online activism in theory and practice*, pp. 255–78. New York and London: Routledge.

Garcia, D. and Lovink, G. (1997). *The ABC of tactical media.* Retrieved May 5, 2010: http://subsol.c3.hu/subsol_2/contributors2/garcia-lovinktext.html.

Garrett, R.K. (2006). "Protest in an information society: A review of literature on social movements and new ICTs." *Information, Communication & Society*, 9(2), 202–24.

Garrido, M. and Halavais, A. (2003). "Mapping networks of support for the Zapatista movement: Applying social-networks analysis to study contemporary social movements." In M. McCaughey and M.D. Ayers (eds.), *Cyberactivism: Online activism in theory and practice*, pp. 165–84. New York and London: Routledge.

Getty Center (2006). *Agitated images: John Heartfield and German photomontage, 1920–1938*. Exhibition at the Getty Center Research Institute, February 21–June 25. Los Angeles: The Getty Center. Abstract and images from the exhibition online, retrieved May 5, 2010: http://www.getty.edu/art/exhibitions/heartfield/.

Giddens, A. (1979). *Central problems in social theory: Action, structure and contradiction in social analysis*. Berkeley and Los Angeles: University of California Press.

Giddens, A. (1984). *The constitution of society: Outline of the theory of structuration*. Berkeley and Los Angeles: University of California Press.

Giles, J. (2005). "Internet encyclopaedias go head to head." *Nature*, 438(15), 900–1.

Gillespie, T. (2007). *Wired shut: Copyright and the shape of digital culture*. Cambridge, MA: MIT Press.

Gladwell, M. (2002). *The tipping point: How little things can make a big difference*. New York: Random House.

Glazer, M. (2006). "Your guide to citizen journalism." *PBS Mediashift* (weblog hosted by the Public Broadcasting Service), September 27. Retrieved May 5, 2010: http://www.pbs.org/mediashift/2006/09/your-guide-to-citizen-journalism270.html.

Godwin, M. (1999). "Who's a journalist? – II." *Media Studies Journal*, 13(2), 38–42.

Golding, P. and Murdock, G. (1978). "Theories of communication and theories of society." *Communication Research*, 5(3), 320–9.

Goldman, A.I. (1999). *Knowledge in a social world*. New York and Oxford: Oxford University Press.

Goodchild, M.F. (2004). "The Alexandria Digital Library Project." *D-Lib Magazine*, 10(5). Retrieved May 5, 2010: http://www.dlib.org/dlib/may04/goodchild/05goodchild.html.

Goodrum, A. and Manion, M. (2000). "The ethics of hacktivism." *Journal of Information Ethics*, 9(2), 51–9.

Graham, M. (2000). "The threshold of the information age: Radio, television and motion pictures mobilize the nation." In A.D. Chandler, Jr. and J.W. Cortada (eds.), *A nation transformed by information*, pp. 137–76. Oxford and New York: Oxford University Press.

Graham, P. (2005). *What business can learn from open source.* Essay based on a talk at OSCON (O'Reilly Open Source Convention), August 1–5, Portland, OR. Retrieved May 5, 2010: http://paulgraham.com/opensource.html.

Gray, C. (ed. and trans.) (1998). *Leaving the 20th century: The incomplete work of the Situationist International.* London: Rebel Press. (Originally published by Free Fall Press, 1974.)

Guerrero, F., Myerson, S., and Jain, V. (2003). "The art of confusion." (Interview with Frank Guerrero of ®™ark.) In J. Richardson (ed.), *Anarchitexts: A Subsol Anthology*, pp. 129–33. Brooklyn, NY: Autonomedia.

Gumpert, G. (1988). "Linguistic character and a theory of mediation." In J.A. Anderson (ed.), *Communication Yearbook 11*, pp. 230–6. Newbury Park, CA: Sage.

Gumpert, G. and Cathcart, R. (1986) *Inter/Media: Interpersonal communication in a media world* (3rd edn). Oxford and New York: Oxford University Press.

Gumpert, G. and Cathcart, R. (1990) "A theory of mediation." In B.D. Ruben and L.A. Lievrouw (eds.), *Mediation, information, and communication: Information & behavior, vol. 3*, pp. 21–36. New Brunswick, NJ: Transaction.

Gusfield, J.R. (1994). "The reflexivity of social movements: Collective behavior and mass society theory revisited." In E. Laraña, H. Johnston, and J.R. Gusfield (eds.), *New social movements: From ideology to identity*, pp. 58–78. Philadelphia, PA: Temple University Press.

Habermas, J. (1981). "New social movements." *Telos*, 49, 33–7.

Hakken, D. (1993). "Computing and social change: New technology and workplace transformation, 1980–1990." *Annual Review of Anthropology*, 22, 107–32.

Hakken, D. and Andrews, B. (1993). *Computing myths, class realities: An ethnography of technology and working people in Sheffield, England.* Boulder, CO: Westview Press.

Halleck, D. (2002). *Hand-held visions.* New York: Fordham University Press.

Halleck, D. (2003). "Indymedia: Building an international activist Internet network." *Media Development*, 12–16. Retrieved May 5, 2010: http://newmedia.yeditepe.edu.tr/pdfs/isimd_04/12.pdf.

Hammond, T., Hannay, T., Lund, B., and Scott, J. (2005). "Social bookmarking tools (I)." *D-Lib Magazine*, 11(4). Retrieved May 5, 2010: http://www.dlib.org//dlib/april05/hammond/04hammond.html.

Hampton, K.N. (2003). "Grieving for a lost network: Collective action in a wired suburb." *The Information Society*, 19, 417–28.

Hardt, M. and Negri, A. (2000). *Empire.* Cambridge, MA: Harvard University Press.

Hardt, M. and Negri, A. (2002). "Marx's mole is dead! Globalization and communication." *Eurozine,* February 13. Retrieved September 1, 2009: http://www.eurozine.com/articles/2002-01-13-hardtnegri-en. html.

Hardt, M. and Negri, A. (2004). *Multitude: war and democracy in the age of empire.* New York: Penguin Books.

Harold, C. (2004). "Pranking rhetoric: 'Culture jamming' as media activism." *Critical Studies in Media Communication,* 21(3), 189–211.

Hartmann, M. (2004). *Technologies and utopias: The cyberflâneur and the experience of "being online."* Munich: R. Fischer.

Hawkins, R.P., Wiemann, J.M., and Pingree, S. (eds.) (1988). *Advancing communication science: Merging mass media and interpersonal processes.* Newbury Park, CA: Sage.

Hebdige, D. (1979). *Subculture: The meaning of style.* London and New York: Routledge.

Helfand, G. (2001). "Q&A with RTMark, media activists: Raging against the corporate machine." *San Francisco Chronicle/SFGate,* June 12. Retrieved May 5, 2010: http://www.sfgate.com/cgi-bin/article.cgi?file=/gate/archive/2001/06/12/rtmark.DTL.

Helft, M. (2010). "Despite changes, many still oppose Google Books deal." *New York Times,* January 28. Retrieved May 10, 2010: http://bits. blogs.nytimes.com/2010/01/28/despite-changes-many-still-oppose-google-books-deal/.

Henning, J. (2003). "The blogging iceberg: Of 4.12 million weblogs, most little seen and quickly abandoned." *Bnet business blog,* October 6. Retrieved May 5, 2010: http://findarticles.com/p/articles/mi_m0EIN/is_2003_Oct_6/ai_108559565/.

Herring, S. (2004). "Slouching toward the ordinary: Current trends in computer-mediated communication." *New Media & Society,* 6(1), 26–36.

Holmes, B. (2007). "Do-it-yourself geopolitics: Cartographies of art in the world." In B. Stimson and G. Sholette (eds.), *Collectivism after modernism: The art of social imagination after 1945,* pp. 272–93. Minneapolis: University of Minnesota Press.

Hopkins, D. (2004). *Dada and Surrealism: A very short introduction.* Oxford and New York: Oxford University Press.

Howe, J. (2008). *Crowdsourcing: Why the power of the crowd is driving the future of business.* New York: Crown Business.

Huesca, R. (2001). "Conceptual contributions of new social movements to development communication research." *Communication Theory,* 11(4), 415–33.

Hughes, R. (1991). *The shock of the new* (rev. edn). New York: Alfred A. Knopf.

Hyde, G. (2002). "Independent Media Centers: Cyber-subversion and the alternative press." *First Monday*, 7(4). Retrieved May 5, 2010: http://first-monday.org/htbin/cgiwrap/bin/ojs/index.php/fm/issue/view/144.

Irr, C. (2003). "On ®™ark, or the limits of intellectual property activism." In M. Bousquet and K. Wills (eds.), *The politics of information: The electronic mediation of social change*, pp. 195–203. Alt-X Press/Electronic Book Review. Retrieved May 5, 2010: http://www.altx.com/ebooks/download.cfm/infopol.pdf.

Ito, M. (2009). "Mobilizing the imagination in everyday play: The case of Japanese media mixes." In L.A. Lievrouw and S. Livingstone (eds.), *Sage Benchmarks in Communication: New Media, vol. 3*, pp. 384–403. London: Sage. (Originally published in K. Drotner and S. Livingstone (eds.), *The international handbook of children, media and culture*, pp. 397–412, London: Sage, 2008.

Jankowski, N.W. and Jansen, M. (2003). *Indymedia: Exploration of an alternative Internet-based source of movement news.* Paper presented at the Digital News, Social Change and Globalization Conference, Hong Kong Baptist University, December 11–12. Retrieved May 5, 2010: http://www.hkbu.edu.hk/~jour/DN2003/Nicholas.html.

Jappe, A. (1999). *Guy Debord* (trans. D. Nicholson-Smith, with foreword by T.J. Clark and new afterword by the author). Berkeley and Los Angeles: University of California Press.

Jeanneney, J.-N. (2007). *Google and the myth of universal knowledge: A view from Europe.* Chicago and London: University of Chicago Press.

Jenkins, H. (2006). *Convergence culture: Where old and new media collide.* New York: New York University Press.

Jenkins, H. and Thorburn, D. (2003). "Introduction: the digital revolution, the informed citizen, and the culture of democracy." In H. Jenkins and D. Thorburn (eds.), *Democracy and new media*, pp. 1–17. Cambridge, MA: MIT Press.

Johnston, H., Laraña, E., and Gusfield, J.R. (1994). "Identities, grievances, and new social movements." In E. Laraña, H. Johnston, and J.R. Gusfield (eds.), *New social movements: From ideology to identity*, pp. 3–35. Philadelphia, PA: Temple University Press.

Johnston, H. and Noakes, J.A. (2005). *Frames of protest: Social movements and the framing perspective.* Lanham, MD: Rowman & Littlefield.

Jones, S.G. (1998). "Information, internet, and community: Notes toward an understanding of community in the information age." In S.G. Jones (ed.), *Cybersociety 2.0: Revisiting computer-mediated communication and community*, pp. 1–34. Thousand Oaks, CA: Sage.

Jordan, T. and Taylor, P.A. (2004). *Hacktivism and cyberwars: Rebels with a cause?* London: Routledge.

Jouet, J. (1994). "Communication and mediation." *Reseaux*, 2(1), 73–90.

Juris, J.S. (2005). "The new digital media and activist networking within anti-corporate globalization movements." *Annals of the American Academy of Political and Social Science*, 597, 189–208.

Juris, J.S. (2008). *Networking futures: The movements against corporate globalization*. Durham, NC: Duke University Press.

Kahn, R. and Kellner, D. (2003). "Internet subcultures and oppositional politics." In D. Muggleton and R. Weinzierl (eds.), *The post-subcultures reader*, pp. 299–314. Oxford and New York: Berg.

Kahn, R. and Kellner, D. (2004). "New media and internet activism: From the 'Battle of Seattle' to blogging." *New Media & Society*, 6(1), 87–95.

Kahn, R. and Kellner, D. (2005). "Oppositional politics and the Internet: A critical/reconstructive approach." *Cultural Politics*, 1(1), 75–100.

Katz, E. (2006). "Introduction to the Transaction edition: Lazarsfeld's legacy – The power of limited effects." In E. Katz and P.F. Lazarsfeld, *Personal influence: The part played by people in the flow of mass communications* (2nd edn), pp. xv–xxvii. New Brunswick, NJ and London: Transaction. (Originally published by The Free Press, 1955.)

Katz, E. and Lazarsfeld, P.F. (2006). *Personal influence: The part played by people in the flow of mass communications* (2nd edn). New Brunswick, NJ and London: Transaction. (Originally published by Free Press, 1955.)

Kaufmann, V. (2006). *Guy Debord: Revolution in the service of poetry* (trans. R. Bononno). Minneapolis: University of Minnesota Press. (Originally published as *Guy Debord: La révolution au service de la poésie*. Paris: Librairie Arthème Fayard, 2001.)

Keane, J. and Mier, P. (1989). "Editors' preface." In A. Melucci, *Nomads of the present: Social movements and individual needs in contemporary society* (ed. J. Keane and P. Mier), pp. 1–9. London: Hutchinson Radius, an imprint of Century Hutchinson Ltd.

Keck, M.E. and Sikkink, K. (1998). *Activists beyond borders: Advocacy networks in international politics*. Ithaca, NY: Cornell University Press.

Keen, A. (2007). *The cult of the amateur: How blogs, MySpace, YouTube, and the rest of today's user-generated media are destroying our economy, our culture, and our values*. New York: Doubleday.

Kelty, C. (2008). *Two bits: The cultural significance of free software and the internet*. Durham, NC: Duke University Press.

Kershaw, S. (2008). "A different way to pay for the news you want." *New York Times*, August 24, Week in Review section, p. 1.

Khamis, S. (2003). "Jamming at work: The politics and play of ®™ark."

M/C Journal, 6(3). Retrieved May 5, 2010: http://journal.media-culture. org.au/0306/04-jamming.php.

Kidd, D. (2003). "Indymedia.org: A new communications commons." In M. McCaughey and M.D. Ayers (eds.), *Cyberactivism: Online activism in theory and practice*, pp. 47–69. New York and London: Routledge.

Kittur, A., Chi, E., Pendleton, B.A., Suh, B., and Mytkowicz, T. (2007). *Power of the few vs. wisdom of the crowd: Wikipedia and the rise of the bourgeoisie*. Alt.CHI at the 25th Annual ACM Conference on Human Factors in Computing Systems (CHI '07). Retrieved August 9, 2010: http:// www.parc.com/publication/1749/power-of-the-few-vs-wisdom-of-the-crowd.html.

Kittur, A. and Kraut, R.E. (2008). "Harnessing the wisdom of crowds in Wikipedia: Quality through coordination." *CSCW '08: Proceedings of the ACM 2008 Conference on Computer Supported Cooperative Work*, San Diego, CA, November 8–12, pp. 37–46.

Klandermans, B. (1991). "New social movements and resource mobilization: The European and the American approach revisited." In D. Rucht (Ed.), *Research on social movements: The state of the art in Western Europe and the USA*, pp. 17–44. Frankfurt am Main and Boulder, CO: Campus Verlag/Westview Press.

Laermans, R. and Gielen, P. (2007). "The archive of the digital an-archive." *Image & Narrative*, 17. Retrieved May 5, 2010: http://www.imageandnarrative.be/digital_archive/laermans_gielen.htm.

Langman, L. (2005). "From virtual public spheres to global justice: A critical theory of internetworked social movements." *Sociological Theory*, 23(1), 42–74.

Lasica, J.D. (2003). "What is participatory journalism?" *Online Journalism Review*, August 7. Retrieved May 5, 2010: http://www.ojr.org/ojr/workplace/1060217106.php

Lasn, K. (2000). *Culture jam: How to reverse America's suicidal consumer binge – and why we must*. New York: HarperCollins.

Latour, B. (2005). *Reassembling the social: An introduction to actor-network theory*. Oxford: Oxford University Press.

Law, J. and Hassard, J. (1999). *Actor network theory and after*. Oxford: Blackwell/The Sociological Review.

Lefebvre, H. (1971). *Everyday life in the modern world* (trans. S. Rabinovitch). New York: Harper & Row. (Originally published as *Vie quotidienne dans le mode moderne*. Paris: Gallimard "Idées," 1968.)

Leibowitz, B. (2003). "Hack, hacker, hacking." In T.F. Peterson, *Nightwork: A history of hacks and pranks at MIT*, p. 4. Cambridge, MA: MIT Press.

Lemann, N. (2006). "Amateur hour: Journalism without journalists." *The New Yorker*, August 7 and 14, 44–9.

Leonard, A. (1999). "Open-source journalism." *Salon.com*, October 8. Retrieved May 5, 2010: http://www.salon.com/tech/log/1999/10/08/geek_journalism/.

Lessig, L. (2001). *The future of ideas*. New York: Random House.

Lévy, P. (1999). *Collective intelligence: Mankind's emerging world in cyberspace* (trans. R. Bononno). New York and London: Plenum Trade.

Levy, S. (1984). *Hackers: Heroes of the computer revolution*. Garden City, NY: Anchor/Doubleday.

Lievrouw, L.A. (1994). "Information resources and democracy: Understanding the paradox." *Journal of the American Society for Information Science*, 45(6), 350–7.

Lievrouw, L.A. (1998). "Our own devices: Heterotopic communication, discourse and culture in the information society." *The Information Society*, 14(2), 83–96.

Lievrouw, L.A. (2001). "New media and the 'pluralization of life-worlds': A role for information in social differentiation." *New Media & Society*, 3(1), 7–28.

Lievrouw, L.A. (2004). "What's changed about new media? Introduction to the fifth anniversary issue." *New Media & Society*, 6(1), 9–15.

Lievrouw, L.A. (2006a). "Oppositional and activist new media: Remediation, reconfiguration, participation." In I. Wagner and J. Blomberg (eds.), *Proceedings of the Participatory Design Conference '06*, Trento, Italy, July 31–August 5, pp. 115–24. Seattle: Computer Professionals for Social Responsibility.

Lievrouw, L.A. (2006b). "New media design and development: Diffusion of innovations v. social shaping of technology." In L.A. Lievrouw and S. Livingstone (eds.), *Handbook of new media* (updated student edn), pp. 246–65. London: Sage.

Lievrouw, L.A. (2008). "Oppositional new media, ownership, and access: From consumption to reconfiguration and remediation." In R.E. Rice (ed.), *Media ownership: Research and regulation*, pp. 391–416. Cresskill, NJ: Hampton Press.

Lievrouw, L.A. (2009). "New media, mediation, and communication study." *Information, Communication & Society*, 12(3), 303–25.

Lievrouw, L.A. and Livingstone, S. (2002). "Introduction." In L.A. Lievrouw and S. Livingstone (eds.), *Handbook of new media* (1st edn), pp. 1–15. London: Sage.

Lievrouw, L.A. and Livingstone, S. (2006). "Introduction to the updated student edition." In L.A. Lievrouw and S. Livingstone (eds.), *Handbook of new media* (updated student edn), pp. 1–14. London: Sage.

Lievrouw, L.A. and Ruben, B.D. (1990) "Introduction to Part I: Theories of mediation – Views of the communication process." In B.D. Ruben and L.A. Lievrouw (eds.), *Mediation, information and communication: Information & behavior, vol. 3*, pp. 3–7. New Brunswick, NJ: Transaction.

Lih, A. (2004). *Wikipedia as participatory journalism: Reliable sources? Metrics for evaluating collaborative media as a news resource.* Paper presented at the 5th International Symposium for Online Journalism, Austin, TX, April 16–17. Retrieved May 5, 2010: http://citeseerx.ist.psu.edu/viewdoc/download?doi=10.1.1.117.9104&rep=rep1&type=pdf.

Lippard, L. (ed.) (1971). "Introduction." In L. Lippard (ed.), *Dadas on art: Tzara, Arp, Duchamp, and others*, pp. 1–12. Englewood Cliffs, NJ: Prentice-Hall.

Litman, J. (2001). *Digital copyright*. Amherst, NY: Prometheus Books.

Livingstone, S. (1990). *Making sense of television: The psychology of audience interpretation*. London: Pergamon.

Livingstone, S. (2009). "On the mediation of everything." *Journal of Communication*, 59(1), 1–18.

Lovink, G. (1997). "The data dandy and sovereign media: An introduction to the media theory of ADILKNO." *Leonardo*, 30(1), 57–65.

Lovink, G. (2008). *Zero comments: Blogging and critical Internet culture.* New York: Routledge.

Lovink, G. and Richardson, J. (2001). *Notes on sovereign media.* Retrieved May 5, 2010: http://subsol.c3.hu/subsol_2/contributorso/lovink-richardsontext.html.

Lovink, G. and Rossiter, N. (2007a). "Proposals for creative research: Introduction to the MyCreativity Reader." In G. Lovink and N. Rossiter (eds.), *MyCreativity reader: A critique of creative industries*, pp. 9–16. Amsterdam: Institute of Network Cultures. Retrieved May 5, 2010: http://networkcultures.org/wpmu/portal/archive/.

Lovink, G. and Rossiter, N. (eds.) (2007b). *MyCreativity reader: A critique of creative industries.* Amsterdam: Institute of Network Cultures. Retrieved May 5, 2010: http://networkcultures.org/wpmu/portal/archive/.

Ludlow, P. (ed.) (2001). *Crypto anarchy, cyberstates, and pirate utopias.* Cambridge, MA: MIT Press.

Ludovico, A. (ed.) (2009). *Ubermorgen.com: Media hacking vs. conceptual art/Hans Bernhard and LIZVLX*. Basel: Christoph Merian Verlag.

Lunenfeld, P. (forthcoming). *The secret war between uploading and downloading: How the computer became our culture machine.* Cambridge, MA: MIT Press. (Excerpt retrieved May 5, 2010: http://www.peterlunenfeld.com/publications/.)

McAdam, D. (2003). "Beyond structural analysis: Toward a more dynamic understanding of social movements." In M. Diani and D. McAdam (eds.), *Social movements and networks: Relational approaches to collective action*, pp. 281–98. Oxford and New York: Oxford University Press.

McAdam, D., McCarthy, J.D., and Zald, M.N. (1988). "Social movements." In N. Smelser (ed.), *Handbook of sociology*, pp. 696–737. Newbury Park, CA and London: Sage.

MacBride Commission (2004). *Many voices, one world: Toward a new, more just, and more efficient world information and communication order*. Report by the International Commission for the Study of Communication Problems for UNESCO. (Introduction by A. Calabrese.) Lanham, MD: Rowman & Littlefield. (Originally published by the United Nations Educational, Scientific, and Cultural Organization [UNESCO], Unipub, and Kogan Page, 1980.)

McCaughey, M. and Ayers, M.D. (eds.) (2003). *Cyberactivism: Online activism in theory and practice*. New York and London: Routledge.

McDonough, T. (2002). "Introduction: Ideology and the Situationist utopia." In T. McDonough (ed.), *Guy Debord and the Situationist International: Texts and documents*, pp. ix–xx. Cambridge, MA: MIT Press (an October Book).

McHenry, R. (2004). "The faith-based encyclopedia." *TCS Daily*, November 15. Retrieved May 5, 2010: http://www.tcsdaily.com/article.aspx?id=111504A.

MacLeod, R. (ed.) (2004). *The Library of Alexandria: Centre of learning in the ancient world*. London: I.B. Tauris & Co.

McLeod, K. (2005). *Freedom of expression®: Overzealous copyright bozos and other enemies of creativity*. New York: Doubleday.

McQuail, D. (2005). *McQuail's mass communications theory* (5th edn). London: Sage.

Madden, M., Fox, S., Smith, A., and Vitak, J. (2007). *Digital footprints: Online identity management and search in the age of transparency*. Washington, DC: Pew Internet and American Life Project, December 16. Retrieved May 1, 2010: http://www.pewinternet.org.

Magnus, P.D. (2009). "On trusting Wikipedia." *Episteme*, 6(1), 74–90.

Maher, V. (2005). *Citizen media is dead*. Blog posting, May 8. Retrieved May 5, 2010: http://www.vincentmaher.com/?p=400.

Manovich, L. (2007). *What comes after remix?* Retrieved May 5, 2010: http://manovich.net/DOCS/remix_2007_2.doc.

Marcus, G. (1989). *Lipstick traces: A secret history of the twentieth century*. Cambridge, MA: Harvard University Press.

Marcus, G. (2002). "The long walk of the Situationist International." In T. McDonough (ed.), *Guy Debord and the Situationist International: Texts and documents*, pp. 1–20. Cambridge, MA: MIT Press (an October Book).

Markoff, J. (2002). "Protesting the Big Brother lens, Little Brother turns an eye blind." *New York Times*, October 7, C1.

Marlow, C., Naaman, M., Boyd, D., and Davis, M. (2006). "HT06, tagging paper, taxonomy, Flickr, academic article, ToRead." In *Proceedings of the 17th ACM Conference on Hypertext and Hypermedia*, Odense, Denmark, pp. 31–40. Washington, DC: Association for Computing Machinery. Retrieved May 1, 2010: http://doi.acm.org/10.1145/1149941.1149949/.

Martín-Barbero, J. (1993). *Communication, culture and hegemony: From the media to mediations* (trans. E. Fox and R.A. White). London and Newbury Park, CA: Sage.

Martín-Barbero, J. (2004). "Cultural change: The perception of media and the mediation of its images." *Television & New Media*, 4(1), 85–106.

Martín-Barbero, J. (2006). "A Latin American perspective on communication/cultural mediation." *Global Media & Communication*, 2(3), 279–97.

Mattus, M. (2009). "Wikipedia – free and reliable? Aspects of a collaboratively shaped encyclopedia." *Nordicom Review*, 30(1), 155–71.

May, T.C. (2001). "Crypto anarchy and virtual communities." In P. Ludlow (ed.), *Crypto anarchy, cyberstates, and pirate utopias*, pp. 65–79. Cambridge, MA: MIT Press.

Meikle, G. (2000). "gwbush.com: Tactical media strike." *M/C Reviews*, April 12. Retrieved May 5, 2010: http://reviews.media-culture.org.au/modules.php?name=News&file=article&sid=1750.

Meikle, G. (2002). *Future active: Media activism and the Internet.* London and New York: Routledge, in association with Pluto Press Australia.

Melucci, A. (1980). "The new social movements: A theoretical approach." *Social Science Information*, 19, 199–226.

Melucci, A. (1989). *Nomads of the present: Social movements and individual needs in contemporary society* (ed. J. Keane and P. Mier). London: Hutchinson Radius, an imprint of Century Hutchinson Ltd.

Melucci, A. (1994). "A strange kind of newness: What's 'new' in new social movements?" In E. Laraña, H. Johnston, and J.R. Gusfield (eds.), *New social movements: From ideology to identity*, pp. 101–30. Philadelphia, PA: Temple University Press.

Melucci, A. (1996). *Challenging codes: Collective action in the information age.* Cambridge: Cambridge University Press.

Mentor [L. Blankenship] (1986). The conscience of a hacker. *Phrack*, 1(7), phile 3. Retrieved April 15, 2010: http://www.phrack.org/issues.html?issue=7&id=3&mode=txt.

Meyer, T.P. (1988) "On mediated communication theory: The rise of format." In J.A. Anderson (ed.), *Communication Yearbook 11*, pp. 224–9. Newbury Park, CA: Sage.

Miller, C.R. (1984). "Genre as social action." *Quarterly Journal of Speech*, 70, 151–67.

Miller, C.R. and Shepherd, D. (2004). "Blogging as social action: A genre analysis of the weblog." In L. Gurak, S. Antonijevic, L. Johnson, C. Ratliff, and J. Reyman (eds), *Into the blogosphere: Rhetoric, community, and culture of weblogs*. Retrieved May 5, 2010: http://blog.lib.umn.edu/blogosphere/blogging_as_social_action_a_genre_analysis_of_the_weblog.html.

Mirapaul, M. (2000). "Now anyone can be in the Whitney Biennial." *New York Times Online*, March 23. Retrieved May 5, 2010: http://partners.nytimes.com/library/tech/00/03/cyber/artsatlarge/23artsatlarge.html?scp=5&sq=Mirapaul%20Whitney&st=cse.

Mische, A. (2003). "Cross-talk in movements: Reconceiving the culture–network link." In M. Diani and D. McAdam (eds.), *Social movements and networks: Relational approaches to collective action*, pp. 258–80. Oxford and New York: Oxford University Press.

Mitchell, W.J.T. (2003). *Me++: The cyborg self and the networked city*. Cambridge, MA: MIT Press.

Monahan, T. (2006). "Counter-surveillance as political intervention?" *Social Semiotics*, 16(4), 515–34.

Monge, P.R. and Contractor, N.S. (2003). *Theories of communication networks*. Oxford and New York: Oxford University Press.

Moore, A.W. (2007). "Artists' collectives: Focus on New York, 1975–2000." In B. Stimson and G. Sholette (eds.), *Collectivism after modernism: The art of social imagination after 1945*, pp. 192–221. Minneapolis: University of Minnesota Press.

Moore, J.T.S. (2003). *Revolution OS*. (Video, 85 min.) Wonderview Productions. Available: http://www.revolution-os.com/.

Morris, A. (2000). "Reflections on social movement theory: Criticisms and proposals." *Contemporary Sociology*, 29(3), 445–54.

Morris, A. and Herring, C. (1987). "Theory and research in social movements: A critical review." In S. Long (ed.), *Annual Review of Political Science*, 2, pp. 138–98. Norwood, NJ: Ablex.

Morris, A. and Mueller, C.M. (eds.) (1992). *Frontiers in social movement theory*. New Haven, CT: Yale University Press.

Morris, D. (2004). "Globalization and media democracy: The case of Indymedia." In D. Schuler and P. Day (eds.), *Shaping the network society: The new role of civil society in cyberspace*, pp. 325–52. Cambridge, MA: MIT Press.

Mueller, C.M. (1992). "Building social movement theory." In A.D. Morris and C.M. Mueller (eds.), *Frontiers in social movement theory*, pp. 3–25. New Haven, CT: Yale University Press.

Naimark, M. (2002). *How to ZAP a camera: Using lasers to temporarily neutralize camera sensors.* Retrieved May 5, 2010: http://www.naimark.net/projects/zap/howto.html.

Nalle, D. (2008). "Netroots Nation: A fly on the wall." *BC: Blogcritics Magazine,* July 18. Retrieved May 5, 2010: http://blogcritics.org/archives/2008/07/18/085517.php.

Negativland (2003). "Two relationships to a cultural public domain." *Law & Contemporary Problems,* 66, 239–62. Retrieved May 5, 2010: http://law.duke.edu/journals/66LCPNegativland.

Negroponte, N. (1995). *Being digital.* New York: Alfred A. Knopf.

Newell, A. and Sproull, R.F. (1982). "Computer networks: Prospects for scientists." *Science,* 215, 843–52.

Neidhardt, F. and Rucht, D. (1991). "The analysis of social movements: The state of the art and some perspectives for further research." In D. Rucht (ed.), *Research on social movements: The state of the art in Western Europe and the USA,* pp. 421–64. Frankfurt am Main and Boulder, CO: Campus Verlag/Westview Press.

Niles, R. (2007). "Lessons from the 'Talking Points Memo' and the U.S. attorney scandal." *Online Journalism Review,* March 20. Retrieved May 5, 2010: http://www.ojr.org/ojr/stories/070320niles/.

Nissenbaum, H. (2004). "Hackers and the contested ontology of cyberspace." *New Media & Society,* 6(2), 195–217.

Norris, P. (2001). *Digital divide: Civic engagement, information poverty, and the internet worldwide.* Cambridge: Cambridge University Press.

Nunberg, G. (2004). "Blogging in the global lunchroom." Commentary broadcast on *Fresh Air,* National Public Radio, April 20. Transcript retrieved May 5, 2010: http://people.ischool.berkeley.edu/~nunberg/lunchroom.html.

OECD (Organization for Economic Cooperation and Development) (2008). *Broadband growth and policies in OECD countries.* Committee for Information, Computer and Communications Policy, Directorate for Science, Technology, and Industry. Prepared for the OECD Ministerial Meeting on the Future of the Internet Economy, Seoul, Korea, 17–18 June. Paris: OECD. Retrieved May 5, 2010: www.oecd.org/sti/ict/broadband/growth.

Offe, C. (1985). "New social movements: Challenging the boundaries of institutional politics." *Social Research,* 52(4), 817–68.

Olesen, T. (2003). "Globalization in movement(s): A review essay." *Social Movement Studies,* 2(2), 229–43.

Olson, H.A. (2002). *The power to name: Locating the limits of subject representation in libraries.* Dordrecht and Norwell, MA: Kluwer Academic Publishers.

Olson, H.A. (2004). "The ubiquitous hierarchy: An army to overcome the threat of a mob." *Library Trends*, 52(3), 604–16.

OpenBusiness (weblog) (2006). *The future of journalism* (interview with Kenneth Neil Cukier), June 24. Retrieved May 5, 2010: http://www.openbusiness.cc/2006/0/24/the-future-of-journalism/.

Orlikowski, W.J. and Yates, J. (1994). "Genre repertoire: Examining the structuring of communicative practices in organizations." *Administrative Science Quarterly*, 39(4), 541–74.

Outing, S. (2005). "The 11 layers of citizen journalism." *Poynter Online* blog, June 15. Retrieved May 5, 2010: http://www.poynter.org/content/content_view.asp?id=83126.

Pasquale, F. (2007). "Conditions for the digital library of Alexandria." *Madisonian.net* (blog on law, technology and society), November 24. Retrieved May 5, 2010: http://www.madisonian.net/2007/11/24/conditions-for-the-digital-library-of-alexandria/.

Paton, D. (1999). "War of words: Virtual media versus mainstream press." *Christian Science Monitor*, December 3, 3. Retrieved May 5, 2010: http://www.csmonitor.com/1999/1203/p3s1.html.

Pavis, T. (2002). "Modern day muckrakers: The rise of the Independent Media Center movement." *Online Journalism Review*, April 3. Retrieved May 5, 2010: http://www.ojr.org/ojr/business/1017866594.php.

Peretti, J. (2001a). "My Nike media adventure." *The Nation*, April 9. Retrieved May 5, 2010: http://www.thenation.com/article/my-nike-media-adventure.

Peretti, J. (2001b). *Culture jamming, memes, social networks, and the emerging media ecology: The "Nike Sweatshop Email" as object-to-think-with.* Unpublished manuscript, MIT Media Lab. Retrieved May 5, 2010 from the Internet Archive: http://web.archive.org/web/20030802192323/xenia.media.mit.edu/~peretti/nike/. (Original Peretti/Nike correspondence is available from the Internet Archive at http://web.archive.org/web/20030811071630/www.shey.net/niked.html.)

Peters, J.D. (1986). "Institutional sources of intellectual poverty in communication research." *Communication Research*, 13(4), 527–59.

Peterson, T.F. *Nightwork: A history of hacks and pranks at MIT.* Cambridge, MA: MIT Press.

Pickard, V.W. (2006a). "Assessing the radical democracy of indymedia: Discursive, technical, and institutional constructions." *Critical Studies in Media Communication*, 23(1), 19–38.

Pickard, V.W. (2006b). "United yet autonomous: Indymedia and the struggle to sustain a radical democratic network." *Media, Culture & Society*, 28(3), 315–36.

Pickard, V.W. (2008). "Cooptation and cooperation: Institutional exemplars of democratic internet technology." *New Media & Society*, 10(4), 625–45.

Platon, S. and Deuze, M. (2003). "Indymedia journalism: A radical way of making, selecting and sharing news?" *Journalism*, 4(3), 336–55.

Plewe, D.A. (2008). "Transactional arts – interaction as transaction." In *MM '08, Proceedings of the ACM International Conference on Multimedia, Multimedia '08*, Vancouver, British Columbia, Canada, October 26–31, pp. 977–9.

Pool, I. de S. (1983). *Technologies of freedom*. Cambridge, MA: Harvard University Press.

Posener, J. (1982). *Spray it loud*. London: Routledge & Kegan Paul.

Poster, M. (1998). "Cyberdemocracy: The Internet and the public sphere." In D. Holmes (ed.), *Virtual politics: Identity and community in cyberspace*, pp. 212–28. London and Thousand Oaks, CA: Sage.

Priedhorsky, R., Chen, J., Lam, S.K., Panciera, K., Terveen, L., and Riedl, J. (2007). "Creating, destroying, and restoring value in Wikipedia." *GROUP '07: Proceedings of the 2007 International ACM Conference on Supporting Group Work*, Sanibel Island, FL, November 4–7, pp. 259–68.

Quattrocchi, A. and Nairn, T. (1998). *The beginning of the end* (with a preface by Tariq Ali). London and New York: Verso. (Originally published by Panther Books, 1968.)

Rafaeli, S. (1988). "Interactivity: From new media to communication." In R. Hawkins, J.M. Wiemann, and S. Pingree (eds.), *Advancing communication science: Merging mass and interpersonal processes*, pp. 124–181. Newbury Park, CA: Sage.

Rainie, L. (2007). "28% of online Americans have used the Internet to tag content." Washington, D.C.: *Pew Internet & American Life Project*, January 31. Retrieved December 15, 2009: http://www.pewinternet.org/Reports/2007/Tagging.aspx?r=1.

Ray, G. (2006). "Tactical media and the end of the end of history." *Afterimage*, 34(1–2), 31–7.

Raymond, E.S. (2001). *The cathedral and the bazaar: Musings on Linux and open source by an accidental revolutionary* (rev. edn). Sebastopol, CA: O'Reilly & Associates.

Rayward, W.B. (1999). "H.G. Wells's idea of a World Brain: A critical reassessment." *Journal of the American Society for Information Science*, 50(7), 557–73.

Rayward, W.B. (2003). "Knowledge organization and a new world polity: The rise and fall and rise of the ideas of Paul Otlet." *Transnational Association*, 1–2, 4–15.

Rayward, W.B. (2008). "The march of the modern and the reconstitution of the world's knowledge apparatus: H.G. Wells, encyclopedism and the

World Brain." In W.B. Rayward (ed.), *European modernism and the information society: Informing the present, understanding the past*, pp. 223–56. Aldershot and Burlington, VT: Ashgate.

Reardon, K.M. and Rogers, E.M. (1988). "Interpersonal versus mass media communication: A false dichotomy." *Human Communication Research*, 15(2), 284–303.

Rheingold, H. (2002). *Smart mobs: The next social revolution.* Cambridge, MA: Perseus Books.

Rice, R.E. and Associates (1984). *The new media: Communication, research and technology.* Beverly Hills, CA: Sage.

Richardson, J. (2003). "The language of tactical media." In J. Richardson (ed.), *Anarchitexts: Voices from the global digital resistance*, pp. 123–8. Brooklyn, NY: Autonomedia.

Rimensnyder, S. (2001). "Mugging for the cameras: Tune in to International Surveillance Camera Awareness Day." *Reason*, September 6. Retrieved May 5, 2010: http://reason.com/hod/sr090601.shtml.

Rogers, E.M. (1986). *Communication technology: The new media in society.* New York: Free Press.

Rogers, E.M. (1994). *A history of communication study.* New York: Free Press.

Rogers, E.M. (2003). *Diffusion of innovations* (5th edn). New York: Free Press.

Rogers, E.M. and Kincaid, D.L. (1981). *Communication networks: Toward a new paradigm for research.* New York: Free Press.

Rolfe, B. (2005). "Building an electronic repertoire of contention." *Social Movement Studies*, 4(1), 65–74.

Rosen, J. (2004). "Top ten ideas of 2004: Open-source journalism, or 'My readers know more than I do.'" *PressThink* blog, December 28. Retrieved May 5, 2010: http://journalism.nyu.edu/pubzone/weblogs/pressthink/2004/12/28/tptn04_opsc.html.

Rosen, J. (2006). "The people formerly known as the audience." *PressThink* blog, June 27. Retrieved May 5, 2010: http://journalism.nyu.edu/pubzone/weblogs/pressthink/2006/06/27/ppl_frmr.html#more.

Rosenzweig, R. (2006). "Can history be open source? Wikipedia and the future of the past." *Journal of American History*, 93(1), 117–46.

Ross, K. (2002a). "Lefebvre on the Situationists: An interview." In T. McDonough (ed.), *Guy Debord and the Situationist International: Texts and documents*, pp. 267–83. Cambridge, MA: MIT Press (an October Book).

Ross, K. (2002b). *May '68 and its afterlives.* Chicago: University of Chicago Press.

Rucht, D. (2004). "The quadruple 'A': Media strategies of protest movements since the 1960s." In W. van de Donk, B.D. Loader, P.G. Nixon, and D. Rucht (eds.), *Cyberprotest: New media, citizens, and social movements*, pp. 29–56. London: Routledge.

Ryfe, D. and Mensing, D. (2008). *Participatory journalism and the transformation of news*. Paper presented at the annual meeting of the Association for Education in Journalism and Mass Communication (AEJMC), Chicago, August 6. Retrieved May 5, 2010: http://www.allacademic.com/meta/p_mla_apa_research_citation/2/7/1/5/8/p271585_index.html.

Sadler, S. (1998). *The Situationist city*. Cambridge, MA: MIT Press.

Sanders, T. (1997). *Into the future: On the preservation of knowledge in the electronic age.* (Video, 60 minutes.) Produced by the American Film Foundation and Sanders & Mock Productions, in association with the Council on Library and Information Resources/Commission on Preservation and Access, and the American Council of Learned Societies. Available: http://www.clir.org/pubs/film/future/order.html.

Sandvig, C. (2007). "Network neutrality is the new common carriage." *Info*, 9(2/3), 136–47.

Sanger, L.M. (2009). "The fate of expertise after Wikipedia." *Episteme*, 6(1), 52–73.

Schiff, S. (2006). "Know it all: Can Wikipedia conquer expertise?" *The New Yorker*, July 31, 36–43.

Schrage, M. (2001). "The relationship revolution." *Merrill Lynch Forum*. Retrieved May 5, 2010 from the Internet Archive: http://web.archive.org/web/20030602025739/http://www.ml.com/woml/forum/relation.htm.

Schramm, W. (1977). *Big media, little media: Tools and technologies for instruction*. Beverly Hills, CA: Sage.

Scott, A. and Street, J. (2000). "From media politics to e-protest: The use of popular culture and new media in parties and social movements." *Information, Communication & Society*, 3(2), 215–40.

Seale, P. and McConville, M. (1968). *Red flag/Black flag: French revolution 1968*. New York: G.P. Putnam's Sons.

Shannon, C.E. and Weaver, W. (1963). *The mathematical theory of communication*. Urbana, IL: University of Illinois Press. (Originally published in 1949.)

Sherman, C. and Price, G. (2001). *The invisible web: Uncovering information sources search engines can't see*. Medford, NJ: Information Today.

Shirky, C. (2005). *Ontology is overrated: Categories, links and tags. Clay Shirky's Writings About the Internet* (personal website). Retrieved May 1, 2010: http://www.shirky.com/writings/ontology_overrated.html.

Shirky, C. (2008). *Here comes everybody: The power of organizing without organizations*. New York: Penguin.

References 273

Sholette, G. (2004). "Interventionism and the historical uncanny." In N. Thompson and G. Sholette (eds.), *The interventionists: Users' Manual for the Creative Disruption of Everyday Life*, pp. 133–42. North Adams, MA: MASS MoCA Publications, distributed by MIT Press.

SI/AFGES (Situationist International and AFGES) (1981). "On the poverty of student life." In K. Knabb (ed. and trans.), *Situationist International anthology*, pp. 319–36. Berkeley, CA: Bureau of Public Secrets. (Originally published as *De la misère en milieu étudiant*. Strasbourg, 1966.)

Silver, D. (2003). "Epilogue: Current directions and future questions." In M. McCaughey and M.D. Ayers (Eds.), *Cyberactivism: Online activism in theory and practice*, pp. 279–92. New York and London: Routledge.

Silverstone, R. (1999). *Why study the media?* London and Thousand Oaks, CA: Sage.

Silverstone, R. (2005). "The sociology of mediation and communication." In C. Calhoun, C. Rojek, and B.S. Turner (eds.), *The Sage handbook of sociology*, pp. 188–207. London and Thousand Oaks, CA: Sage.

Silverstone, R. (2006). "Domesticating domestication: Reflections on the life of a concept." In T. Berker, M. Hartmann, Y. Punie, and K.J. Ward (eds.), *The domestication of media and technology*, pp. 229–48. Maidenhead: Open University Press.

Slashdot (2007, April 29). *Cryptome to be terminated by Verio/NTT*. Retrieved May 5, 2010: http://yro.slashdot.org/yro/07/04/29/134232.shtml.

Smith, P.J. and Smythe, E. (2001). "Globalization, citizenship and technology: The Multilateral Agreement on Investment (MAI) meets the Internet." In F. Webster (ed.), *Culture and politics in the information age: A new politics?*, pp. 183–206. London and New York: Routledge.

Snow, D.A. (2004). "Framing processes, ideology, and discursive fields." In D.A. Snow, S.A. Soule, and H. Kriesi (eds.), *The Blackwell companion to social movements*, pp. 380–412. Malden, MA and Oxford: Blackwell.

Spar, D.L. (1999). "The public face of cyberspace." In I. Kaul, I. Grunberg, and M.A. Stern (eds.), *Global public goods: International cooperation in the 21st century*, pp. 342–62. New York and Oxford: Oxford University Press, for the United Nations Development Programme (UNDP).

Stallabrass, J. (2003–4). "Types and prospects of radical art." *Australian and New Zealand Journal of Art*, 5(1), 2003–4. Retrieved May 5, 2010: http://www.courtauld.ac.uk/people/stallabrass_julian/essays/types_prospects_radical_art.pdf (page references in the text are to this online version).

Stallman, R.M. (2002). The GNU manifesto. In *Free software free society: Selected essays of Richard M. Stallman* (ed. J. Gay, with an introduction by L. Lessig), pp. 31–9. Boston: Free Software Foundation. (Originally published in *Dr. Dobb's Journal of Software Tools*, 10(3), 1985, 30–5.)

Star, S.L. and Bowker, G. (2006). "How to infrastructure." In L.A. Lievrouw and S. Livingstone (eds.), *Handbook of new media* (updated student edn), pp. 230–45. London: Sage.

Star, S.L. and Ruhleder, K. (1996). "Steps toward an ecology of infrastructure: Design and access for large information spaces." *Information Systems Research*, 7, 111–34.

Stein, L. (2009). "Social movement web use in theory and practice: A content analysis of US movement websites." *New Media & Society*, 11(5), 749–71.

Stelter, B. (2010). "A Pulitzer winner gets Apple's reconsideration." *New York Times*, April 17. Retrieved May 1, 2010: http://www.nytimes.com/2010/04/17/books/17cartoonist.html.

Steuer, J. (1995). "Defining virtual reality: Dimensions determining telepresence." In F. Biocca and M.R. Levy (eds.), *Communication in the age of virtual reality*, pp. 33–56. Mahwah, NJ: Lawrence Erlbaum.

Stiglitz, J.E. (1999). "Knowledge as a global public good." In I. Kaul, I. Grunberg, and M.A. Stern (eds.), *Global public goods: International cooperation in the 21st century*, pp. 308–25. New York and Oxford: Oxford University Press, for the United Nations Development Programme (UNDP).

Stimson, B. and Sholette, G. (2007a). "Introduction: Periodizing collectivism." In B. Stimson and G. Sholette (eds.), *Collectivism after modernism: The art of social imagination after 1945*, pp. 1–15. Minneapolis: University of Minnesota Press.

Stimson, B. and Sholette, G. (eds.) (2007b). *Collectivism after modernism: The art of social imagination after 1945*. Minneapolis: University of Minnesota Press.

Sturken, M. and Cartwright, L. (2009). *Practices of looking: An introduction to visual culture*. New York and Oxford: Oxford University Press.

Sunstein, C. (2007). *Republic.com 2.0*. Princeton, NJ: Princeton University Press.

Surowiecki, J. (2004). *The wisdom of crowds*. New York: Doubleday.

Tambini, D. (1999). "New media and democracy: The civic networking movement." *New Media & Society*, 1(3), 305–29.

Tapscott, D. and Williams, A.D. (2008). *Wikinomics: How mass collaboration changes everything* (expanded edn). New York: Portfolio.

Tarleton, J. (2000). "Protesters develop their own global Internet news service." *Nieman Reports*, 54(4), 53–5.

Taylor, A.G. and Jourdrey, D.N. (2008). *The organization of information* (3rd edn). Santa Barbara, CA: Libraries Unlimited.

Teer-Tomaselli, R.E. (2007). Round-table remarks for plenary session, "Fifty Years of Research and Beyond," presented at the 50th anniversary conference of the International Association for Media and Communication Research (IAMCR), held at the headquarters of the United Nations Educational, Scientific, and Cultural Organization (UNESCO), Paris, July 25.

Terranova, T. (2009). "Free labor: Producing culture for the digital economy." In L.A. Lievrouw and S. Livingstone (eds.), *Sage benchmarks in communication: New media, vol. IV*, pp. 219–240. London: Sage. (Originally published in *Social Text 63*, 18(2), 2000, 33–58.)

Thomas, D. (2002). *Hacker culture*. Minneapolis: University of Minnesota Press.

Thompson, J. (2004). "Foreword." In N. Thompson and G. Sholette (eds.), *The interventionists: users' manual for the creative disruption of everyday life*, p. 10. North Adams, MA: MASS MoCA Publications, distributed by MIT Press.

Thompson, M. (2005). "EPIC 2014: The future is now." *Poynter Online*, July 21. Retrieved May 5, 2010. http://www.poynter.org/content/content_view.asp?id=85631.

Thompson, N. and Sholette, G. (eds.) (2004). *The interventionists: users' manual for the creative disruption of everyday life*. North Adams, MA: MASS MoCA Publications, distributed by MIT Press.

Tilly, C. (2004). *Social movements, 1768–2004*. Boulder, CO and London: Paradigm.

Touraine, A. (1971a). *The May movement: Revolt and reform* (trans. L.F.X. Mayhew). New York: Random House. (Originally published as *Le Mouvement de mai ou le communisme utopique*. Paris: Éditions du Seuil, 1968.)

Touraine, A. (1971b). *The post-industrial society* (trans. L.F.X. Mayhew). New York: Random House. (Originally published as *La société post-industrielle*. Paris: Éditions Denoël SARL, 1969.)

Touraine, A. (1977). *The self-production of society* (trans. D. Coltman). Chicago: University of Chicago Press. (Originally published as *Production de la société*. Paris: Éditions du Seuil, 1973.)

Touraine, A. (1981). *The voice and the eye: An analysis of social movements* (trans. A. Duff, with foreword by R. Sennett). Cambridge and New York: Cambridge University Press. (Originally published as *La voix et le regard*. Paris: Éditions du Seuil,1978.)

Touraine, A. (1988). *Return of the actor: Social theory in postindustrial society*. (trans. M. Godzich, foreword by S. Aronowitz). Minneapolis: University of Minnesota Press. (Originally published as *Le retour de l'acteur: Essai de sociologie*. Paris: Librairie Arthème Fayard, 1984.)

Touraine, A. (1992). "Two interpretations of contemporary social change." In H. Haferkamp and N.J. Smelser (eds.), *Social change and modernity*, pp. 55–77. Berkeley, Los Angeles, and Oxford: University of California Press.

Turkle, S. (1980). "Computer as Rorschach." *Society/Transaction,* 17(2), 15–24.

Turkle, S. (1984). *The second self: Computers and the human spirit.* New York: Simon & Schuster.

Turkle, S. (1995). *Life on the screen: Identity in the age of the Internet.* New York: Simon & Schuster.

Turner, F. (2006). *From counterculture to cyberculture: Stewart Brand, the Whole Earth Network, and the rise of digital utopianism.* Chicago: University of Chicago Press.

Turner, R.H. (1969). "The theme of contemporary social movements." *British Journal of Sociology,* 20(4), 390–405.

Turner, R.H. and Killian, L.M. (1957). *Collective behavior.* Englewood, NJ: Prentice-Hall.

Tzara, T. (1971). "Dada Manifesto 1918." In L. Lippard (ed.), *Dadas on art: Tzara, Arp, Duchamp, and others,* pp. 13–20. Englewood Cliffs, NJ: Prentice-Hall. (Originally published in 1918.)

Vamosi, R. (2007). "iPhone hack enables wireless without AT&T." *C|NET News,* July 5. Retrieved May 5, 2010: http://news.cnet.com/8301-10784_3-9739828-7.html.

Van Aelst, P. and Walgrave, S. (2002). "New media, new movements? The role of the Internet in shaping the 'anti-globalization' movement." *Information, Communication & Society,* 5(4), 465–93.

van de Donk, W., Loader, B.D., Nixon, P.G., and Rucht, D. (eds.) (2004). *Cyberprotest: New media, citizens, and social movements.* London: Routledge.

Vegh, S. (2003). "Classifying forms of online activism: The case of cyber-protests against the World Bank." In M. McCaughey and M.D. Ayers (eds.), *Cyberactivism: Online activism in theory and practice,* pp. 71–96. New York and London: Routledge.

Verhulst, S.G. (2007). "Mediation, mediators and new intermediaries: Implications for the design of new communications policies." In P.M. Napoli (ed.), *Media diversity and localism: Meaning and metrics,* pp. 180–219. Mahwah, NJ: Lawrence Erlbaum Associates.

Viégas, F.B., Wattenberg, M., and Dave, K. (2004). "Studying cooperation and conflict between authors with history flow visualizations." *CHI 2004: Conference on Human Factors in Computing Systems,* Vienna, Austria, April 24–9. *CHILetters,* 6(1), 575–82. Retrieved May 5, 2010: http://alumni.media.mit.edu/~fviegas/papers/history_flow.pdf.

Viénet, R. (1981). "The Situationists and the new forms of action against politics and art." In K. Knabb (ed. and trans.), *Situationist International anthology*, pp. 213–15. Berkeley, CA: Bureau of Public Secrets. (Originally published in *Internationale Situationniste*, 11, 1967.)

Viénet, R. (1992). *Enragés and Situationists in the occupation movement, France, May '68*. New York: Autonomedia (in association with Rebel Press, London). (Originally published as *Enragés et situationnistes dans le mouvement des occupations*. Paris: Éditions Gallimard, 1968.)

Wark, M. (2004). *A hacker manifesto*. Cambridge, MA: Harvard University Press.

Wark, M. (2009). "Introduction: The secretary." In G. Debord, *Correspondence: The foundation of the Situationist International (June 1957–August 1960)* (trans. S. Kendall and J. McHale), pp. 5–27. Los Angeles, CA: Semiotext(e).

Warschauer, M. (2004). *Technology and social inclusion: Rethinking the digital divide*. Cambridge, MA: MIT Press.

Wasik, B. (2009). *And then there's this*. New York: Viking.

Webster, F. (2001). "A new politics?" In F. Webster (ed.), *Culture and politics in the information age: A new politics?*, pp. 1–14. London and New York: Routledge.

Weinberger, D. (2006). *Taxonomies and tags: From trees to piles of leaves*. Retrieved May 1, 2010: http://hyperorg.com/blogger/misc/taxonomies_and_tags.html.

Weinberger, D. (2008). *Everything is miscellaneous: The power of the new digital disorder*. New York: Henry Holt.

Wells, H.G. (1938). "World brain: The idea of a permanent world encyclopedia." In *World brain*, pp. 83–8. New York: Doubleday.

Wettergren, Å. (2009). "Fun and laughter: Culture jamming and the emotional regime of late capitalism." *Social Movement Studies*, 8(1), 1–15.

"What's Next?" (1999). *Media Studies Journal*, 13(2), Spring/Summer. (Special issue on the future of journalism and the internet.)

Wieviorka, M. (2005). "After new social movements." *Social Movement Studies*, 4(1), 1–19.

Wilkinson, D.M. and Huberman, B.A. (2008). *Assessing the value of cooperation in Wikipedia*. ArXiv preprint, retrieved October 15, 2009: http://arxiv.org/abs/cs/0702140.

Williams, R.H. (2004). "The cultural contexts of collective action: Constraints, opportunities, and the symbolic life of social movements." In D.A. Snow, S.A. Soule, and H. Kriesi (eds.), *The Blackwell companion to social movements*, pp. 91–115. Malden, MA and Oxford: Blackwell.

Wray, S. (1998). "Electronic civil disobedience and the world wide web of hacktivism: A mapping of extraparliamentarian direct action net politics." *SWITCH* (online journal), 4(2). Retrieved May 5, 2010: http://switch.sjsu.edu/web/v4n2/stefan.

Wright, A. (2008). "The web time forgot." *New York Times*, June 17. Retrieved August 16, 2010: http://www.nytimes.com/2008/06/17/science/17mund.html.

Wright, S. (2004). "Informing, communicating and ICTs in contemporary anti-capitalist movements." In W. van de Donk, B.D. Loader, P.G. Nixon, and D. Rucht (eds.), *Cyberprotest: New media, citizens, and social movements*, pp. 77–93. London: Routledge.

Yates, J. and Orlikowski, W.J. (1992). "Genres of organizational communication: A structurational approach to studying communication and media." *Academy of Management Review*, 17(2), 299–326.

Yates, J., Orlikowski, W.J., and Okamura, K. (1999). "Explicit and implicit structuring of genres in electronic communication: Reinforcement and change of social interaction." *Organization Science*, 10(1), 83–103.

Yes Men (n.d.). *Dow does the wrong thing*. Retrieved May 5, 2010: http://theyesmen.org/hijinks/bhopalpressrelease.

Zittrain, J. (2008). *The future of the Internet – and how to stop it*. New Haven, CT and London: Yale University Press.

Index

Page numbers followed by 't' refer to a table, page numbers followed by 'f' refer to a figure – e.g. 169t, 10f